web 2.0
how-to for educators

Gwen Solomon
Lynne Schrum

International Society for Technology in Education
EUGENE, OREGON • WASHINGTON, DC

web 2.0 • how-to for educators

Gwen Solomon and Lynne Schrum

Director of Book Publishing: *Courtney Burkholder*
Acquisitions Editor: *Jeff V. Bolkan*
Production Editors: *Tina Wells, Lynda Gansel*
Production Coordinator: *Rachel Williams*
Graphic Designer: *Signe Landin*
Copy Editor: *Nancy Olsen*
Editorial Assistance: *Tracy Cozzens*
Proofreader: *Barbara J. Hewick*
Indexer: *Pilar Wyman, Wyman Indexing*
Cover Design, Book Design, and Production: *Kim McGovern*

Library of Congress Cataloging-in-Publication Data

Solomon, Gwen, 1944-
    Web 2.0 how-to for educators / Gwen Solomon, Lynne Schrum.
        p. cm.
    ISBN 978-1-56484-272-5 (pbk.)
    1. Internet in education—Handbooks, manuals, etc. 2. Web 2.0—Handbooks, manuals, etc.   I. Schrum, Lynne. II. Title.
    LB1044.87.S618 2010
    371.33'44678—dc22

                                                    2010022317

First Edition
ISBN: 978-1-56484-272-5
Printed in the United States of America

Cover Image © Neliana Georgieva, Dreamstime.com

ISTE® is a registered trademark of the International Society for Technology in Education.

SUSTAINABLE FORESTRY INITIATIVE Certified Fiber Sourcing
Label applies to the text stock www.sfiprogram.org

About ISTE

The International Society for Technology in Education (ISTE) is the trusted source for professional development, knowledge generation, advocacy, and leadership for innovation. ISTE is the premier membership association for educators and education leaders engaged in improving teaching and learning by advancing the effective use of technology in PK–12 and teacher education.

Home of the National Educational Technology Standards (NETS) and ISTE's annual conference and exposition (formerly known as NECC), ISTE represents more than 100,000 professionals worldwide. We support our members with information, networking opportunities, and guidance as they face the challenge of transforming education. To find out more about these and other ISTE initiatives, visit our website at www.iste.org.

As part of our mission, ISTE Book Publishing works with experienced educators to develop and produce practical resources for classroom teachers, teacher educators, and technology leaders. Every manuscript we select for publication is carefully peer-reviewed and professionally edited. We value your feedback on this book and other ISTE products. E-mail us at books@iste.org.

Contact us

International Society for Technology in Education (ISTE)
Washington, DC, Office:
    1710 Rhode Island Ave. NW, Suite 900, Washington, DC 20036-3132
Eugene, Oregon, Office:
    180 West 8th Ave., Suite 300, Eugene, OR 97401-2916
Order Desk: 1.800.336.5191
Order Fax: 1.541.302.3778
Customer Service: orders@iste.org
Book Publishing: books@iste.org
Book Sales and Marketing: booksmarketing@iste.org
Web: www.iste.org

About the Authors

Gwen Solomon

Gwen Solomon creates, manages, and edits custom websites; writes e-books and advertorials; directs webinars; and advises ed tech companies. She has been the director of the websites techLEARNING.com, Digital Learning Environments, 21st Century Connections, and The Well Connected Educator. She is the author of advertorials such as *Fundamentals of K–12 Technology Programs* and *The Handheld Educator*. Her recent e-books include *Keeping Students Safe Online*, *Netbooks in K–12: Thinking Big by Thinking Small*, *A Guide to Software as a Service*, and *Guide to InFormative Assessment*. Prior to this work, Gwen was senior analyst in the U.S. Department of Education's Office of Educational Technology. Gwen also served New York City Public Schools as coordinator of instructional technology planning and as founding director of New York City's School of the Future. Before that, Gwen was a teacher and computer coordinator.

Lynne Schrum

Lynne Schrum is a professor and coordinator of elementary and secondary education in the College of Education at George Mason University. Prior to that, she served as chair of the Department of Teaching and Learning at the University of Utah. Her research and teaching focus on teacher preparation, appropriate uses of information technology, and preparation of leaders for 21st-century schools. She has written five books and numerous articles on these subjects. Lynne is a past-president of ISTE and currently is the editor of the *Journal of Research on Technology in Education* (JRTE) [2002–2011].

Acknowledgments

Writing the second book in a series is an interesting challenge. We learned a lot in the process, especially from educators who are on the front lines of innovation, and we want to thank them.

First, we thank all of the educators who filled out our survey of Web 2.0 use. We have cited many of them as examples of classroom integration. There are too many to thank individually, but we have cited them in context and so you will find their names mentioned throughout the chapters.

Second, we thank the people who responded to our call for detailed models of Web 2.0 use. Their work comprises Chapter 10, Specific Tools. We thank (in alphabetical order) Steven W. Anderson, Barbara Bray, Steven Burt, Serge Danielson-Francois, Vicki Davis, Esther Eash, Jesus (Al) Garcia, Miguel Guhlin, Mike Hasley, Elizabeth Helfant, Kevin Jarrett, Pamela Livingston, Samantha Morra, Jon Orech, Lisa Parisi, Christine Southard, Bob Sprankle, and Jeff Utecht for their contributions.

Third, the people who helped us produce this book deserve our gratitude as well. We thank the ISTE staff—Jeff Bolkan, Courtney Burkholder, Megan Dolman, Rachel Williams, and Tina Wells. We also thank Patrick Ledesma, a doctoral student at George Mason University, for assisting us in gathering information, checking for permissions, and providing other support.

Finally, we thank our families for their understanding and encouragement and the many others whose work provided inspiration and support.

Contents

introduction

The generation of students in our classrooms today is the first to have grown up with digital tools at their fingertips. They're always "on": texting to friends, meeting on social networks, and interacting with the world in nonlinear fashion. They can get the information they want when they want it, follow an idea in ways that have meaning to them, and jump from one thing to the next as the inspiration hits them. When they go to work in the future, it will be in an environment where reliance on technology is a given and the skills they need are the ability to adapt, learn new skills, and work in ever-changing teams depending on purpose.

Using the tools that students find appealing can make a difference in their learning now and help them prepare for the future. Students can interact with information, create knowledge, and then communicate the results to a real audience. The tools, like the students, are always on, accessible anywhere there is Internet access; many are collaborative. We bring Web 2.0 tools into the classroom, where their importance lies in their potential to change the way we operate. With them we can maximize students' potential.

A definition of any widely used term can be tricky. A Google search for "Web 2.0 definition" returns more than 13 million hits; thus, our goal is to frame just how this term is used in *Web 2.0 How-To for Educators*. Webopedia defines Web 2.0 as follows:

> Web 2.0 is the term given to describe a second generation of the World Wide Web that is focused on the ability for people to collaborate and share information online. Web 2.0 basically refers to the transition from static HTML web pages to a more dynamic web that is more organized and is based on serving web applications to users. Other improved functionality of Web 2.0 includes open communication with an emphasis on web-based communities of users, and more open sharing of information. Over time Web 2.0 has been used more as a marketing term than a computer-science-based term. Blogs, wikis, and web services are all seen as components of Web 2.0.

Some educators have added other qualifications as conditions for being considered Web 2.0 tools. Among these requirements are that the tools must be free, open source, and used online rather than downloadable. Others believe that almost any free tool currently available online can be classified as a Web 2.0 tool.

In general, our plan is to provide readers with information about the tools that educators consider Web 2.0 because they use these applications in classrooms in interesting ways to promote the types of digital-age literacies that we believe all students need to know to spark creativity, engage curiosity, and increase learning outcomes. We hope to introduce educators to a wide range of tools and the ways teachers use them, both in classrooms and professionally.

We should be able to harness these Web 2.0 tools to change education. The web is serendipitous: look up one thing and find another somewhat-related idea and you're off on a learning adventure that can lead to a synthesis of ideas and new thinking on a topic. However, in schools today, students rarely see learning as an adventure, but we know that they enjoy playing with new tools and using them to communicate with others. If only we could take advantage of the tools they like and get them started on the learning adventures we want them to take.

We hear that students are ahead of their teachers in web use. They spend hours texting their friends, meeting up on social networks, and displaying antics on video-sharing sites. Teachers often find it hard to figure out which tools to use (and when to use them), how to use the new tools, how to pull them together in some coherent strategy, and how to integrate them as they direct the learning experience. Students need teachers' guidance to do more than play with these tools, and teachers need easy-to-use applications that are clear about when, why, and how to use them.

challenges for schools

As students and the world change, education faces new challenges and schools are feeling the stresses on their systems. Thomas L. Friedman of *The New York Times* says:

Today, we have fallen behind in both per capita high school graduates and their quality. In the 2006 Program for International Student Assessment that measured the applied learning and problem-solving skills of 15-year-olds in 30 industrialized countries, the U.S. ranked 25th out of the 30 in math and 24th in science. (Friedman, April 21, 2009)

According to the Horizon Report (Johnson, Levine, Smith, & Smythe, 2009) there are five factors at work that need addressing:

❶ There is a growing need for formal instruction in key new skills, including information literacy, visual literacy, and technological literacy.

❷ Students are different, but educational practice and the material that supports it are changing only slowly.

❸ Learning that incorporates real life experiences is not occurring enough and is undervalued when it does take place.

❹ There is a growing recognition that new technologies must be adopted and used as an everyday part of classroom activities, but effecting this change is difficult.

❺ A key challenge is the fundamental structure of the K–12 education establishment. (p. 5)

Fortunately, technology can address some of the issues. Using technology is the way today's students learn outside of school because they are comfortable with the tools. The Pew Internet and American Life Project's *Teens and Social Media* (Lenhart, Madden, Smith, & Macgill, 2007) details that 64% of online teenagers (aged 12–17) engage in at least one type of content creation. Nearly 40% share their own artistic creations online, such as artwork, photos, stories, or videos; 28% have created their own blogs; and 26% remix content they find online into their own creations.

The survey (Lenhart et al., 2007) found that content creation is not just about sharing creative output; it is also about participating in conversations fueled by that content. Nearly half (47%) of online teens have posted photos where others can see them, and 89% of those teens who post photos say that people comment on the images at least "some of the time."

The process of change, especially when it includes adoption of new tools and methods, isn't simple and brings with it another set of challenges: certain requirements in terms of security and bandwidth must be in place. Sufficient funding for initial equipment purchase and ongoing upkeep is needed. Students must have equitable web access. Teachers must get professional development so that they are comfortable with the tools; and, most important, integrating Web 2.0 applications has to be a thoughtful process that relies on best practice, research, and strong pedagogy. Schools have to address these challenges.

Educators can use new tools so that students have new ways to learn both old and new skills. Employing digital tools with time-tested goals and methods improves these teachers' ability to help students develop both basic and higher-order thinking skills. Instructional strategies such as project-based and active learning, constructivism, student-centered approaches, and differentiated instruction are believed to benefit from the advantages technology affords. Similarly, using technology tools may help educators pay closer attention to learning styles, personalization, and formative assessments.

Teachers believe that technology has made a difference. In a poll on the Digital Learning Environments website (www.guide2digitallearning.com) about *Technology's Impact on Learning* (2009), educators were asked how technology has enhanced educational opportunities in their classrooms: 38% said it had increased support for project-based learning; 29% said that it improved critical-thinking skills; and 24% said it resulted in a stronger ability to communicate.

The goal of this book is to offer examples of how educators are using new tools to best advantage and to take a look at which technology investments have long-term value. As tools proliferate, educators have to decide which ones work well to teach a concept, whether using a particular tool is the best way to learn a topic, and if the tool is essential to the process or a distraction.

the eight Cs

Web-based tools can provide new opportunities. Students can learn the skills of communication, collaboration, and creativity. Teachers can take advantage of the connectedness of people and ideas to establish communities of learners to help students acquire new skills. We will see a convergence of tools as using online applications (also known as cloud computing) expands into all aspects of teaching and learning to provide the perspective of tools for contextualized learning.

Although schools are good at emphasizing traditional skills, they may miss capitalizing on student creativity as a way to enhance learning. Web 2.0 tools allow students to write a story and use copyright-free photos to set the scene, illustrate an event, or provide examples. When students use their own photographs, their creativity and seriousness are enhanced. Developing video documentaries is another way in which teachers can tap into the power of student creativity for learning. Photo and video editing and sharing tools are successful because they enhance online collaboration and community as well as provide a real audience for students' efforts.

Communication

Students have traditionally written papers and reports and submitted them for a grade. Computer applications altered the experience to the extent that students could edit one another's work and revise drafts until perfect. Although the web provides access to information and experts, Web 2.0 tools go a step beyond to offer ways of creating, collaborating, and distributing the final product and then interacting with an audience. Students now can post and share their work and get comments from readers globally. The potential of a real audience means that students work harder to perfect what they want to communicate. These tools include blogs, microblogs, and podcasts.

Collaboration

Student collaboration is a complex process, but online tools can be used to transform both the process of working with others and the product that results. Students can post ideas and get feedback from others with whom they are working. They can brainstorm to narrow or expand concepts. They can discuss their ideas, share research, and collaborate on a project. And peer editing takes on new meaning when they can discuss improvements in real time. Tools such as wikis and some productivity applications allow teachers to track changes and watch the progress of individual students in the process.

Connectedness

Digital learners understand the connected nature of people and ideas. Almost anything is within reach. Even adults subscribe to the Six Degrees of Separation theory, which according to Wikipedia is "also referred to as the 'Human Web.'"

> [It] refers to the idea that everyone is at most six steps away from any other person on Earth, so that a chain of, "a friend of a friend" statements can be made to connect any two people in six steps or less.

Young people see that everything is connected; anything worth learning happens interactively, and other people are both their sources of information and their audience in a networked world. In describing his theory of connectivism, Siemens (2004) says:

> A network can simply be defined as connections between entities. Computer networks, power grids, and social networks all function on the simple principle that people, groups, systems, nodes, entities can be connected to create an integrated whole. Alterations within the network have ripple effects on the whole.

What this means for educators is that using students' a priori knowledge is a powerful way to present new content. Linking new information to what students already know to connect past, present, and future concepts gives them a sense that everything and everybody are connected somehow. Using familiar technology tools—with their webs of people and information—makes it just that much easier to reach students, using how they learn to impact what they learn.

Communities of Learners

Although young people use social networks to interact on a personal level, schools can tap into the phenomenon for student learning and professional development. Learning communities are spaces that serve as electronic communities of practice where you find groups of people who have a common topic or theme for learning and who deepen their knowledge and expertise by interacting on an ongoing basis. Schools can create communities of learners in which students' tools, work, peers, and audience are all in one place. Using content management systems or server-based applications, districts can combine lessons, tools, and assessment with a single interface. Communities of learners can also exist at a distance with students, tools, and experts online, accessible either asynchronously or in real time.

Convergence

Of the many definitions of convergence on Wiktionary, the one that offers the best insight into the future of tools is "a trend where some technologies having distinct functionalities evolve to technologies that overlap" (http://en.wiktionary.org/wiki/convergence). How this evolves may be that an individual's browser window or personal start page is the basic element and all applications are contained within it simultaneously as needed. Thus, the user could search for information or e-mail someone from within a collaborative document and include the results, answer, and other information by cutting and pasting.

Similarly, the future will lead to a convergence of skills for students and teachers. For students, the distinctions between basic and higher-order thinking skills will become true digital-age skills in which the ability to analyze and synthesize information, for example, includes the ability to read and comprehend complex ideas or perform mathematical computations as needed.

Educators will similarly demonstrate a convergence of content information, teaching ability, and knowledge of how to integrate technology. For example, the TPACK (Technological Pedagogical Content Knowledge) model of integration emphasizes the intersection of technological knowledge, pedagogical knowledge, and content knowledge. Mishra and Koehler's (2006) framework:

> emphasizes the connections, interactions, affordances, and constraints between and among content, pedagogy, and technology. In this model, knowledge about content (C), pedagogy (P), and technology (T) is central for developing good teaching. However, rather than treating these as separate bodies of knowledge, this model additionally emphasizes the complex interplay of these three bodies of knowledge. (p. 1025)

Contextualization

Much of school learning has been in discrete segments, for example, history divorced from literature. Thus, students do not put the bits of information together to make sense of the world. They can memorize and take tests; they can perform tasks; but the mark of true education is when students can understand new knowledge in the context of what they already know and apply it in new situations. The web, with its ability to link objects and ideas, has the potential—perhaps using tagging and metadata—to allow students to gain the context and perspective of what they learn. Thus, for example, they could see history and literature linked by timeline, topic, theme, or other area for study.

Cloud Computing

The advancement in complexity of computing services and the increase in the need for storage have led businesses, government agencies, and even school districts to outsource services such as data management for greater efficiency. The servers that house the data are all online rather than on site. It is not a great leap from back-office outsourcing to server-based applications for classroom use. Some districts are employing low-cost netbooks with Web 2.0 applications that offer free tools for student learning. Students can use these online applications, store documents online, and find lessons and other students online. The potential, if everything is fully integrated, is that districts will be able to provide an immediate picture of student learning.

Cost-Free (or Almost Free)

Teachers and students have come to expect Web 2.0 tools to be free. In some cases, the tools replace the high cost of licensing software such as applications for word processing, spreadsheets, and presentations. In other cases, new tools are available that don't exist in any other format and so students can learn in new ways with them. Some ask if anything is really free or if there isn't always a cost somewhere to someone. It can be argued that using open-source software for operating systems means requiring staff to train, upgrade, maintain, and troubleshoot. Yet the alternative comes with a cost as well. And many of the tools need no more support than any other software.

Chris Anderson (2009), senior editor of *Wired* magazine, argues that in today's online world, free really is free. He says:

> This triple play of faster, better, cheaper technologies—processing, storage, and bandwidth—all come together online, which is why today you can have free service like YouTube—essentially unlimited amounts of video that you can watch without delay and with increasingly high resolution—that would have been ruinously expensive just a few years ago. (Kindle Location 1249–1253)

things to watch out for

Clearly, today's students live in a world of interactivity and connectedness. They use tools to interact with information and others and to connect the dots of multiple ideas until relationships are clear. So schools must provide the same opportunities as students have outside to engage them and to individualize learning or risk apathy. Anyone used to interacting with objects and others to get information on a daily basis cannot learn by sitting still and listening to someone at the front of the room spout facts.

However, there are challenges. With the proliferation of Web 2.0 tools, the bandwagon effect—in which people flock to the latest and coolest new application and the message to use it spreads virally—can happen before there's a need for the tool, especially in classrooms. The applications are fun to use, the phenomenon of being an early adopter who finds and recommends a tool is exciting, and the novelty of being able to share with the community quickly can delay deeper thinking about a tool's significance for learning.

With the drive to focus on using tools for student creativity, too many opportunities to be pseudo-creative exist. Unfortunately, social software can redefine creativity to be less about originality and more about opportunity. Students can adopt a mixed-tape approach, adapting content from other sources, rearranging the material, and displaying and disseminating it as their own. Similarly, collaboration means combining the peer-reviewed best work of all team members, not allowing the strongest to do the most work. Among the challenges for teachers is creating lessons on intellectual property rights, copyright, and plagiarism to help students understand the ethics of creating digital works. In addition, teachers should focus on teaching media literacy so that students understand such issues as fact versus opinion, multiple sources, accuracy and reliability of information, and narrowcasting.

Educators have to address other questions too. For example, while recent surveys show that students are still ahead of teachers in using the tools, what happens if some students relish using the tools and displaying their work publicly and others don't? Similarly, what happens when students tire of using the tools, and technology no longer serves as motivation or a way to engage reluctant learners?

professional development and leadership

There's a clear distinction between the ways in which teachers and students are comfortable with new technologies. Even where Web 2.0 tools are in use, the percentage of teacher users remains small. According to Dean Shareski (2009), digital learning consultant with the Prairie South School Division in Moose Jaw, Saskatchewan, Canada:

> [T]here is a very small percentage of teachers in my district that have made significant strides to adapt their classrooms to meet the changing needs of our students. ... It's a reality that exists mostly because of an outdated educational system and lack of leadership and political will to make meaningful change. In addition I think our district has a higher proportion of teachers moving in new directions than most. But it's still small.

Yet there are tremendous benefits for educators who use the tools for professional development. They will find a community of other educators online. They can create a network of these educators to share with and learn from and can build a personal learning network to turn to regularly. Online, they have access to best practices and the leader/practitioners and models that can show what strategies make a difference, and they can learn where and when to use them.

The elements that could bring about change are professional development and leadership. Given time, teachers will find their own advantages in learning to use the tools and integrate them into curriculum. A 2009 survey (Bialo & Sivin-Kachala, 2009) conducted by Lightspeed Systems and netTrekker, as part of their *Safe Schools in a Web 2.0 World Initiative*, states:

> The most often cited reasons for adopting Web 2.0 technologies were addressing students' individual learning needs, engaging student interest, and increasing students' options for access to teaching and learning. (p. 1)

Progress is happening in some districts. Bialo and Sivin-Kachala (2009) state that teachers are the key to using digital multimedia resources, online learning games and simulations, and teacher-generated online content; and students are driving the adoption of social networking and student-generated online content. In addition, administrators as well as teachers and students must be on board. The Consortium for School Networking (CoSN) conducted a study (Lemke & Coughlin, 2009) of school district administrators and released the report, *Leadership for Web 2.0 in Education: Promise and Reality*, which found that administrators "understand the significance of Web 2.0 for teaching and learning, but the actual use of Web 2.0 to improve the learning environment in U.S. schools is quite limited" (p. 14).

Although administrators are positive about the impact of Web 2.0 and believe that keeping students interested and engaged is a top priority for its use, they currently limit access to the tools. Thus, "The use of these tools in American classrooms remains the province of individual pioneering classrooms" (Lemke & Coughlin, 2009, p. 11).

New Web 2.0 tools emerge all the time, and those educators at the cutting edge will find them, test them out, and spread the word about the useful ones to colleagues, who will further refine the list of what works for their students and under what circumstances. At some point, use of these tools will reach critical mass as they become increasingly easy to use, transparent, and an essential component of schoolwork. Educators will use sound pedagogical judgment to determine which tools—web-based and traditional—are best to use for student learning and when and how to use them.

purpose of this book

Our first book, *Web 2.0: New Tools, New Schools*, presented an introduction to the Web 2.0 concepts and explored why it is important to use web-based tools. In the few years since the book was published, the world and the web have changed. This book explains how to use the most educationally sound tools we have available now and discusses where we are going with using web capabilities for learning in the future. It also provides explanations, tutorials, and activities to help you get started now and ideas about what you and your students may be able to do in the future.

Using web-based tools is not second nature to many educators. Some were trained to be teachers before the web existed. Others can use web tools for personal tasks but haven't learned how to incorporate them into teaching. Other reasons why online tools aren't in wider use exist as well. If these tools will make a significant difference in student learning, their use must be widespread. Thus, one purpose of this book is to provide a practical guide to integrating Web 2.0 tools into the classroom. Another purpose is to show-case teachers who are using Web 2.0 tools. In the chapters on the major tools, Chapters 1–8, we cite examples from the web and from a 2009 survey we posted online to collect information for this book. (Those examples are cited in the text as electronic communications.) In addition, we invited educators to write analyses of the tools they use. The result is Chapter 10.

Tried and True Tools

In Chapters 1–8 we will explore the top tools as they exist today. These are blogs, microblogs (Twitter), podcasting (and vodcasting), productivity applications (word processing, spreadsheet, presentation tools), social networks, video and photo sharing (visual learning tools), virtual worlds (Second Life environments), and wikis. In some cases, tools overlap categories because people use them in whatever ways work for them. Others prefer to adapt one tool to different activities rather than learn tons of different tools. So the chapters are not hard and fast categories but, rather, ways of explaining the most common tools and their uses.

Tools for Specific Tasks

Some of the tools we know as Web 2.0 applications are more limited in scope, yet they provide capabilities that really make a difference in classrooms. In our online survey of educators, some of these tools were mentioned often enough to warrant discussion about how to use them and how educators are employing them to enhance student learning. Chapter 10 will deal with these interesting applications that readers say make a difference to their teaching and to their students' learning. They include Google Earth, Wordle, Skype, Delicious, and more. Chapter 11 will provide information on an extensive assortment of Web 2.0 tools.

framework for chapters

Each chapter shares a common framework, one designed to make our explanations of using the tools clear and consistent. Borrowing from traditional journalistic terms, we focus on what, why, when, who, how, and where. We begin with *what*, the definition of each tool, and explain *why* it is useful. We discuss *when* teachers use the tool, whether for classroom integration or professional development, or both, and then provide examples of *who* is using the tools and in *what* way. Most of these examples are taken from our online survey of educators who wanted to contribute to this book. Because readers of this book may be teachers or technology coordinators and others responsible for helping teachers to use the tools, we include short tutorials, *how* to use the tools, to help you get started. Finally, we list resources so that you will know *where* to go for more information. Chapter headings are structured as follows:

- ▸ *What* is a … ?
- ▸ *Why* is … a useful tool?
- ▸ *When* do teachers use … ?
  - ▸ Classroom Integration
  - ▸ Professional Development
- ▸ *Who* is using … for teaching and learning?

> ▶ *How* do you get started with … ?

> ▶ *Where* can you find more information about … ?

where to next?

Predicting the near future is always risky, especially in print; but in Chapter 9 we offer you our vision of the direction the technology is going in and the implications of those changes for teaching and learning. We discuss the future of what we call Web X.0 (the "No-Number Web") and learning. The trend we see coming is the integration of tools for greater transparency and ease of use, using smaller devices for anywhere, anytime learning and more equitable access. The focus for students will be on finding, synthesizing, and analyzing information, then using it to create knowledge collaboratively and communicate the results—all online, as cloud computing. District operations will move to the clouds as well.

People describe the early web stages as Web 1.0, focused on finding and displaying information. Web 2.0 focuses on social networking. What's next? Web 3.0, a semantic web about data? Or Web 4.0, ubiquitous, personal, and connective? Or something else?

We predict that the capacities will overlap and consolidate. Let's say there are no Web X.0 numbers for these emerging technologies. The browser or personal launch page will be the base from which anyone can communicate with others; collaborate with a local team or remote group using text, images, video, and sound; work in real time or asynchronously; and find all the other capabilities they want at their fingertips.

To see where the web is going, think about how Apple's iPhone, iPad, or iPod Touch works: there are applications (apps) for everything. Some are free; some that you download to perform the functions you want have a small cost. The main features run in the background so that you can get a phone call or e-mail in the middle of playing a game or watching a video. Third-party developers create these apps, and people pick the ones they need or want. On April 23, 2009, with 35,000 apps available, says the *New York Times* Bits Blog, "One billion apps had been downloaded from app store in just 9 months"

(Stone & Wortham, June 8, 2009). And *PC World* says, "Less than two years after Facebook opened its website to external developers, more than 52,000 applications have been created" (Perez, 2009).

The point isn't the number of tools or where they exist now, but that in the future, students (with teacher guidance) will be able to find and use the kinds of tools that fit their learning styles. If they learn best using games, they will find math and science games that teach the topics and skills. If they like to drill to remember information for an exam, they can use flash cards and even study with someone across the country or around the world. If they want to demonstrate how to do something, they have a choice of writing a blog, preparing a slide show with photos, or creating a video. Or they might choose to use a combination of all the possibilities. The most important aspect is that the tools will be available on a small, lightweight device with constant web access.

The future web will have almost limitless features and functions available whenever a person wants, and they may be integrated rather than continue to be a collection of many tools to do discrete tasks. Students will take their tools with them on a small, lightweight netbook, handheld device, or cell phone and use them throughout the day.

What will be important for users, especially in teaching and learning? The web will be personal and individualized and allow for collaboration and communication as the primary features. It will consolidate, seamlessly, other web tools as apps, gadgets, and widgets so that using any of them will be transparent. It will be ubiquitous and portable and have metadata as its underlying organizing principle so that links among objects and ideas are clear. But there will be a great deal more about the future in Chapter 9. First, let's see what Web 2.0 tools are working now, where and how they are working, and how to get started.

Before we begin, we want to stress that tools are just ways of accomplishing what needs to be done. They may contain the elements of motivating students and keeping them engaged in work, but, ultimately, they have to pass the sniff test regarding how they impact learning. And while we talk about tools a lot in this book, the point is how they contribute to increased student achievement in learning both basic and advanced skills.

1

blogs

what is a blog?

Blog is a portmanteau of the words *web log*. It is a type of website developed and maintained by an individual using easy-to-use online software or a hosting platform with space for writing. Blogs feature instant publishing online and invite audiences to read and provide feedback as comments.

A blogger updates the page regularly with ideas, advice, suggestions, and other types of commentary. Entries appear in reverse chronological order, so the most recent entry appears at the top.

Blogs are primarily text, but they can include features such as videos, photos, charts, graphs, music, and other audio enhancements, such as podcasts. They contain links to other online locations and are often discussions of topics found at these links. Readers can write comments and engage in discussion with the blogger about the topic posted.

In the real world, blogs are extremely popular because they give a voice, platform, and audience to anyone who has an idea and wants to express it. Blogs have gained both respect and notoriety for such things as radical opinions, breaking news stories, insights into contemporary events and ideas, and political writing.

Educator-written blogs are often thoughtful, well-reasoned discussions of ideas. Because they are public, teachers who write blogs can gain a reputation as thought leaders and develop a following of other educators who read, think about, and comment on their posts.

Blogs offer considerable educational benefits for students as well. Because they are predominantly a written medium and are on public display, students have to learn to write carefully, think about their ideas, and communicate effectively.

Although having students communicate globally sounds beneficial, risks are involved; districts may want to use content management systems with internal blogging capability, or blogs designed specifically for education, such as ePals (www.epals.com), 21Classes (www.21classes.com), Class Blogmeister (classblogmeister.com), and Gaggle (www.gaggle.net).

why are blogs useful tools?

Blogs encourage writers and responders to develop thinking, analytical, and communication skills. Some characteristics of blogs make them excellent teaching tools.

Blogs are brief. They are usually relatively short posts of just a few paragraphs that are crafted to communicate an idea clearly and concisely. Because readers don't want to read long, rambling treatises on their monitors, students learn how to get to the point.

Things happen fast. Publishing is instantaneous. Students click Submit to see their blog online at once and feel that they've accomplished something. They can get feedback quickly, too.

Visual elements enhance them. Students can include images, video, and sound to enhance the meaning and to create and sustain interest. Blogs can link to other websites (and have them open in a new window) to provide more information, a related idea, or even a starting point for the writer's ideas.

Students become responsive to one another. Students think about their peers' ideas and ways of expressing them and then comment. Teachers can direct students to focus on the ideas or on the writing, or both. Thus, readers develop analytical skills and writers learn to be better writers and communicators.

The evidence exists forever. Blogs are stored online and remain as a portfolio of a student's ability to write, think, and communicate. Because they appear in reverse chronological order, the latest example is first. They are searchable, so refinements in student thinking can be identified.

when do teachers use blogs?

Classroom Integration

Classroom integration and writing instruction are natural uses for blogs. In the classroom, blogs are similar in concept to personal journal writing because they are often short, informal pieces of writing that can deal with personal topics and ideas. Even when they focus on serious topics, they are personal expressions of thoughts and ideas and contain opinion as well as facts. Although writing is most often the purview of English and language arts teachers, all subjects can involve written explanations of ideas and strategies. Blogging motivates students to tackle writing across the curriculum. The result can be that they think more clearly and organize their ideas more easily.

The difference between blogs and journals and essays lies in the public nature of blogging. With handwritten or typed journals, students write on personal topics and show selected entries to the teacher. With blogs, students write on topics—personal or assigned—with the understanding that a potential audience of at least classmates and parents, and possibly people from anywhere, can read it.

Their knowledge of an authentic audience means that students will work on their writing more than when the teacher is the only reader. In addition, their audience can engage with, and challenge, the blogger about the ideas presented using the comments box. Therefore, those ideas must be well reasoned. Teachers can use blogs for students to develop an ongoing conversation about a topic, theme, or concept.

The goal of writing teachers has always been to engender good writing habits in students. The writing process has been the traditional means to that end, and process writing involves engaging students in creating thoughtful expressions of ideas. The traditional steps include brainstorming, prewriting, organizing, writing, editing, and revising.

Brainstorming allows students to generate ideas around the topic and narrow the field to the most appropriate. Prewriting is guided discovery; students begin to focus on a concept and assemble ideas. Organizing involves formulating a central focus for writing and developing the details most likely to express that focus effectively. Writing is the main part of the process in that it means students explain the topic using the organization they developed and adding the details that make it clear and easy to understand. This part of the process also involves revising until a first draft is reached. Editing and peer editing refine that process even more; students learn to say what they mean by presenting it and getting feedback. The final step is to revise based upon recommendations.

The limitations of traditional tools have made the process complex, slow, and less than elegant. The nature of blogging changes the process; the tool's capabilities make it possible for students who engage in blogging to develop writing and thinking skills they couldn't achieve easily before.

Creativity

Freed of the constraints of solitary writing with the teacher as the sole judge of worth, students use blogging to post ideas that will be refined with the help of their peers over time because of the feedback loop possible with the comments feature. They can be creative when they know they can get feedback for their ideas and ways of communicating. They can use multimedia elements to enhance how creative the blog appears, with images, video clips, sound, and links.

Collaboration

One of the new skills students will need in the future is that of collaboration and the ability to work with colleagues to produce work that has shared authorship. Using the comment feature of blogging for peer review can help students develop the trust and ability to provide and accept constructive criticism in their learning community.

Communication

Blogging over time provides students with the ability to communicate effectively and to reinforce the experience. They share ideas and in the process must learn how to express them in exactly the words that their readers will understand. If they do not, peers will pose questions that serve to help them learn how and where to improve and refine their communication skills.

Connections

The public nature of blogs provides students with a wider world than the teacher as reader. Their audience can include people in the community and beyond and peers can be students around the world. Understanding that their words can have a global impact encourages students to hone the craft of writing.

Critical Thinking

Writing for an audience means thinking about the ideas first and then writing the ideas so that others understand what you mean. To accomplish this, students need to develop a logical set of facts, ideas, and persuasive arguments.

As always, putting ideas into words refines the writer's ability to think. Thus, writing is thinking critically.

Reading

Being part of a learning community in which students read one another's blogs adds the skill of information literacy: discerning fact from opinion, following the logic of others, commenting effectively, and being able to engage in well-reasoned discussions with others.

Digital Portfolios

Because blogs are archived, the audience—students, teachers, parents, and other readers—can review the change in thinking, analytical ability, writing style, and other intellectual development over time. Blogs can serve as digital portfolios of student work to demonstrate growth in skills of communication, collaboration, and critical thinking—all through a student's writing.

Professional Development

When educators write about their work or the ideas in education, they are performing reflective practice and developing their thinking about their craft. The audience becomes a personal learning community or network with whom they can share and learn and grow as practitioners.

English as a Second Language

Margaret McKenzie, district coordinator for English for Speakers of Other Languages (ESOL) for the Cobb County School District in Marietta, Georgia, set up a blog (http://flesolcobbcentral.typepad.com/esol) as a means of communicating with the more than 200 ESOL teachers and other stakeholders in the district.

> The blog allows me to not only post the official ESOL Department professional learning opportunities but [also] the latest news and research on strategies and resources for ESOL students and teachers. The blog assists me in helping teachers to be current in the ever-changing world of ESOL. (M. McKenzie, electronic communication, August, 2009)

The blog is a way to help teachers improve. The category "Strategies" provides information for teachers on current research-based strategies. The category "Spotlight" has teacher-submitted samples of successes. Some of the examples include student work. Says McKenzie, "It constantly changes as I learn more about what all of our teachers want and need."

Online Professional Reading Group

Susan Quinn, at C. M. Russell High School in Great Falls, Montana, started an online professional reading group (http://gfpsprg.blogspot.com) for teachers to use to get recertification credit. She posts links to articles on the blog and formulates discussion questions. Teachers read articles, mostly focusing on school reform, and discuss them online.

The district did not have any online professional development (PD) in place, and Quinn would often hear teachers complain that they could not find PD that fit their schedule. So she lobbied to try an online option. She read through the articles and formulated questions to pose for discussion. She tried to create questions that force teachers to examine their own practice and discover how the concepts in the reading can be immediately applicable in the classroom.

> Teachers really appreciate not only the flexibility of this option but also the other benefits of online learning—differentiated processing time, sharing ideas with colleagues they wouldn't normally see, and time to process professional literature that might otherwise be overlooked. (S. Quinn, electronic communication, August, 2009)

who is using blogging for teaching and learning?

At-Risk High School Students

Cindy Jones Woods-Wilson worked with high school teachers and students as part of her PhD study of blogs as learning tools in a high school science class for at-risk learners. She set up the blog for students and assigned e-mail pseudonyms as log-ins to avoid any of the usual boy/girl social interactions. This took place with 11th graders at Ponderosa High School in Flagstaff, Arizona.

Three times a week, for 45 minutes each time, and for five weeks, the students responded to a prompt she had posted. She kept track of where the teacher was in her curriculum, and the prompt was based on the curriculum students were learning. The prompts were posted the night before they were needed.

The students said how much the chance to "talk" about the topics anonymously helped them learn. In addition, the anonymous blogging provided a tremendous learning experience. The girls liked that they had a chance to "speak" without embarrassment. Several of the "oh-so-quiet" boys wrote the same. The teacher was amazed at the learning (C. J. Woods-Wilson, electronic communication, 2009).

Language Arts/Journal Writing/ Making Connections/Reader's Response

Lauren Kelley, from John Wallace Middle School in Newington, Connecticut, wanted to give her students a real-world platform from which to support their state testing and district curriculum, with an emphasis on making reader-to-text connections. She also wanted a way to infuse technology into the classroom in an innovative, fun way that would motivate students. To accomplish this, computer resource teacher Terri Buganski helps Kelley's students participate in a Reader Response blog using 21Classes (www.21classes.com).

The students are put into groups of three or four within which they share their thoughts and opinions. Each student reads a different novel. The groups' membership changes every two weeks. This allows for increased social interactions among all the students. The students are required to have at least four entries and four comments based on their peers' entries.

Each student's posting is required to contain at least five "I" statements. This requirement is in direct alignment with state testing and the curriculum. Students are asked to make connections with the book, the characters, the setting, and more. Kelley says, "This activity impacts learning because our students are not only more willing, but also more excited to express their ideas using this type of platform."

The students respond very positively toward this activity. They express excitement about using technology to interact and communicate with their peers. According to Kelley, "It has been such a success in this one class that my other class is already buzzing about wanting to participate in blogging" (L. Kelley, electronic communication, August, 2009).

Spanish Independent Reading

Carmen Maria Villalta Ochoa, from the Academia Britanica Cuscatleca in Santa Tecla, San Salvador, uses blogs with her sixth and seventh grade Spanish and humanities students for diary entries and independent reading reports to discuss their work and be involved more in the subject.

Independent reading is part of students' daily assignment; they read for the first five minutes and when they finish each book, they write about it and others have a chance to comment on what they say and add more if they have already read it. Villalta Ochoa says, "We have had good results as more are reading the books they have commented about and they are continuously writing their comments" (C. Villalta Ochoa, electronic communication, August, 2009).

Eleventh Grade Health Unit on Child Development

Fern Entrekin, learning technologies coordinator, and Dusty McMillan, health instructor, from Milton Hershey School in Hershey, Pennsylvania, created a blogging activity for their 11th grade health education students' unit on Child Development and Parenting. Students visit a Head Start class for children aged 3 to 5. In the past, they wrote a paper about their visit. Now, they write a blog to allow other students, their peers, instead of just the teacher, to share their observations and provide feedback. They use the school's eSchool Builder course management program for privacy and security. The object of the activity is to encourage discussions surrounding physical, social, linguistic, and emotional development of children newborn to age 5.

The students blog about what they learned about child development firsthand by interacting with 3-year-olds. Both the visit and the blog are real-world experiences, and students take ownership of their own learning. They were given directions on how to navigate to, and create, their blog and then respond to classmates' blogs.

Blogs are a 21st-century method of communication. When students know they are writing for an audience wider than just their teacher, they tend to be more thoughtful about their writing. In addition, we felt it was important for our students to learn and recognize the difference between a social blog and a professional blog. Students were encouraged to use academic writing and part of their grade depended on the use of correct grammar and spelling. (F. Entrekin, electronic communication, August, 2009)

Students observed the children and discussed what they had learned from the experience. For example, one of Entrekin's students wrote about the two children she spent time with: "One was all about action and being active and the girl just wanted to be calm and talk and play with instruments. I'd never figure that I would learn so much from two kids I've never met before."

Compiling Research for a Project

Instead of taking notes on note cards or in spirals for their sophomore research paper, Melissa Lynn Pomerantz's students at Parkway North High School in St. Louis, Missouri, make their entire process public through blogging. The project is created online, and the information-gathering aspect using blogs is unique.

Pomerantz's reasons for doing research with blogs include

- An organizational strategy (through tags)

- An easy way for formative assessments (if I have their notes, they don't have them to work on)

- An interactive format (students and others can comment on blogs, providing encouragement, incentive, and direction)

- An easy way to check electronic sources (students link to all electronic sources in blog post)

- An effective way to share sources with other students (hyperlinks)

- An effective way to create a class community that is also a part of the larger world community

(M. L. Pomerantz, electronic communication, August, 2009)

Students blog about their research using one blog post per source. They take notes; use meaningful tags to help them organize; and practice summary, paraphrase, and direct quotation. They evaluate their sources and their findings and apply those findings to their central research question. They read their classmates' posts and comment on them, making suggestions for connections and other readings through hyperlinks, asking meaningful questions, and offering insightful questions. Adult volunteers comment on the blogs, and students respond to the comments, engaging in an academic discussion with people outside of their class and school.

Pomerantz finds major impacts on learning, including

- ▶ Engagement: students are excited to get feedback from others on their work

- ▶ Community building: students work together for a common goal and are happy when they can help other students

- ▶ Accountability: students know their work is available for anyone to see and so take more pride in it

- ▶ Ethical researching: students know they are linking to the original material, so cutting and pasting is not an option

(M. L. Pomerantz, electronic communication, August, 2009)

Science: Save an Animal

Kifi Kanagy's fourth and fifth grade students at Grandview Elementary School in Windsor, Colorado, use a blog for a project on animal extinction. This is the question they have to address: If we are only allowed to save one endangered animal, why should we save your animal? They had to write a paragraph explaining their position and providing compelling arguments. Their classmates provided many replies to each other's blogs (K. Kanagy, electronic communication, August, 2009).

Geography: Travels with Kyle

Sycamore Creek Elementary School in Raleigh, North Carolina, has a blog for their mascot, Kyle the crocodile, and his family of stuffed toy crocodiles (www.kylecrocodile.com). It is used to expose students to the world outside of their immediate surroundings.

Teacher Matthew Clobridge explains this is a year-round school, so at any time one-fourth of the students and staff are on break and can take Kyle, Kirby, Katie, or Carlyle Crocodile with them on trips. Students have shared their travels to many places around the world. One crocodile has been stationed with a helicopter pilot in Iraq, another is on a trip through Asia with a FedEx pilot, and one went to the presidential inauguration.

Students are asked to take pictures and blog about their trip. They also ask questions about the location of their trip for students back at school to research and post on the blog. Students back at school respond to the blog post through the comments, or they work as a class with their teacher to answer the questions as a class.

> Before taking the crocodiles on a trip, students are provided with a "croc care" sheet that explains what they are to do while on their trip. We try to ensure that no matter where the crocodiles travel, there is an educational benefit to it. (M. Clobridge, electronic communication, August, 2009)

how do you get started with blogs?

Creating a blog is relatively simple. We've included the six steps to creating a blog using Blogger, along with a screen capture of the start screen.

1. Go to Blogger (www.blogger.com/start) and sign in (Figure 1.1).

2. Fill out the form with your contact information.

3. Name your blog (you can change this later).

4. Enter a blog address (URL).

5. Choose a template (you can change this later).

6. Write your first ever post (you can delete this later)!

► **Figure 1.1.** Blogger start screen, www.blogger.com/start

Five Rules for Blog Commenting

Commenting on someone else's blog post is simple: read the post, write your comment, type your name, and click Submit. Doing it well takes practice.

❶ Read the blog post carefully.

❷ Consider its strengths and weaknesses.

❸ Start with the strengths.

❹ If you have something nice to say, say it—and give specifics.

❺ If you have criticism, say it nicely. (Constructive criticism is helpful, not vindictive.)

Six Assessment Points for Student Blogs

❶ How well did student writing address the curricular topic and/or discussion theme?

❷ How well reasoned was the logic of what students wrote?

❸ How well developed was the writing?

❹ To what extent was their writing analytical about the topic?

❺ How well did they communicate their thinking?

❻ To what extent did their blog generate real discussion?

Starting Over

IF YOU'RE NOT HAPPY with your blog, you can delete it and start a new one later.

A Word about RSS

RSS (Really Simple Syndication or Rich Site Summary) is a way to get regularly changing web content delivered rather than going to individual sites. Bloggers, websites, and other online publishers syndicate their content as RSS feeds. Readers subscribe so that they can use an RSS reader to get the content they want regularly.

Blogger Jim Hollis writes:

> How does [RSS] apply to education? Well, motivation is a key ingredient in learning and we, as educators, should do whatever we can to try to increase intrinsic motivation in learning. If we acknowledge that choosing "what" we want to learn and "when" we want to learn it are two factors that increase intrinsic motivation, what can we do to increase the positive influence of these two factors in the classroom? (Hollis, n.d.)

For example, Mary Schwander at New Hope-Solebury High School in New Hope, Pennsylvania, has students gather resources for a research assignment. In the process, they subscribe to RSS feeds on their topic so that they are updated as new information becomes available. Mary writes:

Using databases subscriptions, students assign RSS feeds to certain keyword searches. It helps them in gathering resources and is much like having a personal librarian helping them to get information. (M. Schwander, electronic communication, August, 2009)

where can you find more information about blogs and blogging?

Blogging Tools

Blogger (Google):
www.blogger.com

Bloglines:
www.bloglines.com

Blogspot:
www.blogspot.com

CoverItLive:
www.coveritlive.com

LiveJournal:
www.livejournal.com

TypePad:
www.typepad.com

WordPress:
www.wordpress.com

Blogging Tools for Education

ePals:
www.epals.com

21Classes:
www.21classes.com

Class Blogmeister:
www.classblogmeister.com

Gaggle:
www.gaggle.net

Information

7 Things You Should Know About Blogs, EDUCAUSE Learning
Initiative (2005):
www.educause.edu/ELI/7ThingsYouShouldKnowAboutBlogs/156809

Education Blog Directory:
www.blogged.com/directory/education

Blogs in Plain English:
A video for people who want to know what is important about blogs:
www.commoncraft.com/blogs

2

microblogs—twitter

what is a microblog?

In the annals of advertising lore, products whose names become the generic term for a category enjoy tremendous branding and promotion opportunities. In the world of microblogging, or sending short messages quickly to multiple readers on various devices, Twitter has become the generic term. It is a cross between blogging and text messaging with a character count limitation.

Twitter is a free microblogging service that allows its users to post comments of up to 140 characters, called tweets, and read the tweets posted by others. Its power to connect people makes it a social network, and its word limit means that people must make their ideas clear and concise. Users can write anything as long as it falls within the 140-character limit. The prompt for each message is "What are you doing?" People have generated creative shortcuts to communicate well beyond text messaging codes and employ services such as TinyURL (www.tinyurl.com) to abbreviate long links into ones that leave room in the 140-character limit to say something about them (Figure 2.1).

People follow others by reading one another's tweets. They can make their tweets available to anyone, limit their audience, or make messages private. They have control and can decide who should follow them. Users can log in to send and receive tweets on the Twitter website or use the communications protocol Short Message Service (SMS) on any mobile device that has web access to e-mail, texting, or instant messaging.

Twitter has taken off in all directions, proving its worth in sales, marketing, customer service, public relations, even nonviolent ("velvet") revolutions. In particular, we saw its communication potential expand when Iranians were protesting election fraud in 2009. Twitter worked because it operates differently from other web-based tools.

> [P]eople can use [Twitter] to communicate with each other from a multitude of locations. ... You do not have to visit the home site to send a message, or tweet. Tweets can originate from text-messaging on a cellphone or even blogging software. Likewise, tweets can be read remotely, whether as text messages or, say, "status updates" on a friend's Facebook page. (Cohen, June 21, 2009)

Twitter advocates often turn to online applications and desktop clients such as Twhirl (www.twhirl.org), Twitterific (http://iconfactory.com/software/twitterrific) for Macs, or Twitteroo (http://rareedge.com/twitteroo) for PC users to view tweets rather than rely on the Twitter site. Many more third-party applications and add-ons exist, including some that allow scheduling of tweets. Examples are Twuffer (www.twuffer.com), SocialOomph (www.socialoomph.com), and FutureTweets (www.futuretweets.com). Because Twitter has a flexible architechure, add-on applications can include additional

▶ **Figure 2.1.** ISTE's Twitter account

features well beyond the basics of Twitter itself. For example, Twhirl is a desktop client that shortens long URLs (using digg.com, bit.ly, snurl, twurl, or is.gd); displays notifications for new messages; connects to multiple Twitter, laconi.ca, Friendfeed, and Seesmic accounts; cross-posts updates to Jaiku, Facebook, MySpace, LinkedIn, and other social network services; and auto- matically finds tweets mentioning you, noted by @username.

why is twitter a useful tool?

Twitter has become a popular tool for educators to connect with one another to get advice or information quickly, share points of view, or just stay in touch. Although the messages are short and sweet, the power is in how it connects individuals and enables educators to assemble a group of people to turn to for instant advice and leads on where to get needed information. Even the short statements that do no more than let others know what one is doing helps people get to know those in their personal learning networks.

Jon Orech in "Why I Tweet" (2009a) blogs about the reasons he twitters:

> I cannot tell you how much I have learned and been able to
> share since joining Twitter. ... If I need materials or a question

answered, my PLN (Personal Learning Network) is right there. …
There are stimulating discussions … Also, whenever I have a new
blog post, I can post it on Twitter, and be sure to get constructive
feedback from colleagues … I am content with using it as a means
to connect with people whose opinions and ideas I value.

While Twitter is popular with educators, some are also using Edmodo
(www.edmodo.com), a private communication platform designed specifically
for teachers and students to share notes, links, and files. Teachers can send
alerts, events, and assignments to students and chat with individual students,
groups, or the whole class. Educators can set privacy controls and use a public
component that allows them to post items to a public timeline and RSS feed.

Eldon Germann, a Canadian educator, uses Edmodo to create assignments
and share files with students as well as for class instruction, discussion, and a
digital sharing forum. Students embed video, audio, files, and messages. Two
similar tools that educators use are Posterous (www.posterous.com) and Plurk
(www.plurk.com).

Posterous is a simple blogging tool for users to post text, photos, and other
media by sending an e-mail message to post@posterous.com. The service
processes and posts that information. It handles multiple image uploads and
can syndicate posts to Facebook, Twitter, Flickr, and other sites.

Plurk is another free social networking and microblogging service that claims
to be "a social journal for your life" so that users can share information with
"friends, family and fans." Updates are visible on a timeline on the user's
home page and sent to other users who have signed up to receive them. Users
can respond to other users' updates from their timeline through the Plurk
website, by instant messaging, or by text messaging.

Teachers can search for one another by name, e-mail address, or location; or
they can choose from the extensive lists of educators arranged by interest on
the Twitter4Teachers wiki (http://twitter4teachers.pbworks.com). You can
add people whom others find interesting and create an online community
of people who share such things as subject area to create a personal learning
network. In practice, many people use Twitter to share news, link to interesting articles and ideas, point to their blog posts, inform about online events,
and promote themselves as thinkers.

web 2.0 wisdom

Nine Reasons to Twitter

Laura Walker

1. **Together we're better.** Twitter can be like a virtual staffroom where teachers can access in seconds a stream of links, ideas, opinions, and resources from a hand-picked selection of global professionals.

2. **Global or local: you choose.** With Twitter, educators can actively compare what's happening with others on different continents. GPS-enabled devices and advanced web search facility allow searches that tell you what people are tweeting within a certain distance of a location, so if the other side of the world isn't your bag, you can stick with your own patch.

3. **Self-awareness and reflective practice.** Excellent teachers reflect on what they are doing in their schools and look at what is going well in order to maintain and develop it, and what needs improvement in order to make it better. Teachers on Twitter share these reflections and both support and challenge each other.

4. **Ideas workshop and sounding board.** Twitter is a great medium for sharing ideas and getting instant feedback. You can gather a range of opinions and constructive criticism within minutes, which can help enormously, whether you are planning a learning experience, writing a policy, or putting a job application together.

5. **Newsroom and innovation showcase.** Twitter helps you stay up-to-date on news and current affairs, as well as on the latest developments in areas of interest like school leadership and technology.

6. **Professional development and critical friends.** One of the best things about training days is the break-out time between sessions, when teachers can get together to talk about what they are working on or struggling with. Twitter enables users to have that kind of powerful networking capacity with them all the time. It's just a matter of finding the right people to follow.

▶▶▶

▶▶

7. **Quality-assured searching.** Trust the people you follow. Hone and develop the list of people whose insights you value. Once your Twitter network grows past a critical mass, you can ask them detailed questions and get higher-quality information back than a Google search would generally provide.

8. **Communicate, communicate, communicate.** Expressing yourself in 140 characters is a great discipline. You can become better at saying what needs to be said in my professional communications with less waffle and padding (even without txtspk).

9. **Getting with the times has never been so easy!** Twitter is anything but complicated! You simply visit Twitter.com and create your account. A little light searching using key words for your areas of interest will soon yield a list of interesting people to follow. There are plenty of websites offering advice on getting started and how to avoid a few common beginners' faux-pas. Your biggest challenge is likely to be getting twitter.com unblocked on your school network if your main usage will be at school.

Laura Walker is director of e-learning at a UK mixed secondary comprehensive.

when do teachers use twitter?

Classroom Integration

Although most educators who are on one of the microblogging sites use it to be in touch with peers, classroom uses are emerging as well. For example, the ability to feel connected can mean that students have a voice and an audience. They can reach out to others in their class, school, or community, or get answers from experts in their network. For students who are hesitant to write much, tweeting can provide an introduction to the power of communication and motivate learners to hone their writing skills. Writing fewer words to communicate a thought is harder to do than writing many words and requires thinking carefully about exactly what one wants to say.

No one wants to promote writing only short statements. However, students can start with something easy to handle: one thought in one sentence, then develop more sentences to build on that thought.

Students often think they don't really know enough to write for an audience. Using Twitter requires such short answers that students are more willing to write something, secure in the knowledge that they aren't allowed long answers. Getting their ideas down improves their confidence. Exchanging ideas with others and providing and getting feedback improves their confidence even more.

Interactivity is one way of engaging students and keeping them motivated to work. Twitter provides interactivity in that students can explain, clarify, and compare their thinking as part of a collaborative project. As they send tweets back and forth about the topic, they provide feedback to one another and are engaged in thinking analytically about the subject and explaining these thoughts effectively. Thinking and communicating promote increased understanding and remembering.

In addition, microblogging is ubiquitous because it makes use of the Short Messaging Service (SMS) on cell phones and other handhelds. Educator Doug Belshaw says:

> I think Twitter could be ideal for reminding students about homework, trips and such things, especially as they can enter their mobile phone number to be alerted when one of their "friends" updates their account. The advantage is that you don't need to know the phone numbers of students to get messages onto their device: they are the ones who authorize their mobile phone from the website and they subscribe to your Twitter feed. (Belshaw, February 15, 2007)

In some schools, a system of advisories, home bases, or student groups monitored by a caring adult provides the support for students emotionally for the years students are enrolled. In such an environment, Twitter can be a useful tool to reach out to trusted peers. Students can identify who should receive these messages.

Professional Development

Educators connect with one another using microblogging's short, quick message system to ask questions and share information. For example, tweets such as Wesley Fryer's May 14, 2009, "Can you recommend some software to use for e-portfolios?" gave him a place to start looking for products with the knowledge that each answer was a recommendation (W. Fryer, electronic communication, August, 2009).

Similarly, Miguel Guhlin tweeted that same day, "ARRA Ed-Tech Grant Opportunity—July 9 Deadline http://tinyurl.com/of293r" to provide valuable information to the community (M. Guhlin, electronic communication, August, 2009).

Jon Orech in "Why I Tweet" (2009a) says that Twitter is a way to reach his Personal Learning Network:

> Last month my supervisor told me I needed to develop a card for teachers to learn to use Word '07 when we make the transition next year. Instead of reinventing the wheel, someone from Texas was right there. Another time, I needed help on using VoiceThread and another friend was there with answers and samples.

who is using microblogging for teaching and learning?

Although microblogging helps educators stay in touch with their personal learning networks, using microblogs for classroom use is an emerging application. Some early examples provide good models.

Gathering Real-World Data

In the first of "Twenty-Nine Interesting Ways to Use Twitter in the Classroom," Doug Belshaw, teacher and e-learning staff tutor in Doncaster, England, suggests that you "Put a shout out to your Twitter network for them to tell you (and your students) something" (Belshaw, 2010).

His suggestions include location for a geography lesson, temperature for science, an interesting historical fact, an opinion, or anything else. He says, "This makes learning based on up-to-date information and real people (with a real story behind it!)."

Students can also set up a learning network that is made up of anyone from classmates to others around the world to work on content. Geographical constraints limit the worldliness by preventing immediate responses from very distant time zones where peers may be asleep. Of course, it can work to advantage if answers to questions are requested from all ends of the earth to prove a point.

For example, you can use Twitter to help your students gather data. You can put out a call for your followers to tweet one piece of information specific to their location. You might ask for the price of milk or other staple, the temperature at a specific time of day, or other data. You'll have to wait 24 hours if you want to collect this information from around the world.

In math, if you ask about an item that can be purchased, you could convert the answers from the local currency to dollars (or the reverse) where needed, create a chart, and compare the costs of the item around the world.

In science, if you ask for the temperature at a given time, your students could convert all the answers to Celsius or Fahrenheit, create a chart, and look for the location on Google Earth to decide what season it is in the responders' locations.

GeoTweets: Inviting Your Network into the Classroom

Tom Barrett, a teacher in Nottingham, England, has been using Twitter for classroom activities in math and geography. For his math lesson on probability, Tom asked teachers on Twitter to provide a word or two to tell his class about the probability that it would snow the next day and to say where they are located. He linked the responses he got to a world map to help students see that technology can bring us into direct contact with a range of people from around the world (tbarrett, 2008a).

The children had been using the words "certain, probable, possible, unlikely, impossible" to describe their statements. Tom asked them to position "1 in 4" or 25% on their own scale and to give a word that best describes the chances of snow where they were.

Barrett says:

> A few moments before the children came in from lunch, I asked my network to challenge the children to find them in Google Earth, to search and discover their location from a few scraps of info via Twitter. Well, the challenges rolled in and in a couple of hours we had 25 different people to track down. As you can imagine we had lots of fun exploring the world and the real time challenges from real people—that is the power of bringing Twitter into the classroom. The children's efforts were driven by a real purpose and I always think that with such a context, we focus on the learning going on, not just the tool. (tbarrett, blog post, 2008b)

Twalter-Egos

Alan Parkinson, curriculum development leader at the Geographical Association, Norfolk and Sheffield, England, created fictional characters in Twitter that could be used as an educational resource. He says:

> As my Twitter alter-egos, I have come up with the phrase "twalter-ego" to describe them. … The idea is to build up a character profile over time before "releasing them" on the students, who could then be asked to engage with the characters in a number of ways. (Parkinson, blog post, February 21, 2009)

The sequence of activities was to

- ▸ Go through previous tweets and collate information on the background to the characters

- ▸ Prepare questions to ask them

- ▸ Suggest the next few weeks' activity that might happen

- ▸ Create some new interactions between the characters that have been mentioned so far

- ▸ Produce a resource that the character could have created for a particular audience and shared via a social web tool

- ▸ Write a letter to/from the character on a related issue

- ▸ Create a new character who interacts with the character that has been created: a neighbour/colleague/relative (depending on the nature of the original character)

(Parkinson, 2009)

Six Tips for Classroom Microblogging

1. Establish goals for the project.

2. Explain the concept of microblogging.

3. Practice brevity.

4. Pick a topic that is simple enough to communicate in 140 characters.

5. Time your tweet so that there is enough time to gather answers before you need them.

6. Display the answers in a Twitter client to avoid seeing tweets on other topics.

Tweetstory

Kevin Mulryne, e-learning specialist at National College for School Leadership in Coventry, England, suggests Tweetstory in Slide 4 of "Twenty-Nine Interesting Ways to Use Twitter in the Classroom" (Mulryne, 2010). Tweetstory, he says, is "great for editing skills, story structure, etc." He asks, "Where will your network take the story?"

Mulryne explains how to set up a Tweetstory in a few short steps:

- ▸ Choose your theme and genre (fairy tale, sports story, adventure, etc.).

- ▸ Create a standard story opener and tweet this to your network.

- ▸ Ask your network to continue the story in tweets, collaborating with the previous tweets and following them via Twitterfall (www.twitterfall.com) or a trending hashtag ("#tag").

Students follow the tweets, choose the best ones, and edit them into a coherent story.

how do you get started with twitter?

Go to Twitter.com and click Join for Free. Type your full name, a username (it will check for availability), a password, and an e-mail address. You'll have to type in the captcha code word (the strangely written word that people can decode but computers can't), and click Create My Account.

Click on Settings. Create a profile and upload a picture (optional). Also optional, check the Protect My Updates box so that people won't be able to read your tweets unless you authorize them.

Send people to your Twitter page: twitter.com/username. Send a tweet by typing in the What Are You Doing? box at the top. You can use up to 140 characters. Your latest post will appear at the top of your page.

Add people: Log into your account, go to a person's Twitter page, and click Follow. (Use the search box on your page to find people.) Read the tweets of people you've added on your page. See who others are following by moving your mouse pointer over the pictures in the sidebar on their pages. You can click on the pictures to go to their pages and add them to your list. (They will be notified.)

where can you find more information about microblogging?

Sue Waters's wiki with information about using Twitter:
http://suewaters.wikispaces.com/twitter

Are You Twittering? Here's How I Use Twitter, by Sue Waters:
http://theedublogger.edublogs.org/2008/04/02/are-you-twittering-heres-how-i-use-twitter/

Twitter4Teachers:
http://twitter4teachers.pbworks.com

22 Ways to Use Twitter in the Classroom:
www.ideastoinspire.co.uk/twitter.htm

Twitter Handbook for Teachers, by Tomaz Lasic:
www.scribd.com/doc/14062777/Twitter-Handbook-for-Teachers

podcasts and vodcasts

what are podcasts and vodcasts?

Have you listened to a broadcast of your favorite television show on your iPod? Have you longed for the opportunity to revisit a favorite television program from the 1980s? Want to listen to a weekly travel show with Rick Steves? Planning a trip to China and want to listen to an expert historian talk about the country's history? Or perhaps you are looking for gardening tips. With a few simple clicks, you can download an audio file (a podcast) or an audio-video file (a podcast or vodcast) that meets your interests or needs at the very time you want it. There are many directories of what is available: PodcastDirectory.com (www.podcastdirectory.com), Podcast Alley (www.podcastalley.com), and iTunes (http://itunes.com) are just a few examples.

Definitions

A **PODCAST** is an audio or video netcast (streamed or non-streamed).

A **VODCAST** is a video podcast.

Wikipedia's definition clearly indicates the audio *and* video capabilities of a podcast: "A podcast (or netcast) is a series of digital media files (either audio or video) that are released episodically and often downloaded through web syndication. The mode of delivery differentiates podcasting from other means of accessing media files over the Internet, such as direct download, or streamed webcasting. A list of all the audio or video files currently associated with a given series is maintained centrally on the distributor's server as a web feed, and the listener or viewer employs special client application software known as a podcatcher that can access this web feed, check it for updates, and download any new files in the series. This process can be automated so that new files are downloaded automatically."

Although the technology has been available for as long as the Internet has been around, it really began to catch on in popularity in the early 2000s. The most common audio file format used is MP3 or MP4. For a simple video explanation, visit CommonCraft's "Podcasting in Plain English" (http://commoncraft.com/podcasting). One podcast site (podcastalley.com) reports statistics (as of August 2009) regarding the numbers of podcasts as 66,088 types of podcasts, a quarter of a million comments about podcasts, and more than 4 million unique podcast episodes. This site also has users vote and then highlights the top 10 podcasts each day, as well as the 5 newest ones as they are posted. Interestingly, the word podcast was named the New Oxford American Dictionary's Word of the Year in 2005! By the way, you can receive a Merriam Webster's Word of the Day by podcast (www.learnoutloud.com/Podcast-Directory/Languages/Vocabulary-Building/MerriamWebsters-Word-of-the-Day-Podcast/19450).

Podcasts can be differentiated from regular MP3 files by virtue of their ability to be syndicated. This is referred to as Real Simple Syndication (RSS). This involves special client software the user installs, often called podcatchers (for example, Apple's iTunes), that automatically searches for and downloads the new files you have specified. Once these files are on your computer, or other device, you can use them offline when you are ready to use them. You also can retain them for as long as you choose.

A vodcast is a video podcast; in essence, it is an on-demand production that contains video and audio information. These can be downloaded as a file, or received as streaming video, delivered live as they are being produced.

why is a podcast a useful tool?

Your class may be participating in an Antarctica adventure in which scientists post podcasts as events occur. Your students may be following the scientists as they track animals and gather flora and fauna from the frozen environment. You can set your podcatcher to check for new postings routinely, and then it will alert you after each new adventure has become available. This of course saves considerable time and effort; you no longer have to check each day for new and appropriate materials.

The possibilities are truly endless in society these days; many people, including ourselves, pursue their interests and entertainment through podcasts on a daily basis. Interestingly, educators have discovered endless uses for education, too, and podcasting has become one of the most frequently used Web 2.0 tools.

when do teachers use podcasts?

While the use of podcasts has been very popular for purposes of entertainment, educators soon began to see value for teachers and their students as well (Lum, 2006). Podcasts are now being used at all levels of education, from preschool through higher education (Harris & Park, 2008). The best news is that podcasts really are simple to create or use, and have provided teachers and students with a tool that is user-friendly, flexible, and convenient. Students are able to create podcasts to demonstrate their understanding of material, present research, and express their points of view.

Classroom Integration

Educators are using podcasts and vodcasts in many ways. First, they take advantage of the huge number of prepared and freely available "casts," on a wide variety of subjects, for professional development and curriculum integration. Second, many teachers are now moving to the next step and are finding ways to have students at all levels demonstrate their knowledge, understanding, and questions by creating their own podcasts and vodcasts. Many schools that in the past may have had student-developed, -created, and -produced news shows have moved those shows into the digital age by creating them as pod- or vodcasts. Family members can stay up-to-date and involved by means of these tools.

Of course, students have been producing audio programs for generations, typically using tape recorders or reel-to-reel machines. What makes podcasts better, educators say, is that they are easier to edit than splicing a tape because they are recorded digitally on a computer. Perhaps the biggest difference, though, is that podcasts are available to a worldwide audience. Anyone anywhere can subscribe to them and have them automatically downloaded to their computers when a new installment is posted.

In general, Harris and Park (2008) identify four uses of podcasts. "Teaching driven" allows educators "to provide a repeat or summary of a lecture given and also to provide timely academic material, such as law-related news" (p. 549). "Service driven" offers the opportunity to provide detailed information to families and others by offering podcasts on policies, events, or student academic activities. Podcasts can also be useful as "marketing tools" to promote the school or district to potential students, or for parent to take a virtual tour of the facilities and community. "Technology-driven" podcasts refers to the ability of teachers to assist with instruction about podcasts and not examine podcasts' effectiveness in any of these uses.

Students investigating, designing, creating, and teaching: what could be more educational or valuable to our students? Three unique ways of using podcasts in the classroom have emerged. First, many prepared lessons and support for lessons exist for students of all ages and in all content areas. Teachers of very young children can find podcasts of stories, dramatic events, musical instruments, art, and information on science experiments. All are readily available.

An enormous number of choices can be found at Kids Podcasts website (http://kids.podcast.com) and fit into a planned curricular unit. For example, elementary students at Willowdale Elementary School in Nebraska create podcasts for kid-to-kid learning of literature, geography, and math, with such titles as "Did You Know?" and "Vocabulary Theater" packed with grade-perfect learning. Students can hear about Revolutionary War history from fellow fifth graders (http://millard.esu3.org/willow/radio/listen.html). Or they can listen to National Geographic's introductions to the orangutans of Borneo or the penguins of Antarctica (www.nationalgeographic.com/podcasts) or a 60-second science tidbit from Scientific American (www.sciam.com).

The Science Show for Kids provides five-minute audio podcasts on burning science questions through iTunes.com. Bookwink (www.bookwink.com) provides video booktalks (3 minutes each) about new books for Grades 3 through 8. And Storynory (www.storynory.com) offers podcasts of familiar stories (*Jack and the Beanstalk* or *Little Red Riding Hood*) as well as less familiar ones. Happily, these stories come with full English text so that beginning readers or English language learners (ELL) can see the words as they are spoken. The Inkless Tales Podcasts for Kids (http://inklesstales.wordpress.com) provides retelling of familiar and ethnically diverse stories. For example, in the well-known story *Princess and the Pea*, the princess is rather passive. In the new version on this website, she is filled with spirit and is active.

Other examples abound. Podcast tours are available for museums, battle-grounds, and other important locations. The Blazing Guns and Rugged Hearts podcast, created by the Kansas Historical Society (www.kshs.org/audiotours/blazingguns/tours.htm), prepares those students lucky enough to visit this location and provides information to those who are unable to take a tour. Or perhaps your students would like to take a real tour of Gettysburg National Military Park (www.nps.gov/gett/historyculture/gettysburg-podcast-tours.htm) or the Smithsonian Museums (http://museumpods.com/id31.html).

Poetcasts bring poetry to anyone who wishes to learn how to enjoy this literary form (www.learnoutloud.com/Podcast-Directory/Literature/Poetry), and Learn Out Loud writing (www.learnoutloud.com/Podcast-Directory/Education-and-Professional/Writing) helps writers in a wide variety of activities. Classical music podcasts are available to introduce music in a fun and engaging manner; these could easily be used as signals to transition from one activity to another (www.npr.org/rss/podcast/podcast_detail.php?siteId=14946301). Are you looking for math or science or geography? Podcasts on these content areas, and more, are all easily found from national content organizations.

Students are now becoming the creators of their own learning through their own design and development of podcasts. Podcasts have changed the ways in which educators conceptualize their content and pedagogical strategies. For example, Jonathan Bergmann, from the Woodland Park School District in Colorado, reports completely redesigning his chemistry course with the use of podcasts.

Why would a teacher want to use podcasting as a teaching tool? Research has shown that active writing, with an authentic audience, makes learners more committed to their activity, more engaged, and more willing to revise their work (Dalton & Proctor, 2008; Jenkins, Clinton, Purushotma, Robinson, & Weigel, 2006). With a podcast, writing can include images, spoken words, and written texts. It can also include moving images if the creation is a vodcast. Learners are then able to share what they have created and demonstrate their understandings of the content. It also requires that the students plan, organize, rehearse, and then produce their podcast, which also requires using effective oral presentation skills. The Very Spatial Geography Site (http://veryspatial.com) also offers podcasts to make geographical events (for example, natural disasters) useful to non-geographers.

When you let students create their own podcasts, you do want to make sure that they are safe. One site, kid-cast.com, calls itself a kid-safe place. It prides itself on safety, on allowing children to create their own podcasts, and on giving them a voice of their own. Each upload is rated: E for everyone; E10+ for those 10 and older; T for teens; and T16+ for those over 16. Each podcast sent to the site is reviewed to make sure the content and the rating are appropriate. Kids.podcast.com is another site for students to create their own podcasts. Some are in languages other than English, which is also a way to incorporate English language learner (ELL) strategies into your classroom.

Creating podcasts is not limited to learners of a certain age. At the Point England School in New Zealand, they have been creating podcasts since 2005. Their first program was called Korero Point (Pt.) England, or KPE; and since that time, they have gone on to win the ComputerWorld Excellence Award, in 2006. Most of their creators are between 9 and 11 years of age, and they use their podcasts to let people throughout the world know about books written by New Zealand authors (http://tamaki.net.nz/index.php?family=6,41,1456, 1471,2936,3021). All their podcasts and vodcasts are archived and serve as models for others who are getting started.

The potential of students making their own podcasts has recently created a new interest in using cell phones in the classroom, rather than just automatically banning them. Using students' cell phones, podcasts can be created and uploaded, certainly with oversight from the teachers. Andrew Trotter (2009) reports in *Education Week* that some classes are allowing the use of cell phones so that students can use their personal cell phones to make podcasts, as well as to take notes and maintain a school schedule. This is one possible way to reach a true 1-to-1 access for all learners.

Finally, podcasts are being used to expand and extend the notion of school. One school, Empire High School in Vail, Arizona, provides students with computers, and the students get their lessons, do their homework, and listen to podcasts of their teachers' lectures. At Cienega High School, also in Vail, students who have their own computers are able to take digital sections of traditional required classes, such as English, history, or science.

Professional Development

Thousands of educational opportunities exist for professional development, and it is best to consider them in two different ways. First, educators tend to be lifelong learners. They value learning and continually improve themselves in current events, in global issues, and in just learning about the world in which we live. They are also responsible for staying current in their content areas. Thus, on a personal level, podcasts offer an opportunity to improve their knowledge about a wide range of topics.

Educators, like others, are using podcasts to learn languages, history, music, and more. Some find them on noneducational-specific places such as Digital Podcast (www.digitalpodcast.com) or iTunes (www.apple.com/itunes/), where they find topics of interest to themselves, of course. In addition, educators are finding podcasts to be a source of incredible opportunities to improve their professional practice, no matter where they happen to live. Professional development on demand is an extremely popular resource for busy teachers!

Perhaps the most well-known educational source is The Education Podcast Network (http://epnweb.org), where one can find an enormous array of information. Their website states their mission and goal: "The Education Podcast Network is an effort to bring together into one place, the wide range of podcast programming that may be helpful to teachers looking for content to teach with and about, and to explore issues of teaching and learning in the 21st century." They appear to accomplish this. Want to learn how to teach with a Smartboard? Listen to information on using the tool effectively (http://epnweb.org/index.php?request_id=2024&openpod=7#anchor7). Interested in improving your students' literacy skills? Listen to the Creative Writing podcast (http://epnweb.org/index.php?request_id=1401&openpod=4#anchor4). Are you curious about ways to encourage your learners to take an interest in renewable energy? Have we found a podcast for you (http://epnweb.org/index.php?request_id=3056&openpod=9)! Another type of program offers support for using technology, effective teaching, and learning with ICT in the primary classroom (http://epnweb.org/index.php?request_id=409&openpod=1#anchor1).

Another organization, Russell Educational Consultancy and Productions (Recap), has set itself the goal to collect, verify, and make publically available a wide variety of professional podcasts (http://recap.ltd.uk/podcasting). For example, http://recap.ltd.uk/podcasting/colleges/ offers links to a number of university podcasts. The Imperial College of London (www.imperial.ac.uk) provides information on solving world hunger, Nobel lectures, updates on China, and many more (http://recap.ltd.uk/podcasting/colleges/imperialcollege.php). Or you can visit the Bowdoin College Music Department (http://academic.bowdoin.edu/music) and listen to famous music programs and interviews with conductors and performers, or revisit old masterworks (http://recap.ltd.uk/podcasting/colleges/bowdoinmusic.php). Recap also has a blog for those who want to talk about their use of, and recommendations for, podcasts (http://recap.ltd.uk/podcasting/weblog/blog.html).

Fordham University has long supported a Podcast for Teachers website and now that has evolved into The Teachers' Podcast (www.teacherspodcast.org), Figure 3.1.

The Teachers' Podcast is hosted by Kathy King and Mark Gura. Here you can find podcasts of interesting articles, discussions of all things educational, and a way to subscribe to their future podcasts. You also have access to archives of

▶ **Figure 3.1.** The Teachers' Podcast homepage

past years' podcasts. One of the benefits of this network is the current events and timely podcasts. For example, as soon as California education leaders began to compile digital resources, they had links to that information. This site also has links to webinars that are readily available.

Siobhan Curious's blog (http://siobhancurious.wordpress.com/2009/01/11/ listening-and-learning-mark-smilowitzs-classroom-teaching-podcasts/) heaps high praise on one type of professional development podcast. The blog states:

> The Classroom Teaching podcast is the work of Mark Smilowitz, a Judaic Studies middle school teacher, originally American, now working in Israel. Each podcast explores a nugget of educational theory, replete with concrete, everyday examples drawn from Smilowitz's and others' classroom experience. Smilowitz's clear, friendly, and no-nonsense tone makes you want to be a teacher like him before he's said more than a few sentences. And although he's talking about teaching students younger than mine, in an educational context very different from mine, I'm finding his mini-essays on classroom management, student questions, and, especially, the role of the teacher very inspiring and reassuring. (S. Curious, blog post, January 11, 2009)

Another educator, Steve Decker, offers a website, Teaching for Today: Educational Insights with Steve Decker (http://web.mac.com/stevedecker1/ educational_insights_with_steve_decker/Welcome.html), which also includes podcasts. He states, "Educational Insights is a program intended to promote and enhance educational methods and instructional practices. Teachers, aspiring educators, and parents will hopefully be inspired by program content."

A PBS station, WETA, produces Reading Rocket, a popular show that teaches students to love reading, and helps them learn. To support teachers learning how to teach reading, they post pod- and vodcasts online for teachers to watch experts (www.readingrockets.org/podcasts/classroom) provide strategies, examples, and experiences. These can be used with preservice teachers, as a professional development activity for a school, or for a teacher to review alone. Titles include The ABCs of Teaching Reading, Classroom Strategies, and more. The ESL Teacher Talk podcasts assist teachers of students who are learning English by offering interviews and strategies from experienced teachers, and it is available through iTunes or www.ESLteachertalk.com.

In addition to learning from podcasts, educators at all levels are using podcasts for communicating with various audiences. Podcasting thus offers school districts the potential of expanding knowledge in the areas of instruction, curriculum, parental engagement, and distance driven instruction. For example, one podcast is Eric Langhorst's "Speaking of History" podcast (http://speakingofhistory.blogspot.com). This eighth grade American history teacher from Missouri routinely creates episodes about history and social studies. The goal is not only to extend his students' learning beyond the classroom, but also to be a way of reaching out to parents and families. Even more exciting, the students are the ones who author and produce these podcasts that their families can then enjoy.

Teachers are not the only educators using podcasts for professional development; they are also tools for school leaders. Michael Waiksnis, principal at Sullivan Middle School in South Carolina, writes a blog about his uses of technology in his capacity as a school leader (http://edleaderweb.net/blog). He states:

> Podcasting—This is another way to communicate with your
> school stakeholders. I have a principal's podcast. The audience is

still growing and I plan on continuing it this year. To gauge the amount of interaction, I always include a trivia question for a small prize. We always get parents calling in, so I know someone is listening. There are many direct uses of podcasts in the classrooms as well. I have seen them used as a culminating activity on a research project. I have seen them used in conjunction with photo story. There are many other uses as well! (M. Waiksnis, blog post, August 10, 2009)

who is using casts for teaching and learning?

Debbie Prunty and Jean Nelson, teachers in the Oconomowoc Area School District of Oconomowoc, Wisconsin, have their students create a vodcast on a current event in the news. They report that 80% of the lesson is really the research and writing; the other 20% is the creation of the vodcast by recording, adding graphics, and then publishing it in the correct MP3 format. Their students develop their story as a news report and must include the background, data from a survey or interview if appropriate, and their own opinion on the topic.

DreamExtreme Podcast (www.dreamextreme.us/podcast) is an amazing podcast produced by sixth graders in David Cosand's Kennedy Elementary class in Medford, Oregon. The students plan and produce full podcasts covering class news, movie reviews, fashion, sports, and more. And in June 2009, 16 pupils at Chepping View Primary in High Wycombe, Buckinghamshire, England, won a national radio award for their podcasts.

Brett Moller's 21st Century Education podcast (http://blog.brettmoller.com) is an exemplar of the way in which his students have entire language units created around the design, editing, and production of episodes for seventh grade learners. Turkey Foot Middle School in Kentucky has student-created math podcasts to assist learners (www.myteacherpages.com/webpages/SDue/podcasts.cfm), and the TIE network under the auspices of Georgia Public Broadcasting (www.tienetwork.org/component/option,com_remository/Itemid,0/func,select/id,46/) offers student-created podcasts.

Sue Palmer (www.classroom20.com/profiles/blog/list?user=hkn1p2e92if4) reflects on her use of podcasts in the classroom. Earlier in 2008 she asked for examples of podcasts on the classroom 2.0 Ning. One respondent discusses the ways that students are required to create podcasts and make them available (www.ahs.osd.wednet.edu-a.googlepages.com/podcasting). The respondent said:

> I teach high school. The school I teach at uses independent learning plans so students do this on their own. I have them do a 30-second movie review using Audacity and then they do a commercial and then they do something of their choosing. I also signed up for a Grand Central (it's free) http://grandcentral.com telephone number and you can post podcasts through a phone right to Blogger and other web pages. My web page www.ahs.osd. wednet.edu-a.googlepages.com/podcasting has some really good examples, resources. (Brenda, blog comment, March 27, 2008)

And Matt Montagne, who works at the Castilleja Independent School in Palo Alto, California, has his students create radio broadcasts. He reports:

> The purpose of our student radio show is to give the students the opportunity to interact with a global audience. Our live radio shows are broadcast twice a month and are also recorded and posted online as podcasts. All radio broadcasts are done from our homes, with students connecting via Skype. In many cases our guests are bridged in via cell phone/Skype out and a new platform called "HiDef Conferencing." We also have several planning sessions each month and these are done from our homes as well. By connecting with guests on various topics our students are exposed to a variety of viewpoints and perspectives that they would not get from traditional mediums. They're also learning how to collaborate and interact with people across the U.S. and the world. Of course they're developing presentation skills, writing skills, collaborative writing skills, teamwork, etc. My role in this project is simply to be a conduit for the students. I have a deep network of educators/individuals across the globe, and I tap this as a tool to connect the students with them. Search the iTunes music store for, "Gator Radio Experience" and you'll

see the body of work that the students have created. Visit http://gatorradio.blogspot.com for more information on our project. (M. Montagne, electronic communication, August 2010)

how do you get started with casts?

We recommend getting started creating your own podcasts and then bringing in the students to create curricular activities that include them. One place to start is About.com's "How to create your own Podcast" (http://radio.about.com/od/podcastin1/a/aa030805a.htm). It will walk you through the steps regardless of the type of computer or software you are using.

You will want to learn the following steps:

1. How to record your audio and save it to an .mp3 file

2. How to create an RSS file that holds the "directions" for sending your file when a user's program like iPodder requests it

3. How to write the "directions" that are inside the RSS file

4. How to upload the RSS "feed" and your .mp3 file

5. How to validate that the file is written correctly and will send the file correctly

Specific directions are available at About.com: Radio (http://radio.about.com/od/podcastin1/a/blpodcast1hub.htm).

An innovative school in New Zealand has been involved in one podcasting project for some time. Dorothy Burt, e-learning facilitator, Manaiakalani, Auckland, has created a graphical representation (Figure 3.2) for thinking about the creation of podcasts, for you as the instructor or for your learners. KPE stands for Korero Pt. England, mentioned earlier in the book.

Listening
to podcasts

Publishing
the podcast

Reflecting
on podcasts

Editing
the podcast

**Podcasting with
KPE teaching
and learning
activities**

Reading
a book

Recording
the podcast

Summarizing
the plot

Rehearsing
the podcast

Writing
the script

▶ **Figure 3.2.** Creating podcasts (Korero Pt. England)

You may find the sidebar "Five Easy Steps for Creating Podcasts" helpful. You and your students may want to add to this list after you create your first set of podcasts.

One school district in Texas has a novel approach to teaching how to create podcasts. They asked teacher participants to bring 10 pictures representing themselves: their hobby, pet, places they like to go, food they like, favorite things, and so forth. They then asked them to make a podcast about themselves to post on their web page. The technology specialist, J. J. Pool, said, "This is how we taught them the process so they could use it in the classroom. We did it this summer in a one-day workshop for which they received a comp day during the year. To see one of these, go to www.hjisd.net and click on [Campuses, then] Sour Lake Elementary, click on Classrooms, then Third Grade, then Mrs. Britt. She has hers up and ready to look at."

Five Easy Steps for Creating Podcasts

Allisyn Levy

1. Have students write a script for their podcasts. This could be a rough outline or a multi-draft, finished paper, but it must show that the student(s) have thoughtfully planned out and practiced their podcast.

2. After approving their script, I teach students how to use a USB microphone and iMovie to record their podcast. I like iMovie because I can use it for an audio-only podcast or for video as well, and I'm able to hand over the editing to the students because of its ease of use. In iMovie, simply click on the Audio tab and use the record/pause button. Be sure your settings reflect an external microphone as your input if you are using one.

3. Have students take turns being the "audio engineer" and record themselves. This is a great way for them to hear their own mistakes or the quality of their voice, fluency, etc., and be self-motivated to improve. Once they have a recording they are happy with, save the file. We are ready to make any quick edits.

4. To edit a podcast, I teach students to focus on the beginning and ending of the podcast. They want to pad both ends of the recording with at least five seconds of silence. This applies to video recording as well. We can edit this down later, but it ensures that none of their words will be missed. It's also a nice place to add a bit of intro/outro music. iMovie makes it extremely easy to import music from a CD or from iTunes in that same Audio tab. Be creative!

5. Finally, once the students are happy with their podcasts, you can Export (now under the Share menu) your podcast and play it for the class, burn a CD, or post it online.

Allisyn Levy is the director of BrainPop Educators.

where can you find more information about casts?

An excellent resource for learning about podcasts is PoducateMe (www. poducateme.com/guide). This easy-to-use website provides clear information about finding and using podcasts. It also has detailed instructions about how to create and share a podcast, including a discussion on the types of hardware and software you might need.

Software Audacity Garageband Podguide Generator:
http://teachdigital.pbworks.com/podcasting

Tech Tutorials & Resources:
www.evalamar.com/tut_Podcasting.htm

Learn how to plan a podcast or vodcast for your classroom:
www.ehow.com/how_2029095_plan-podcast-class-lecture.html

Read an explanation of how to teach using Podcasts at Teach Digital.
Curriculum by Wes Fryer:
http://teachdigital.pbworks.com/podcasting

4

productivity applications

what are productivity applications?

If we asked you to name some of the things that computers help you do every day, you might talk about the types of things you could not do without their assistance. Asked what software you use the most, you might say word processing, spreadsheets, databases, presentation tools, and collaborative calendars. A large proportion of organizations and individuals choose to purchase these items as a suite of products created by the same company so that the software works well together in an integrated fashion. These products are of course available for both Mac and Windows platforms.

This chapter is devoted to introducing you to the same types of tools, and more, that are considered Web 2.0. In general, these tools mirror the typical productivity tools you have on your own computer, except that they are available for free, stored on the company's servers, and reachable by the computer owner or, for those with access, from any computer connected to the web. These tools have added advantages over the software on your computer in that they are stored securely online and only those invited to participate in a particular conversation or collaboration may do so. They are available from anywhere with an Internet connection, and multiple people can edit at the same time. Google Docs are tied to a Google account that is linked to a specific e-mail address.

If you asked 100 individuals what their favorite productivity applications online are, it is probable that there would be 100 different answers based entirely on what each person uses and likes the most. These tools typically include word processing, spreadsheets, project management, form generators, sketch tools, and presentations. While all of these are completely accessible from any browser, sometimes you also want to keep them on your own computer. Happily, you can also download your files to your own computer to keep, if you so choose. You and others can create something collaboratively and then publish these documents.

These tools have been termed the Get Things Done (GTD) tools! And any description would also include other tools, such as a calendar system, task management, project management, and to-do lists. Google Docs, for example, also has a wide variety of templates to get you started on many of the most common activities (http://docs.google.com/templates?category=7&sort=hottest&pli=1).

You can join more than three million viewers in watching a Common Craft video called Google Docs in Plain English at www.youtube.com/watch?v=eRqUE6IHTEA/. "Say goodbye to messy e-mail attachments" (Figure 4.1).

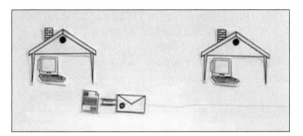

▶ **Figure 4.1.** Google Docs in Plain English

why are productivity applications useful tools?

The answer to this question is relatively simple: imagine if we took away, for a month, the traditional productivity tools that reside on your computer. You would have difficulty doing your job, conducting your personal and professional activities, and perhaps even staying connected with your support system. Let's consider one suite of these tools, Google Docs, because it offers the largest suite of tools currently available.

In addition to word processing, a spreadsheet and a presentation tool are built into the Google Docs system. But Google Docs does not stop there. You can also create a calendar (http://calendar.google.com). You can draw, create 3-D models, and more, with SketchUp (http://sketchup.google.com). You can have your favorite website, newspapers, and other locations bring you materials as they are updated in Google Reader (http://reader.google.com). You can conduct polls and create forms easily and for free, too (http://docs.google.com/support/bin/answer.py?hl=en&answer=87809). And Google Sites (http://sites.google.com) allows even beginners to create and publish websites.

Google Docs versus Zoho

Although Google is perhaps the most well known, there are other comprehensive programs. For example, Zoho (www.zoho.com) offers some of the same tools: word processor, spreadsheets, project management, presentation tool, and a poll tool. Many people find these to be less complex than the Google versions, but you will need to determine which are more comfortable for you and your students to use.

EduRatings 2.0 (http://er2.weebly.com) allows educators to rate the Web 2.0 tools, and it offers some interesting tidbits of information. Under the category of Office Applications (http://er2.weebly.com/office-applications.html), some 24 individuals have voted. Of those, 18 voted for Google Docs and 6 voted for Zoho (as of April 2010). One educator stated, "How did I function before Google Docs? I use it for everything—both as a personal tool, office productivity tool, and collaborative environment for student projects and web publishing." However, another educator disagrees: "The Zoho suite of applications is tops. It puts Google Apps in the shade for depth, breadth, and innovative features. The best parts for teachers and classes are the collaborative and sharing features."

Some More Useful Productivity Tools

Here are some examples of other programs that will help you grasp the wide variety of possible tools:

EditGrid (www.editgrid.com). This online spreadsheet allows real-time update and collaboration.

eFax (www.efax.com). Perhaps this is most helpful when you find yourself with e-mail but no fax machine or you wish to make something available to others. This program allows you to receive the fax through a temporarily assigned phone number. You can receive for free, but there is a small price for sending.

Gliffy (www.gliffy.com). Gliffy is a collaborative tool for creating graphical representations online and in teams. The products, charts, graphics, or diagrams can be published online.

Instapaper (www.instapaper.com). Instapaper is handy when you want to read something but are unable to do it at the time you come across the material (a web page or other document). Once you have registered, you will just click a "read later" button to be able to access it from your computer, a phone, or offline.

iRows (www.irows.com). This is another option for spreadsheets that can be stored online and collaboratively constructed. This tool does allow the creation of charts and saves in a variety of formats.

Mayomi (www.mayomi.com). This free flash-based mind-mapping tool, similar to Inspiration or Kidspiration, is a very good way to help students prepare to write a report or organize their information.

Scanr (www.scanr.com). Scanr is an exciting product if you happen not to have a scanner just when you need one. You can use your camera phone or digital camera. Imagine being at a library when you want to capture detailed information or a graphic.

SlideShare (www.slideshare.net). This service has two distinct benefits. First, you can go to the site and search for presentations that others have created on a topic of interest. It is an excellent way to get started learning about themes or content; once you join, you are also able to download some of the presentations. Second, you can post your presentations and then access them from any computer that is online. This makes it easy to create presentations as well as share and receive feedback.

Sproutliner (www.sproutliner.com). Sproutliner allows individuals or groups to create lists, tasks, and project management activities and keep track of who has completed their assignments.

ThinkFree Show (www.thinkfree.com). This is an exceptional Java-based presentation tool that feels similar to PowerPoint. You can create presentations and then show them, or even save them, to view in PowerPoint.

30 Boxes (www.30boxes.com). Simple, with a quick learning curve and sharing that is easily arranged, 30 Boxes might be the calendar of choice for your students. With this one, you can also include an RSS subscription to monitor items of interest or items you wish your students to hear or read.

YourDraft (www.yourdraft.com). If you are in a hurry and wish to draft a collaborative start or individual start on a paper or project, this may solve your problem. You can allow others to edit or just read your materials, and no registration is necessary.

More Reasons Why Teachers and Students Use These Tools

Imagine this situation: You and your colleagues create a paper, presentation, or report. You pass the file around, each adding the date or your initials, or both. After several iterations, you are not really sure which is the latest version, whose tracking or changes have been accepted and incorporated, or who has made the final decisions on the document. But assuming you end with the correct version, you show up with your thumb drive only to discover that the best version is not the one you have with you! The correct one is really on your home computer or on the thumb drive in your other coat pocket!

If this has happened to you, or you know someone for whom this occurred, you might begin to understand the lure of Google Docs. One of the authors was in this situation and instead of the above scenario used the Web 2.0 tools effectively. Four people who had never met created a slide show for presentation to an audience in the U.S. Senate building. Each person added her slides, made comments on them, checked for redundancy and adequate coverage, and then when the time for the presentation arrived, it was readily available online, in its final form. To be sure, each of us had downloaded the presentation and had it on a thumb drive, *just in case!* Had we been delivering the presentation online, we might have chosen to narrate the show; or if we had been delivering it live, the audience might have been able to simultaneously participate in an online chat. The potential is enormous.

Another reason for the enthusiastic embrace of these online productivity tools may be the fiscal reality. Schools often spend a significant portion of their technology budget on software and upgrades. Beyond the cost of the software itself, technical and professional development dollars must be expended with each software upgrade. With Web 2.0 tools such as Google Docs, these expenses are no longer necessary. The upgrades are automatic, and the end user is typically not even aware as minor changes are made. Everyone involved is using the same system at the same time.

Most of these tools also include protections and a high level of privacy. The creator of a document allows or invites others into the collaborative process as necessary. The control assures that no one sees a document until its authors are ready; or, conversely, drafts can be made public for comment and discussion across a wide group, if desired.

Educators have found that some things about these tools are not perfect. For example, some of the formatting is not as easy as in the commercial products. Also, as the teacher, identifying individual contributions of collaborative projects requires preplanning. Students may be assigned colors or taught to add their names so that their contributions can be identified. Although these are relatively minor issues, it is important that an educator preview the tools before planning a student project with them. One advantage is that there is a history of revisions so that teachers can see the changes over time since the file was created.

when do teachers use productivity tools?

Classroom Integration

Teachers and other educators have begun using these tools for a variety of activities, and as they become more familiar, they see other ways for students to benefit from them. In general, the goal and purpose has been to make public the types of development, creativity, and other activities that their students typically do individually. These tools have also afforded educators a way in which to promote and encourage collaboration authentically in the development of projects and papers.

On the Classroom 2.0 Ning (www.classroom20.com/forum/topics/wiki-or-google-docs) this appeared:

> My school has been using Google Apps for almost a year now, and we are really liking it. Docs are great for creating content with group members and getting feedback—the draft/brainstorm stages, while Sites have been great for "publishing" or displaying content and creating a showcase of learning. (Allison, blog comment, April 13, 2009)

Jill Malpass (http://jmalpass.blogspot.com/2009/03/using-google-docs-in-classroom.html) writes in her blog about the ways she has used Google Docs and says their school has accomplished many educational goals by getting started with the tools. She describes how her school received funds for a Web on Wheels (WOW) cart with 28 laptops designed to use Web 2.0 tools with learners. She got started in an interesting fashion.

> Ms. Pritchard created a form that she posted on her website for band parents to complete. It was a questionnaire regarding e-mail addresses and other contact information. I clicked on the link to the form, completed my information and submitted. I got a message that my information had been added to her spreadsheet. Instead of spending hours compiling a contact list from hand-written information, the band director created one form, added it to her website, and notified band parents to access the link. In essence the band parents collaboratively completed her contact list for her. This was amazing to me! I was instantly interested in finding out more about Google Docs. (J. Malpass, blog post, March 30, 2009)

She went on to explain that her use of the tools has increased. For example, she stated that for her, it "means that teachers can create short quizzes by using a form and posting a link to their website. Students can take the quiz by clicking on the link and signing into their Google account. When their answers are submitted, the teacher's spreadsheet will show the date, time, and username of each submission."

Ana Balboa-Guenthner (www.classroom20.com/main/search/search?q=Zoho+Writer) asked Kevin how he integrates science and technology with his middle school science students.

> This year I did a collaborative writing assignment with my middle school science class on Zoho Writer. Everyone contributed to an on going story about how to remember pi (3.14...) I taught them the Peg system to remember numbers by changing them to letter and words. This way, the students contributed to the story from home as an assignment.

> I also use WizIQ to tutor some of my students from home. I also tutor my MathCounts students on WizIQ as it has an interactive white board. I will be teaching a class on WizIQ next month on how teachers can use the Peg system in class. (Kevin, blog comment, May 26, 2008)

His goal of encouraging participation outside of the classroom is one that is shared by other educators who have come to depend on these tools.

One teacher, Graham Balch (http://graham.balch.googlepages.com/biology) described his use of Google Pages:

> I have used it as an online syllabus and as you can see all my lessons are online as well as my homework assignments. I also put my tests and quizzes on there (password protected) so that other teachers who use my website as a resource can also get the tests and quizzes once I give them the password. (Mr.Balch, blog comment, May 24, 2009)

Professional Development

Teachers are learning to use these tools in authentic ways. Susan Stein, Johns Hopkins University School of Education, reports using Google Docs in their graduate program in administration and supervision. She communicated with the authors (August, 2009) that "cohorts process information and post onto a common document for submittal to the instructor" routinely.

Ken Messersmith, University of Nebraska at Kearney, uses Google Docs with his teacher education students who are studying about classroom diversity. He described how he divides students into cooperative learning groups and has each group read a different book on the topic of diversity. Then using Google Docs they discuss their book for three weeks, and then they create a document to share with other students. He said:

> The collaborative nature of Google Docs allows the discussion to take on a chat-like character when two or more students are discussing at the same time but also allows asynchronous discussion to meet the varying schedules of students. (K. Messersmith, electronic communication, August, 2009)

Bruce White, Thames Valley District School Board, London, Ontario, Canada, provides professional development to teachers in his district. He uses Google Docs to prepare the workshop outlines and the content for the workshop and to modify the resources as the course is taught. Participants have access to the document and add to it as they use the resources. Teachers then use Google

Docs in their classrooms with their students. He also described a laptop project for which the resources, lesson plans, support, and training material are all posted to Google Docs. He reports that the teachers are very enthusiastic about their access and the ability to add to all professional resources.

Jennifer Weible, from the Punxsutawney High School, in Punxsutawney, Pennsylvania, uses Google Docs for creating group documents or projects, writing position papers on authentic learning problems, working with other teachers to plan inservice programs, creating strategic plans for the district, and working together on group projects for online classes.

Ms. Lyman, from William Tennent High School in Warminster, Pennsylvania, describes her school's use of Google Forms and states everyone "LOVED them!" They use the forms for feedback on professional development, questionnaires, and anything for which they need information that can be easily tabulated. She added, "One teacher is trying to get Google Forms unblocked for students to take quizzes from her Wikispace this way." Her story brought up an important consideration. In many districts the tools are automatically blocked from students; thus, their potential may not be realized. Ms. Lyman explained:

> I am trying to educate administration to realize that Google Docs is a wonderful way for students who have computers but may not have MS Office products to still use word processing and spreadsheet capabilities. I would like to see our elementary students use Google Docs in the classroom and then we begin teaching the MS Office suite in middle/high schools. Google Docs is a little less intimidating and they can use it at home if they have an Internet connection. (C. Lyman, electronic communication, August, 2009)

As an example of working with adult learners, Michael Wesch from Kansas State University describes his efforts to create a three-minute video (http://mediatedcultures.net/ksudigg/?p=119). He calls his project a video ethnography. The goal was to present information about how students learn and what they need to learn, as well as their goals, hopes, dreams, and what kinds of changes they will experience in their lifetimes. He used Google Docs for the students to write a survey for other students, and within a week they had 367 contributions to the document. The process would not have been possible without this type of shared brainstorming and editing. Ultimately, the entire class put together a video of the results of their survey.

who is using productivity tools for teaching and learning?

Productivity tools offer classroom teachers the potential for effective strategies. For example, global activities, which promote project-based learning and international perspectives, become easier when tools facilitate the conversations, collaborations, and interactions. It is worth considering that students have the possibility to develop their own authentic questions based on their interests about other cultures. There is also evidence that students become engaged when they share their work with other students who serve as a real audience. A wide variety of ideas for educational experiences are available at 4Teachers.org's Project Based Learning site (http://pblchecklist.4teachers.org/checklist.shtml). Clearly, finding the educational goals and purposes for using these tools will be the first step.

Michele Whaley, a teacher in the Anchorage, Alaska, School District reports on her use of Google Docs tools with her students:

> **Methodology training Google Docs.** Last year, a Russian teacher in Alaska and another in California encouraged their students to become acquainted over Google Docs. Both teachers wanted students to practice using the vocabulary to truly communicate with students who didn't know them. This year, a new project began. Students in three schools (an additional one in Moscow, and possibly two more in Siberia) are sharing pictures of their schools and comments about what is important to them at school. Again, the purpose is for students to truly use the vocabulary to communicate.

> **Skyping.** Teachers in the Anchorage area are gathering to learn a new methodology once monthly. Because we are so far from the experts, the experts are calling in on Skype. Being able to see the faces and hear questions on both ends makes a huge difference in the amount that we are able to learn.

Google Docs. Students honed their short passages about themselves so as to post them on Google Docs. By reading about the other students and directing questions to them, they were able to truly use the language for communication with others who didn't know them and who were interested in people from another area. The teacher has to present the vocabulary and help students to word-process their information. The teachers must also collaborate on the method, the rubric, and a schedule of connections so that students experience communication. I would be willing to share the original teacher agreement pages, as well as student work pages (no students are identified) and possibly a link to the virtual school photo essay document—it's still in progress. (M. Whaley, personal communication, August, 2009)

Beth Richards, Division of Accountability and Achievement Resources in New York, reports that students in her district are doing many activities using these tools:

Using 2.0 tools students can collaborate on projects. For example, students working in collaborative groups can prepare for a presentation. The students are more interested in the assignment. They don't have to find a home to work in, they can work at any time that is convenient, they can share ideas, peer edit work, reach out to other peers for assistance and submit to the teacher for review and comment. Students are more inclined to do the project because they are constructing their own knowledge, researching and developing ideas for a broader audience. Their work is done in an environment they are very comfortable in. (B. Richards, electronic communication, August, 2009)

Peg Weimer, from Paul VI Catholic High School in Fairfax, Virginia, described that in her school "Google Docs is used as both a collaborative tool and electronic storage. Students across the curriculum are producing digital photo stories to summarize information, construct meaning, teach a process, and create infomercials" (electronic communication, August, 2009).

Karline Clark, from Douglas High School, in Box Elder, South Dakota, described how she uses Google Docs with her high school students:

I set students into groups of three. Each group picked a topic of interest to research and present. Students set up a Google Docs and Presentation for their group; they collaborated to put their research, links, pictures, and URLs together. They then used Google Presentation to put their research into a presentation for the class. The best example was when a student that was home sick for the day collaborated with his group via the Internet to complete the project on schedule. It continues to grow and evolve every time I use it! (K. Clark, electronic communication, August, 2009)

Cheryl Lyman, from William Tennent High School in Warminster, Pennsylvania, has her students respond to articles and requires them to summarize and provide their opinion. Only students in the class can respond, and they may respond to each other's discussion. This opens the way for collaboration, and they are sharing these technology tidbits, something she says she does not have time to do in class each week. She summarizes:

While it has taken me a little bit of time to get this project moving, it has been VERY EASY and I am beginning to see myself as more of a facilitator to my students' learning while they are collaborators to each other and myself! It is exciting to see them engaged in their own learning—heads aren't down anymore and they are doing work outside of the school walls. (C. Lyman, electronic communication, August, 2009)

Tara Seale, a ninth grade English teacher at Bryant High School in Bryant, Arizona, reports on a day devoted to digital citizenship, netiquette, and the school's core values for ninth graders. She stated that the students meet in advisory groups and do some small group activities, then "break into groups around the core values and the students choose the Web 2.0 tools they want to use to send a message (movie, poster, comic, etc.). Google Apps drive the whole site and allowed us to receive feedback quickly and easily" (T. Seale, electronic communication, August, 2009).

Using the tools is not confined to traditional classroom settings. David Gibson, from Stowe, Vermont, describes the Global Challenge Award and his efforts to create global work teams of high school students. They create four student teams (two U.S. teams and two from outside the U.S.) that use a variety of tools to create a solution to global warming. Teams may submit their goals as either a global business plan or technical innovation plan, or they may just work on content "Explorations." These efforts are judged, and teams may earn letters, certificates, and cash or prizes. Gibson said, "The students form their own teams using a custom Web 2.0 application, then use a wiki-style content system, electronic portfolio, and a variety of tools such as Skype, SketchUp, Google Docs, etc., to perform the activity" (D. Gibson, electronic communication, August, 2009).

More information on Global Challenge activities is available at:

www.globalchallengeaward.org

www.globalchallengeaward.org/for_teachers.html

www.globalchallengeaward.org/display/public/Program+Overview

how do you get started with productivity tools?

We are using Google Docs as our example in getting started because it is the most popular, but also because the use of others will be very similar in terms of what you will need to do.

To begin your adventure of using online productivity tools, start by reviewing this PowerPoint presentation produced by Google Docs (http://docs.google.com/present/view?skipauth=true&id=ddnctvgt_170cbskvf68). Once you are ready to begin, there are a few steps to take.

First, you need to create an account for your classroom. Your students will need to have an e-mail address. If your school provides e-mail addresses all within the same domain name, then you can sign up as a team (www.google.com/apps/intl/en/business/). However, it does cost to use this method. Otherwise, you can sign up as individuals, again making sure that all your students have an e-mail address. Once you have the e-mail addresses, you simply create a Google account (Figure 4.2). Students must be 13 to use Google Docs at school. Additionally, you will want to start with your own account to gain familiarity with the tools. We encourage you and your colleagues to begin by creating documents and sharing them collaboratively with your department, team, or group.

Once you have your account, you can begin just as you would in a word processor. From a Google Docs list, you can select New and at that point you will be able to create a word processing file, a spreadsheet, or a presentation.

To share that document, you will click on the Share tab and enter the e-mail addresses of the individuals with whom you wish to share. These individuals do not have to have a Gmail account to receive your information, but to access the document they do need to have a Google account tied to a specific e-mail address. You can assign permission at two levels; someone can be a Viewer (where they can see the most recent version but they cannot make changes), or they can be a Collaborator (where they can have access to the most recent version and can make changes, and also view past versions). There is a 200-person limit per document (which does seem like quite a large number!), and there is a limit to how many individuals can be editing simultaneously. For documents and presentations, that limit is 10; for the spreadsheet, 50 can edit at one time. A document on how to use Google Docs was created using (no surprise) Google Docs (http://docs.google.com/View?docid=dcdn7mjg_72nh25vq). It provides some excellent information to expand your understanding about using these tools. You may also want to listen to a podcast, Google Docs in Education (www.twentyfortech.com/?tag=google-docs-in-education).

Figure 4.3 provides a view of the entry page once you have established a Google account. You can see all the things you can do from this screen.

Another excellent reason to use these types of systems is that they have an interface that is similar to the one many people are familiar with. For example, similar icons to commonly used word processing programs are used, and a mouse-over produces reminders for the icons. Figure 4.4 shows the familiar layout of the document toolbar.

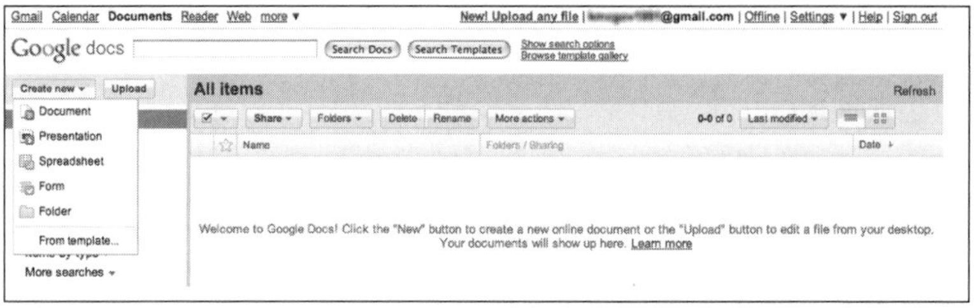

▶ **Figure 4.3.** Interface of Google Docs

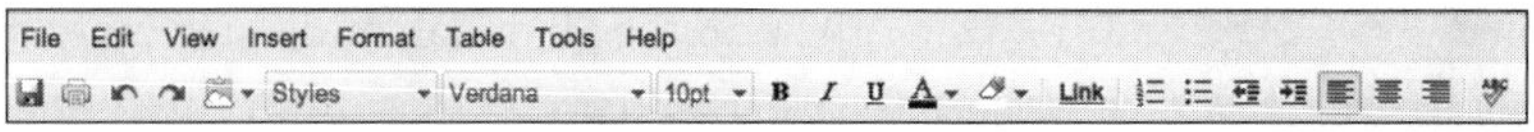

▶ **Figure 4.4.** Toolbar from Google Docs

where can you find more information about productivity tools?

Try this crib sheet for using Google Docs in education:
www.google.com/educators/learning_materials/WR_cribsheet.pdf

Watch a video on ways that teachers and principals are using Google Docs in their professional practice:
www.google.com/educators/p_docs.html

View this video of teachers and principals talking about Google Docs in education:
www.youtube.com/watch?v=TYPjJK6LZdM

Here's a tutorial on using these tools in educational settings:
www.youtube.com/watch?v=urrvY0YQWE4

Don't miss the Common Craft video on Google Docs:
http://vodpod.com/watch/497154-google-docs-in-plain-english

5

social networks

what is social networking?

Educators have always had communities of practice; in the past, though, a teacher's community may have been the teachers in a particular school, or all the math educators in a district. The point of communicating with others is to learn, develop, and expand all that we know; to share ideas and information; or just to enjoy social interactions.

One definition comes from Green and Hannon (2007):

> Social networking refers to the aspect of Web 2.0 that allows users
> to create links between their online presence such as a webpage
> or a collection of photos. These links may be through joining
> online groups or by assigning direct links to other users through
> lists of "friends" or contacts. (p. 13)

It is widely accepted that learning has a strong social component and that this learning often is situated in our relationships with others (Lave & Wenger, 1991). With the advent of electronic communications and communities, the possibilities have expanded so that people affiliate by interests, questions, or ideas rather than geographically or by happenstance.

Many examples of social networking are evident on the web. These include communities discussing medical issues, playing games, and planning a trip to the moon. Educators often engage in discussions about learning, pedagogy, curriculum, assessment, and standards. In fact, the web is filled with millions of individuals who are looking to meet others who share their interests and goals.

According to one explanatory website (www.whatissocialnetworking.com), some networking communities focus on particular interests, and others do not. The websites without a main focus are often referred to as "traditional" social networking websites and usually have open memberships. This means that anyone can become a member, no matter what their hobbies, beliefs, or views are. However, once you are inside this online community, you can begin to create your own network of friends and eliminate members that do not share common interests or goals.

Wikipedia says:

> A **social network service** focuses on building and reflecting of social
> networks or social relations among people, e.g., who share inter-
> ests and/or activities. A social network service essentially consists
> of a representation of each user (often a profile), his/her social
> links, and a variety of additional services. Most social network
> services are web based and provide means for users to interact
> over the internet, such as e-mail and instant messaging.

Some of the things that distinguish and support the way social networking works in this environment include the fact that comments or artifacts are tagged as a way to categorize content. Those tags can be created and managed collaboratively, and that adds to the collective development of knowledge. This system of classification is termed *folksonomy* (Wikipedia reports this term comes from *folk* and *taxonomy*) and is also known by the terms *collaborative tagging*, *social classification*, *social indexing*, and *social tagging*. Additionally, the possibility exists for the software to offer recommendations to individuals based on their usage, and people are able to identify so-called "friends," which then allows individuals to stay current with what those friends are doing or saying.

The concept and adoption of social networking has become so important that now institutions are creating courses on social networking and Web 2.0. What's interesting is that it's not just a presentation or learning event but an actual full course. One institution, the University of Arizona, will have its students learn about Web 2.0 products and social networking from a business standpoint to give leadership, communication, and community-building skills. But in establishing this course, the university's press release reports that the final project will have each student work with a separate group of students from a local high school to organize into micro-communities.

why is social networking a useful tool?

Humans are social creatures, and educators as well as students want to communicate with others. MySpace and Facebook are usually the first social networks people think of. Thousands of individuals have joined these networks from all parts of the world and all walks of life, and one can find discussions on just about any topic. The main types of social networking services are those that contain category divisions (such as former school-year or classmates), the means to connect with friends (usually with self-description pages), and a recommendation system dependent on trust. Popular methods now combine many of these, with Facebook widely used worldwide. Across the globe, other networks have emerged, too: MySpace, Twitter, and LinkedIn are the most widely used in North America; Nexopia is popular in Canada; and Bebo, Hi5, MySpace, and StudiVZ are used more in Germany. Others you may have heard of include Decayenne, Tagged, XING, Badoo, Skyrock, Friendster, Multiply, Orkut, Wretch, Xiaonei, and Cyworld. Each of these has people who are passionate about their particular service, but in general they all work in similar ways.

Not surprisingly, "Young people are in the vanguard of social networking practices" (Livingstone, 2008, p. 461). According to one report (ACMA, 2007), in Australia, in families with 8- to 17-year-olds, 72% of girls and 52% of boys had their own online social networking profile, and 42% said they had posted their own materials online. A study by the National School Boards Association (2007) explored the online behaviors of U.S. teens and tweens and found the following:

> 96% of students with online access used social networking tech-
> nologies, such as chatting, text messaging, and blogging, and
> visited online communities such as Facebook, MySpace, and
> Webkinz; 81% said they had visited a social networking website
> within the past three months; and 71% said they used social
> networking tools at least weekly. Further, students reported that
> one of the most common topics of conversation on the social
> networking scene was education. (p. 1)

Dodge, Barab, and Stuckey (2008) argue that they are analogous to

> third spaces … informal public spaces such as coffee houses,
> affording novelty, diversity, and learning. Unfettered by school
> protocol or family emotions, third spaces allow groups to meet in
> generous numbers, and while no individual constitutes the third
> space, close friendships can be developed unlike those found at
> home or school. (p. 229)

Educators have been reluctant to use social networking tools in the classroom, or to even encourage students to participate in them (Ferdig, 2007; Green & Hannon, 2007). Instead, the idea emerged that if individuals or groups of individuals could start their own social network, they might be able to better organize, protect, and define the goals of that "space." Thus, in 2005, Ning (www.ning.com) was started as an online platform for people to create their own social networks. The term Ning is Chinese for peace, and the number of Nings has expanded quickly. Many other educational social networking sites have also appeared; in general, they all share similar characteristics and features. These are some of the advantages of all social networking sites:

- Small groups can collaborate on projects.

- Students can post questions and concerns.

- The site can be used to retain teacher notes, videos, podcasts, and other classroom activities.

- Students who are absent can catch up on work.

- Students can develop, collaborate, and retain their own efforts over time.

- Access can be granted to families and others to share the information.

Other educational social networking examples abound. For example, Librarything (www.Librarything.com) is a social network of almost 1 million people who love books. Participants catalog their own books and are then connected to others, for conversation and recommendations, who read what they do. They call it the world's largest book club. Perhaps Rushkoff (2005) said it best: "It's the simplest lesson of the Internet … it's the people, stupid. We don't have computers because we want to interact with machines; we have them because they allow us to communicate more effectively with other people" (p. 74).

Tapscott and Williams (2006) summed up the nature of social networking:

> While the old web was about websites, clicks, and "eyeballs," the new web is about communities, participation and peering. As users and computer power multiply, and easy-to-use tools prolif- erate, the Internet is evolving into a global, living, networked computer that anyone can program. Even the simple act of participating in an online community makes a contribution to the new digital commons—whether one's building a business on Amazon or producing a video clip for YouTube, creating a community around his or her Flickr photo collection, or editing the astronomy entry on Wikipedia. (p. 19)

There are many ways that people are connected on social networking sites. Some sites use profile matching, which requires individuals to enter personal details that are either matched against the profiles of others or searchable by others. Some are personal networks that have shared contacts systems: databases of contacts and contacts of contacts. These are often geared to plain sociability (e.g., Friendster) or are for business contacts (LinkedIn).

One other type of matching is an affinity system that allows people to register their membership of groups. Thus, you may be a member of the 1989 high school graduating class from Thomas Jefferson High School, or you may be someone who worked at Apple from 1990 to 1995. Then, others who match those requirements can be found in a simple search on one criterion (Owen, Grant, Sayers, & Facer, 2006).

when do teachers use social networking?

Social networks have been focused on supporting relationships between teachers as well as between teachers and their students. Moreover, these networks are now used for learning, professional development of educators, and content sharing. A variety of sites have evolved specifically to provide the type of content that encourages and supports teacher-specific activities and needs. For example, Ning for teachers (www.ning.com), Learn Central (www.learncentral.org), School Net Global (www.schoolnetglobal.com), Gold Star Café (www.goldstarcafe.net), Learnhub (http://learnhub.com), and other sites are being built to foster relationships via educational blogs, e-portfolios, and formal and ad hoc communities. Social networks also encourage communication through chats, discussion threads, and synchronous forums. These sites also have content-sharing and rating features.

Perhaps one of the most popular places for educators is Classroom 2.0 (www.classroom20.com). It offers a feature that allows users to select the level of privacy needed. It also includes a forums feature, a feature to personalize pages, embedded blogging, groups, chat options, and an easy way for students to embed media. This site has guides for beginners, forums to exchange information, a network for creating collaborative projects, and an easy way to start new discussions. There are also archives of podcasts, lessons, and interviews, as well as other items of particular interest to educators.

Classroom Integration

Teachers are known to do whatever will help their students learn. And students these days are using the tools seamlessly and smoothly. The National School Boards Association (2007) reports that almost 60% of students who use social networking talk about education topics online; and, surprisingly, more than 50% talk specifically about schoolwork. Yet the vast majority of school districts have stringent rules against nearly all forms of social networking during the school day, even though students and parents report few problem behaviors online.

One study (Crook, 2008) suggests the relationship between Web 2.0 tools and learning:

> A second significant reason for educators to turn to Web 2.0 is that it seems to fit with certain experiences emphasised in contemporary theories of learning and modern thinking about how best to design the conditions of learning. Within the psychology of learning, there are four influential but overlapping frameworks (this term more appropriate than "theories"). These are: behaviourism, constructivism, cognitivism, and the socio-cultural perspective. (p. 30)

It is worth asking if teachers believe that students will learn better and develop better skills when being taught by traditional methods or if they believe students will learn better and develop new and unique skills when teachers create a learning environment that includes Web 2.0 social networking tools. There is some evidence that the large number of humans engaged in Web 2.0 may be the key to innovative thinking and problem solving (Surowiecki, 2004). The most straightforward reason for using Web 2.0 for teaching must be recognition that young people are already engaged by Web 2.0 applications. So, for pupils, there will be familiarity with a style of interacting and inquiry that arises from browsing within these spaces, even when the young learner has not been an active producer. In a recent research study, Green and Hannon (2007) found that teachers, parents, and students agree on the types of learning that come from the use of these digital tools, especially social networking, as shown in Table 5.1:

Table 5.1 | DIGITAL SKILLS

Social / Personal	Cognitive / Physical	Technical
▶ Communication	▶ Multitasking	▶ Hand–eye coordination
▶ General knowledge	▶ Logical thinking	▶ Technical confidence
▶ Creativity	▶ Problem solving	▶ Web design/content creation
▶ Collaboration	▶ Trial-and-error learning	
▶ Self-esteem		
▶ Parallel processing		
▶ Persistence		
▶ Peer-to-peer learning		
▶ Risk taking		

Source: *Their Space: Education for a Digital Generation,* p. 36

In addition to the obvious goal of supporting instruction, learners' needs and interests, and the attainment of digital-age skills, educators, of course, want to improve their practice. One educator said:

> For me, social networking is a revelation as an educator. For years, teaching was an isolated experience. Learning more so, lonely and in a dark room. Further, the power was in the hands of "experts" who the learners could only mumble verbatims thereof. … Finally, production, performance, presentation, product, OBJECTIVES are happening and energizing all learners. This is the goal of true education, to share with others, ourselves. And in that process, burn brighter (learn). Social networking allows that to happen. It is like for years, we were just reading about driving, now in the classrooms, we can drive/demonstrate/ do/experience. This is social networking, or the future of it. Not merely chat but performance, high speed performing vehicles … purring cars. (ddeubel, blog comment, August 30, 2007).

CHAPTER 5

Professional Development

Teachers are very happy to share their favorite websites and their reasons for joining together through social networks and electronic learning communities. The examples of such networks abound, and the difficulty is in choosing some to feature. Let us state that your favorite may not be here, but we encourage you to check out the following, too.

BLC/MELC Middle School Teachers in Action

The Maryland Electronic Learning Community has as part of its network a Baltimore Learning Community of Middle School Teachers in Action (http://www.cs.umd.edu/hcil/blc/partners.html). Their goal is to develop a library of multimedia learning resources and facilitate interaction among teachers. This began with five schools and 35 teachers but is being expanded to high schools as well. It includes an extensive collection of video clips, lesson plans with metadata tags, and content organized by topic that is also aligned to the Maryland learning outcomes. It even includes a feature similar to social bookmarking in that teachers can document their favorites in a public fashion, on an individual "bookshelf," and can enter their own materials into the community digital library. It is searchable so that you might find other teachers' recommendations and then examine other things used by those with whom you have some affinity.

TERC MSPnet

TERC has long been involved in teacher professional development and now has taken another step. For some time TERC has supported a Math Science Partnership in a variety of ways. The TERC MSPnet (Math Science Partnership Network) provides the MSP program with a web-based, interactive electronic community. Its goal is to build capacity and expand each educator's level of knowledge regarding the MSP projects, but in addition, they strive to increase the development of the entire learning community. They call their network "An Electronic Community of Practice Facilitating Communication and Collaboration" (http://mspnet.mspnet.org).

DO-IT

National Center on Accessible Information Technology in Education offers another electronic community and a promising practice in creating a completely accessible electronic community, DO-IT (Disabilities, Opportunities, Internetworking, and Technology). It is designed to allow educators, students, and mentors an opportunity to exchange information. The center provides computers, assistive technology, and Internet connections for the homes of disabled college-bound teens who have been accepted into the DO-IT Scholars program. Participants have many different types of disabilities, including those that affect the ability to hear, see, speak, learn, and move. The community offers many ways to interact to accommodate all disabilities. It can be found at www.washington.edu/accessit/articles?1179/.

Kansas Future Teachers

Some faculty members at postsecondary teacher education institutions have found authentic ways to introduce preservice to the tools and to take the first steps in building a sense of the professional learning community. As part of their students' responsibilities, students participate in an electronic Ning with inservice teachers. In Kansas this is called Kansas Future Teachers (http://kansasfutureteachers.ning.com), and the teachers from the trenches join with students in the discussions. Cyndi Danner-Kuhn, who runs this program, states, "The Teachers from the Trenches add the real meat and guts to the discussions." She welcomes others to join her conversation and has as a goal helping new teachers (who are expected to know and use new tools easily) to understand the complexity of, and rationale for, using such tools in pedagogically strong ways.

Additional Nings and Communities

Some Nings are for all educators to join and share, for example, Fireside Learning: Conversations about Education, which invites educators to "sit by the fireside and share your thoughts" (http://firesidelearning.ning.com). English educators hold a virtual book club through the English Companion Ning (http://englishcompanion.ning.com) and have been finding ways to support their own personal and professional growth.

Educators who have specialized responsibilities also are using the features of social networking to improve their professional activities. Teacher-Librarians and other educators (http://teacherlibrarian.ning.com) have created a way for them to work, share, and help each other. Teachers of English as a Foreign Language have a place to learn ways to improve their practice at EFL Classroom 2.0 (http://eflclassroom.ning.com).

Some of these social networks are comprehensive, such as the ISTE network of communities for those educators who wish to interact with other technology-using educators (www.iste-community.org), or the ones that national organizations run for content-specific educators. For example, the National Council of Teachers of English (http://ncte2008.ning.com), National Council for the Social Studies (http://ncssnetwork.ning.com), or Art Educators Ning (http://arted20.ning.com).

Others are more narrowly focused:

- High school math teachers (www.classroom20.com/group/highschoolmathteachers)

- Middle School Portal for math and science teachers (http://msportal-2.ning.com)

- Secondary art teachers (http://naea-secondary-teachers.ning.com)

- Middle school science teachers (http://scienceteacher.ning.com)

- Synapse for biology teachers worldwide (http://thesynapse.ning.com)

- Texas history teachers (http://texashistoryteacher.ning.com)

- Math teachers who use interactive whiteboards (http://smartboardrevolution.ning.com/group/highschoolmathteachers)

Twitter

Administrators also use social networking sites for both communication and personal growth. Michael Waiksnis, principal of Sullivan Middle School in South Carolina, said this about his Twitter network:

> It is basically an informal personal learning network. I have learned more from it than most other forms of professional

development. We share ideas, links, resources, just about everything. If you have a question, you send it out and just wait for the
responses. You build up a large amount of "followers" (people
who follow you on twitter) by sharing as well as receiving. I have
been doing it for a few months and the amount I have learned is
tremendous. I also have a school Twitter account. I use this as a
way to send quick updates on the happenings at my school.
(M. Waiksnis, personal communication, August, 2009)

who is using social networking for teaching and learning?

It is challenging to select a few of the many examples of ways that teachers are
using social networking in classrooms to improve student learning, to support
inquiry and self-directed learning, and to expand the students' horizons.
The examples do run the gamut of what is possible and are offered for two
reasons. First, it is quite a tribute to our fellow educators to see the wide range
of ideas and creativity that they have come up with. Second, we hope that you
will be inspired and encouraged by something that you read here and, also,
recognize the similarities that bind all of these projects. You may decide to try
to adapt one of the ideas you read here, or you may figure out a way to change
something to fit your curriculum. Whichever works for you, we hope you will
try a project that fits your and your students' style and educational goals.

Educators have created a wide variety of ways to involve their students in
social networking. One teacher uploaded a song to the Ning and asked the
children to interpret the lyrics. A math teacher has been using the Ning to
post homework and share a "puzzle of the week." In addition, the teacher
has been embedding VoiceThreads into the Ning to share test preparation tips
and for student mathcasts. Through a Ning, United States college students are
connecting with adult learners of English from a language school in Spain.
This teacher said, "I like [the Ning] better than Blackboard for certain tasks.
I definitely feel more connected to my students than before, which I think
is essential in foreign language teaching (to reduce students' anxiety)"
(P. Munday, blog comment, February 22, 2009).

Project Peace (http://projectpeace.ning.com) is one social community designed to teach English through students' singing, promoting peace. Their stated goal is "Project Peace is a place for educators and students to sing, learn English, and help make this world more peaceful." Teachers join the network, and then their students create videos, podcasts, and other projects to post online along with others from around the globe.

English Companion (http://englishcompanion.ning.com/group/teachingwith technology/forum/topics/introducing-ning-to-students) is an English education Ning set up to foster the use of Nings in classroom curriculum and to help teachers begin the journey of integrating these tools into the classroom. One teacher, Susanne Nobles, Fredericksburg Academy, Fredericksburg, Virginia, said:

> I am just now finishing a Ning unit with my seniors and got some feedback from them about how it went. They LOVED it! They felt very comfortable with how the Ning is set up and works because of their experience with other social networking sites, so I think showing it to them then giving them some time to play on it (get their personal pages set up, write on each other's walls, maybe do a quick first blog post) would start things off well. We are a laptop school, so I do this in my classroom, but I think for this first day in a non-laptop school, you should bring them to the lab to get started all together. I think they will understand the site pretty quickly. (S. Nobles, blog post, March 15, 2009)

One of the results of becoming known in the educational social networking community is that one activity often results in other opportunities. After Susanne Nobles posted the results of her activities, she received a message from another teacher:

> Hi Susanne. I was wondering if you and your students would be interested in participating in a nationwide SAT Vocab Video Contest @ MIT university. If not, perhaps you have some educator contacts you could direct me to. You can view contest details at BrainyFlix.com. Please let me know. Thanks. (Jack, blog comment, March 2009)

FieldFindr (http://fieldfindr.ning.com) aims to connect global volunteers with teachers and their students. Teachers can create posts if they are looking for volunteers or people who have expert knowledge to enrich their classes' study of immigration, peace studies, playgrounds, and the Holocaust. Teachers can also search for other collaborators through posted comment.

The International Classroom (http://internationalclassroom.ning.com) is an invitational social network created specifically for students aged 12 to 14 to be able to safely connect and share their experiences and cultures.

The French Connection (http://stjesfrench.ning.com) is an invitational Ning linking sixth grade classes in the United States and France for French language study.

Rolling on the River (http://rollingontheriver.ning.com) is centered on the study of rivers and other bodies of water. It is "a resource for global collaboration" where users can "share information, find global partners, and learn more about rivers, lakes, and oceans through participation and collaboration." Teachers also share web resources, and videos of the projects are available on this site to inspire teachers and learners.

Museum Pods: the Social Media Network (http://museumsweb2.ning.com) is a portal to connect students with museums, their staff, and artists. It exploits one of the great aspects of Nings: the multimedia nature of interaction. It has videos of artists discussing their works and processes, links for a podcast from the Columbia Museum of Art and other art-related podcasts, notices of art-education events and professional development opportunities, and additional groups that focus on topics related to ongoing projects and answer questions.

Greenovation (www.greenovationnation.com) is designed to "energize education and inspire action." Many teachers have gone to Greenovation to engage their students or the entire school in a project designed to consider the environment. The website has a counter to record the kilowatt hours saved due to their efforts, and it also has a contest to engage students: "If you could dream up the ultimate energy-efficient classroom of the future, what would it look like? Lutron Greenovation invites you to take a good look at your entire school—from the classroom to the science lab to the lunchroom and beyond—and tell us your big, bright ideas for improving energy efficiency."

Digiteen (http://digiteen.ning.com) is a place for teens to communicate in a Ning that focuses on what it means to be a digital teenager today. It also offers a private and safe place for teens to post their own social information because the pages are protected and only available to those the teen allows. For an example of how one teen put together what was learned, check out the SlideShare production at www.slideshare.net/Gemma58284/digital-citizenship-1589336?type=presentation/.

Flat Classrooms (http://flatclassrooms.ning.com) is designed for transforming learning through global collaboration. It was started for the purpose of "Fostering new ways of learning using Web 2.0 and global collaborative 'flat classroom' ideals and practices." Here, teachers find projects from classrooms around the world or post their ideas of connections they would like to start.

One thing seems certain: once a teacher starts down the road of including these tools in teaching, it seems to take off in unanticipated directions. Tara Seale reports:

> I have discovered that in an English classroom, Nings are useful in engaging students who are involved in a lengthy, difficult read. My 9th grade English students participated in a Ning called Verona Lifestyles (http://veronapages.ning.com), which I created specifically for the class as we read Romeo and Juliet. Students signed up and became a member of the Ning as a character of the play. My students responded to and posted blogs and forum comments on the Ning while in character. Not only did the Ning activity increase the students' interest in the play, but students were forced to closely read the play to understand the complexity and motivations of their character in order to create a believable persona. Incorporating this fun, engaging, and creative activity balanced out the difficulty students were having in trying to interpret the archaic language of the play, kind of a reward for their hard-work. (T. Seale, electronic communication, August, 2009)

A middle school teacher, Sondra (http://education.ning.com/group/
middleschool/forum/topics/1027485:Topic:22084), reports:

> We are just starting to experiment with Nings in some middle
> school classrooms. The first to try it was a 7th grade English
> teacher who wisely invited only 21 of his 84 students to join the
> Ning. These students read a "challenging" novel, *The Red Scarf
> Girl*, and used the Ning to discuss it. The teacher is now planning
> to expand the Ning to include all students in his "cluster." He
> will assign each student to one of twelve different science fiction
> novels, and create groups in the Ning to discuss each book. Last
> year we used blogs for his Science Fiction Genre Study Groups.
>
> The Ning idea is contagious! Now the Social Studies teacher who
> works with the same "cluster" of 84 students is planning a SS
> Ning! This cluster is unique in our school because the students
> are part of a 1-to-1 pilot program; each leases his own iBook from
> our school. The students take the iBooks from class to class and
> may take them home.
>
> We also have a 6th grade teacher who is planning on introducing
> a Ning within the next few weeks. This will raise interesting
> issues around access, as these students do not have their own
> iBooks. We do have mobile carts of 14 iBooks which teachers
> can schedule for classroom use, and we have two computer labs.
> (Sondra, blog post, January 17, 2008)

An example of how students might participate in networking projects is
offered by Owen, Grant, Sayers, and Facer (2006):

> A Year 13 student of English literature writes an essay on one of
> her Jane Austen set readings. Before she submits it for marking
> by her teachers she decides to submit her essay for peer assess-
> ment using a fan fiction web resource. Twenty-four hours later the
> student has constructive feedback from five other Jane Austen fans
> and she is able to improve her essay. (p. 8)

Sometimes the Ning is the place for thinking out loud. Peter Dawson reaped many responses when he set out "to establish some working projects with like-minded primary teachers around the world" (http://globaleducation.ning.com/group/primaryteacherscollaborating/forum/topics/717180:Topic:5608):

> Also, there's a teacher in this Ning, Elaine Wrenn, who used to do a project called Communities Around the World. I think there was a theme each month like playgrounds and kids compared their playgrounds around the world. I wonder if we could do something simple like that ... and post pictures to a Flickr group for discussion purposes. Maybe teachers then could record the discussions and we could post them online somewhere for other classes to listen to. (L. Gray, blog comment, July 11, 2007)

Paul Harrington commented:

> A European Project that we are involved in called Play to Learn that is targeted at looking for similarities and differences between the way children play both in school and at home—communication via blogs, skype and podcasting—but I think that using VoiceThread could be really good for a project like this. I look forward to your thoughts ... we are in South Wales UK. (P. Harrington, blog comment, September 24, 2007)

Here is one more example of the ways in which the Ning supports educators connecting to each other to expand their students' curricular experiences. Nerine Chalmers (http://flatclassrooms.ning.com/profile/NerineChalmers) works at the Qatar Academy Primary School, Doha, Qatar. She wrote about her class's project. Students in Grade 5, in their field of investigation for the IB Primary Years Programme (PYP) Exhibition, are interested in investigating the notion that "a balance of work and recreation contributes to the well being of our community." They wish to create a survey and then get "responses from students in different parts of the world, as well as from students living in countries facing upheaval and challenge. If students at your school would be interested in responding, please let me know. Thank you." The opportunities are obvious and exciting.

how do you get started with social networking?

It is always an adventure to try a new Web 2.0 tool. Happily, social networking tools are almost foolproof. From Ning (www.ning.com) click on the Get Started Now button and choose a plan (www.ning.com/chooseplan). The first 30 days are free. After choosing a plan, you will see the screen in Figure 5.1:

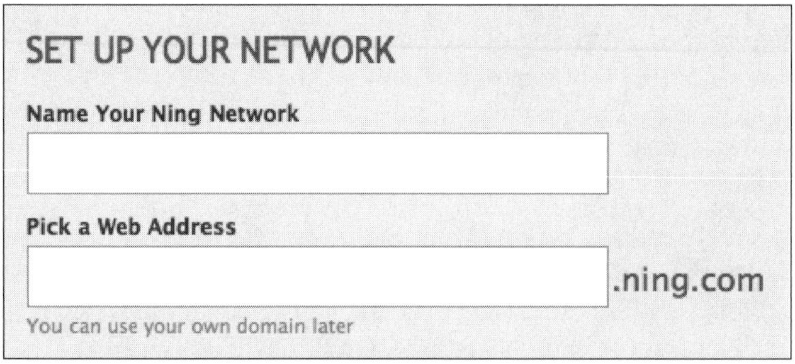

SET UP YOUR NETWORK

Name Your Ning Network

Pick a Web Address

.ning.com

You can use your own domain later

▶ **Figure 5.1.** Create a Ning Network

Enter the name for your ning, and pick a name for your website. That is all it takes. Next you will want to consider how your network will work. The following list will help you determine the ways you want your network to operate. Before you start, you might want to plan a color scheme, find graphics that represent your network, and create a few introductory and welcoming messages.

Some Things to Think About Before You Get Started with a Ning

- ▶ Your Ning network can either be open or closed. If it's closed, members can join only by your invitation.

- ▶ Ning allows you to edit comments posted by members (e.g., the students in your classroom) of the network. Therefore, teachers can remove inappropriate comments and materials.

- Because it is a social networking site, Ning may be a blocked site at your school district. Check with your tech support person to get the site opened.

- Although most unwanted ads are filtered, every now and then an irritating (and sometimes inappropriate) ad could pop up on your screen. A fee-based premium network allows you to restrict ads.

- If you decide a Ning is not appropriate for use with students, you might want to consider an alternative format. A Ning can be a strong communication tool for team building or staff development.

- Ning does have an age restriction: students must be 13 or older to join. If your students are younger than 13, consider using a Ning as a mode of communication with the parents or guardians of the students in your classroom.

- Finally, you may want to establish rules for your students in working with the Ning in the classroom. It also makes sense that you inform the parents about your plans and about the rules. Later, once the students have become adept at working with Nings, you and they may want to revise the guidelines, or customize them.

We found the following rules for participating in a classroom Ning in a posting by Michael Umphrey, but when he was contacted, he wrote the following:

> I don't think I can give you permission—not because I mind if you use it but because my part in it doesn't really rise to the level of making it my intellectual property. A teacher asked permission to use it on her Ning, and I told her that I'd created it in a few minutes by copying, pasting, splicing, and editing a few documents from the web, without enough investment to even note where the pieces came from.

Thus, we present the rules here as an example of the way things evolve in our social web, and as a good place to start.

Umphrey's Ning Rules for Students

The school standards of language and conduct apply to this forum.

1. **Respect.** We are polite, kind, and appropriate at all times. Remember that many students and Mr. Umphrey will view your comments.

2. **Inclusion.** Anyone is welcome to comment or join a discussion as long as he or she is respectful.

3a. **Learning** (in this forum). It's OK to have fun in this space, but if others are having a learning conversation, either add to it positively or make your comments in a new post.

3b. **Learning** (in class dialogues and blogs). These are places to reflect and learn. You are encouraged to: ask questions; answer questions; share your learning; synthesize ideas; plan projects or assignments; and reflect on the process of learning.

4. **Safety.** In general, be reserved about revealing private details on websites. You don't need to use your full name, but use enough of it so that everyone in English 11 will know who you are. Though this is a password-protected site, it is digital information that anyone could copy, forward, save to hard drive, and so forth. Anything you type into a digital forum may last forever, so respect your own and others' privacy.

5. **Decorating your personal space.** Arrange your personal site to your taste, but keep it wholesome. It may be your choice to walk on the dark side, but one of the purposes of this site is to add to the world's light. Please, no gross, disgusting, immoral, or irreverent photographs. Also, don't put up a background that makes your text hard to read. Communication is a primary purpose of this site, and design should enhance, rather than obstruct, communication.

▶ ▶ ▶

▶▶

6. **Formality.** The level of usage here is "informal standard English"—
which is what is used in business, government, and education for
everyday work. No texting abbreviations. Use complete sentences and
standard spelling.

I'll ban people who ignore these rules. When a person is banned, the
program deletes all the person's content and it cannot be recovered.

This quotation from Owen, Grant, Sayers, and Facer (2006) summarizes this
chapter extremely well:

> We are increasingly witnessing a change in the view of what
> education is for, with a growing emphasis on the need to support
> young people not only to acquire knowledge and information, but
> to develop the resources and skills necessary to engage with social
> and technical change, and to continue learning throughout the
> rest of their lives. In the technological arena, we are witnessing
> the rapid proliferation of technologies which are less about
> "narrowcasting" to individuals, than the creation of communities
> and resources in which individuals come together to learn, collab-
> orate and build knowledge (social software). It is the intersection
> of these two trends which, we believe, offers significant potential
> for the development of new approaches to education. (p. 7)

We want to provide our students with engaging, important, and valuable
information and content; and we also want to help them see where and how
they fit into the larger world. This chapter offered an overview of social
networking and the ways in which it is having an impact on our learners,
and on our teachers.

where can you find more information about social networking?

For a good overview, try this video on Social Networking in Plain English:
www.youtube.com/watch?v=6a_KF7TYKVc

Go to Examine, a website that describes all aspects of social networking:
www.whatissocialnetworking.com

Join more than 28,000 other educators at Classroom 2.0:
www.classroom20.com

Explore your options on Social Networking for Teachers:
http://socialnetworking4teachers.wikispaces.com

Or, go to this site for educators:
www.teachade.com

Perhaps bringing about social change is of interest. Try this educational community:
www.teachingforchange.org

6

visual learning tools—videos and photos

what are visual learning tools?

Today's students view and communicate information through personal screens that include computer monitors, cell phones, handhelds, and television. They learn and spread information using new media such as YouTube, photo sites, and online presentation tools that feature visual displays.

The old adage is that a picture is worth a thousand words; for today's young people, the picture is all. When words matter, it is often in text messages or 140-character communiqués such as Twitter.

With so much emphasis on visual media, students need skills to understand the power of the various media and skills to use media to communicate. And many students are visual learners for whom seeing—whether tutorials or diagrams or videos—helps them learn.

Visual or media literacy involves both the ability to understand and interpret and the ability to create visual messages: students must develop the skill to process and analyze information delivered through images as well as understand the impact images have on a viewer. They should understand that text and images affect readers differently.

Students have always learned by reviewing photos, maps, diagrams, charts, graphs, and tables. However, because there are more ways now than ever before to get information visually—including web-delivered images, videos, and presentations—and because visual communication is so commonplace for this digital generation, students must develop the ability to think critically about the image presented and decode its meaning. They should be aware of the effect the image was designed to produce, and they should analyze the extent and ways in which it successfully accomplishes the intended effect, both while watching visual media and while creating it.

why are visual learning tools useful?

Students must learn how to create meaning and communicate with visual tools. They can create digital media projects using video clips, video podcasting, and screencasting (screen capture with audio narration). Teachers can use images and visual presentations in the curriculum and encourage students to create presentations that develop the skills of inquiry, creativity, and higher-order thinking. Students should be able to create a product that demonstrates their knowledge of the subject matter, the ability to communicate that information visually, and the ability to make an impact on the audience. Skills include using visual means creatively to convey or enhance meaning.

The Partnership for 21st Century Skills (2004) includes media literacy as an essential skill, demonstrated by the ability to analyze media and create media products.

They state that to analyze, students should be able to:

- ▸ Understand both how and why media messages are constructed, and for what purposes

- ▸ Examine how individuals interpret messages differently, how values and points of view are included or excluded, and how media can influence beliefs and behaviors

- ▸ Apply a fundamental understanding of the ethical/legal issues surrounding the access and use of media (p. 5)

They further state that to create media products, students should be able to:

- ▸ Understand and utilize the most appropriate media creation tools, characteristics and conventions

- ▸ Understand and effectively utilize the most appropriate expressions and interpretations in diverse, multi-cultural environments (p. 5)

When students can work on a curricular project, they can sharpen their ability to discover relationships among ideas and to develop new concepts and insights. When they can collaborate with others, they have a feedback loop for their ideas and a relationship with others that promotes using higher-order thinking skills. When they can communicate and share ideas with a real audience, they take ownership of their work and develop a commitment to learning. Using photos and videos for this purpose enhances the process, and the two most important methods are digital storytelling and the making of documentaries. Students can also share information through the creation of slide shows or screencasts, using text, audio, and visual elements.

when do teachers use video and photo tools?

Classroom Integration

Digital Storytelling

When students can organize their thoughts logically, find just the right words to express them, and communicate their ideas to others, they are demonstrating the ability to think logically. Teachers can help students improve thinking skills by encouraging them to write creatively and express themselves visually. An effective way to do this is with digital storytelling using free photo-editing tools.

Storytelling is a tradition in which ideas and customs are handed down from generation to generation. Digital stories derive their power from adding the elements of images and design to create a story that communicates in powerful ways. Digital stories are compelling forms of expression because it is so easy to make them look like they were created professionally, share them with a wide audience, and store them in e-portfolios.

Teachers encourage students to take, edit, post, and include their own photos in their work and to use others' photos that are stored online at sites such as Flickr (www.flickr.com) using Creative Commons attributions (http://creativecommons.org).

Being visually creative enhances the power of narrative. It is easy for students to add visual elements to their stories; they can import their photos, design their documents, enter their story text, and share their digital stories by printing them or saving them as digital files to post to a web page.

Video Documentaries

Students have traditionally watched videos to learn, but being the creators of visual information is now possible with today's tools. When students create knowledge from information, collaborate with others, and do hands-on learning, they engage with the subject matter and learn, understand, and remember it. They create and collaborate, research and share, and take ownership of their learning. When, in addition, students use videocameras and video-editing tools, teachers can motivate students to learn. For example, making history come alive in the classroom can be a challenge, but creating video documentaries encourages students to learn about the past.

Documentary filmmaking in the classroom can produce positive effects. Students can demonstrate their individual strengths and master the skills of researching, reading, writing, and speaking as they build critical skills such as problem solving, collaboration, and the ability to gather and analyze data. With such project-based learning, students can be motivated to do their best work and be proud to share what they've created—a professional-quality documentary.

For teachers, documentary filmmaking can offer a very natural formative assessment tool. They can evaluate student learning from the perspective of applying skills rather than from remembering facts for tests. In addition, creating a documentary changes students from being spectators of history or literature, for example, to being active participants. Students study curriculum by filling in gaps, solving the mysteries, and exploring and understanding rather than memorizing. They are engaged in gathering evidence and analyzing and interpreting with the goal of presenting a story.

The ultimate achievement is for students to post their videos on a video sharing site so that it is available not only to other students, the teacher, and parents but also to the world. YouTube is the most common, but some districts block its use. Alternately, they can post on sites such as TeacherTube (www.teachertube.com).

Whether in photographs or video, students learn to create, collaborate, and communicate effectively with digital tools. Jakes (2005) gives examples of the power that visual learning has in *Making a Case for Digital Storytelling*:

> ▶ A student who never talks in class develops a digital story about being afraid to talk. He describes how he likes being talked to, how he is misunderstood and lonely, and how he had to develop a new identity. He shows how this was accomplished through the Internet, and as a result, he found some true friends. For a student who says nothing, he has much to say.

- ▶ A student who is physically challenged and is selectively mute tells a story and makes a breakthrough by recording the voice-over.

- ▶ A student who has Asperger's syndrome actually tells a story about his favorite hobby.

- ▶ A student reconnects with her estranged siblings through her digital story.

- ▶ A student tells of the importance of her childhood drawings as representations of her life, and what she wants that life to become.

- ▶ And there are other stories—tales of first-loves, of the death of loved ones, of personal sacrifice, of accomplishment, of the importance of a place, of challenges overcome, of important moments in a life, and of the value of parents and grandparents.

If you want to get a sense of how the making of documentaries works, Melissa Lynn Pomerantz's blog (http://nhsglobalwarmingdocumentary.edublogs.org) provides a firsthand account of how the entire process of creating video documentaries worked in her classroom. Pomerantz and her students blogged about the process while her English/communication arts class created a video documentary of a research project online. She also made screencasts using Jing as tutorials for the students. Her blog provides the screencasts, pedagogical reflections, model entries for students, and ideas for improving the project. It includes written and video exit interviews about the project (M. L. Pomerantz, blog post, May 24, 2008).

Teachers use visual tools to demonstrate topics to students and can learn to create their own tutorials using screencasting software. For example, Amy Mayer from Conroe ISD in Conroe, Texas, uses screencasts made with Jing to show teachers how to create free, unlimited teacher accounts on Animoto, which they use in many subjects including language arts, science, and math (A. Mayer, electronic communication, August, 2009).

Patrick Ledesma, school-based technology specialist at Holmes Middle School in Fairfax County, Virginia, relates that one educator, who is getting her high school math certification and currently teaches Algebra I to special education high school students, learned how to teach a difficult concept in multivariable calculus, not from her professor, not from the county math specialist, but from a high school teacher who posted a video of himself teaching it on YouTube. He explained it in a way that the others had not, and now she can pass that style of teaching on to her students (P. Ledesma, personal communication, August, 2009).

Digital Images and Copyright

Copyright laws govern how we use the creative work and information of others in any form. People can copy material under some circumstances if they cite the reference or get author or copyright holder permission, or both. Fair Use provisions of the law allow teachers and students to use these materials for educational purposes; again, with certain restrictions. In creating digital stories, students often include images created by others that are stored online.

Creative Commons (http://creativecommons.org) is a nonprofit organization. According to Wikipedia:

> [It is] devoted to expanding the range of creative works available for others to build upon legally and to share. The organization has released several copyright licenses known as Creative Commons licenses for free to the public These licenses allow creators to communicate which rights they reserve and which rights they waive for the benefit of recipients or other creators.

Photo and Video Tools

Because there are so many tools and so many uses for visual tools, we list a few here for the purpose of understanding the variety of options.

Flickr (www.flickr.com) is a photo hosting site where people upload, tag, and store their photos, share them with others, and browse the many images and photos posted. Users can add comments and annotations.

Jing (www.jingproject.com) allows users to snap a picture or make a quick video of anything on a computer screen and then share it.

Microsoft's Photosynth (http://photosynth.net) takes a collection of photos of a place or object, analyzes them for similarities, and displays them in a reconstructed three-dimensional space.

Photobucket (http://photobucket.com) is a video site that provides free, web-based versions of Adobe's video remix and editing tools.

Photoshop.com (www.photoshop.com) is a free version of Adobe's photo-editing toolkit available online for users to upload, organize, edit, and share photos online.

Photo Story (www.microsoft.com/windowsxp/using/digitalphotography/ PhotoStory/default.mspx) is Microsoft's free downloadable software that allows users to create a presentation from digital photos with narration, effects, transitions, and music.

Picasa (http://picasa.google.com) is Google's software for organizing and editing digital photos. Rather than editing, organizing, and storing photos online, it is available for people to download and use on their computers.

SlideShare (www.slideshare.net) is a website to share presentations; users can upload, view, and share their work, and have it converted to Flash for viewing.

TeacherTube (www.teachertube.com) is a public video sharing website similar to YouTube for teachers to share videos and tutorials online. Students can also post videos for educational purposes.

Ustream (www.ustream.tv) is a web streaming site that lets people broadcast their own channels on their own or other site.

VoiceThread (www.voicethread.com) is a collaborative, multimedia slide show site that holds images, documents, and videos and allows people to navigate pages and leave comments in a variety of ways.

Windows Live Movie Maker (www.download.live.com/moviemaker) is downloadable video creating and editing software that is a part of Microsoft's Windows Live.

YouTube (www.youtube.com) is a public video sharing website. Google provides YouTube Remixer, an online video editor on YouTube that is powered by Adobe Premiere Express. Users can remix videos on YouTube or enhance them with titles, transitions, and effects.

who is using video and photo tools for teaching and learning?

In addition to digital storytelling tools and tools to create video documentaries, educators are using many other creative tools in classrooms today. Here are some examples.

Family Stories

Digital storytelling is popular because students learn a great deal from being immersed visually in a topic. Often that topic involves personal matters. Dan Erikson, a fifth grade language arts teacher at Poly Drive Elementary in Billings, Montana, uses VoiceThread to advance writing skills with an authentic purpose, hone oral reading fluency, and involve families with a school project.

Students learn the story behind five or six family photos by interviewing family members, and then they prepare a narration. They scan the photos (if not already in digital format), upload them to VoiceThread, and record their narration. Students learn something about their family history and background, which often includes historical events and geography. They also learn to transform oral stories into a written narration, digitize and manipulate images on a computer, and upload images and sound to the Internet. Accounts are set up so that each student's family can access, and contribute to, the project (D. Erikson, electronic communication, August, 2009).

Engaging Reluctant Writers

Edwina Martin from the Kansas City Missouri School District helps teachers to engage reluctant writers in reading and language arts classes. Students use Toondoo (www.toondoo.com) to create cartoons that express information and opinions. She says, "The excitement in creating the entire cartoon: background, choosing characters, drawing them and selecting all other aspects helps students learn to synthesize information and demonstrate their abilities."

They do research and write outlines to establish what information will be shared, create storyboards of ideas and points to be made, and select precise vocabulary appropriate to the social issues they choose in order to persuade others (E. Martin, electronic communication, August, 2009).

Teaching Languages: The Written Word

Allyssa Andersen from the Traver School in Lake Geneva, Wisconsin, uses visual tools with her eighth grade Spanish students. For example, students take pictures of places in their community to create digital stories using VoiceThread, and they make cartoons with Goanimate (http://goanimate.com), creating both of these projects entirely in Spanish.

Alyssa says:

> Students take the material we're learning and make it their own by using their own pictures, experiences, and ideas. I go through what I want the kids to do and show the site. I give checklists of what they'll need to start the project and then I use a rubric to assess.

Each student has a wiki page for work samples, such as their VoiceThread presentation and animation. She adds, "This is one of the first times that I've not had kids complain about writing (they needed to write their scripts in Spanish) because they just wanted to get to the 'fun stuff' and put it all together. They have great pride in their creations" (A. Anderson, electronic communication, August, 2009).

Teaching Languages: The Spoken Word

Sue Allen from Hempfield High School in Landisville, Pennsylvania, helps Spanish teachers use Voki (www.voki.com) so that students can create an avatar and a piece of dialogue in the target language and post it for other students to peer review it. They embed the Voki avatars in a Moodle (an open-source course management system) table.

The students create the Voki avatar and record the audio using the telephone. They post the code for their Voki to a shared Google spreadsheet that the teacher used to create the table in Moodle. Students are able to create a sound file and review each other's work and comment. Allen says, "For some this was the first time that they had heard themselves speak in Spanish" (S. Allen, electronic communication, August, 2009).

Chemistry

Elaine Plybon, who teaches at the Texas Virtual School, uses Animoto (http://animoto.com) to make short videos. This adds excitement about upcoming units of study. "Students post comments on the discussion thread about things they learned about me by watching the video." She continues, "As a science teacher, I also use this opportunity to point out how different things look from different perspectives and that there is always more to a picture than revealed at first glance" (E. Plybon, electronic communication, August, 2009).

Her video from 2009 is at http://animoto.com/play/Ejod6VmZa1NG0uoWV0 WmyA?autostart=true.

Students in her former "real" classroom used Animoto for a get-to-know-you activity as well as for oral project presentations. For the get-to-know-you activity, students gather approximately 10 photos or images that describe something about them. They produce an Animoto short and post it on the discussion board, and other students post one thing they learn about that person from watching the video.

Mathematics

Jim Moser, math teacher at The Principia School in St. Louis, Missouri, uses Jing and Photo Story 3 to create tutorials. Students use them to create podguides in which a student explains how to do a mathematical process through a slide show or video clip using Jing or Photo Story.

He believes that students have to really understand something in order to teach it. So they break down mathematical processes to step-by-step instructions, and it helps them understand the concept better. They create podguides using a computer and a camera, or just using a computer. It helps them learn how to teach others, and it solidifies concepts for them. Examples include sixth grade podguides on lattice multiplication and creating perpendicular bisectors (J. Moser, electronic communication, August, 2009).

Marine Biology

Goosehill Primary School in Cold Spring Harbor, New York, is collaborating with the Cold Spring Harbor Fish Hatchery. According to Lydia Bellino, principal, each of the seven first grade classes has its own turtle, and students are charting their turtle's growth and working with a marine biologist. They exchange e-mail comments and questions with the biologist. They often use Jing to capture images related to the communication. When the marine biologist visits the school, teachers photograph and video parts of the presentation so that students can revisit the information and add audio.

Students learn how to hold the baby turtles, feed them, measure and record the growth, set up the tanks, and more. Because these are first graders, the teachers are the primary users of Jing, but the students understand its use and direct where and what they want to highlight. The students record their learning to accompany the images and share with the kindergarten children, which makes it a bit like a science mentoring experience. (L. Bellino, electronic communication, August, 2009).

how do you get started with video and photo tools?

With the large number of options for photo- and movie-editing around, there are many choices. For the purpose of simplicity, we chose to focus on one photo-editing tool, Picasa, and one video-editing tool, Windows Live Movie Maker. Both are downloaded and manipulated on a computer rather than online and are most often used on PCs; however, Macintosh users have free photo- and video-editing software included on their computers (Picasa is available for Macs).

Steps for Digital Storytelling

▶ Brainstorm and develop a topic and purpose for writing.

▶ Discuss expectations and assessment of digital stories.

> ▶ Create a storyboard or outline for the story line.

> ▶ Discuss how images can help communicate a story and enhance the message.

> ▶ Use a digital camera to capture photos or find photos online that are free and available to use (attribute photos that were online).

> ▶ Identify elements of digital stories.

> ▶ Use editing tools to edit images and create the digital story.

Six Elements of Digital Stories

❶ Voice: Write in the first or third person

❷ Character: List the traits your main character demonstrates

❸ Setting: Describe where the story takes place

❹ Conflict: Show a disagreement or struggle

❺ Visual: Use photos or other images to enhance the story's meaning

❻ Pacing: Set the stage by using rising action, create drama using conflict, and use falling action to lead to resolution

Photo Editing with Picasa

Download and install Picasa on your computer (Figures 6.1 and 6.2). Watch as Picasa scans your hard drive and displays folders with your images. Note for Macintosh users: Picasa displays photos from the iPhoto Library as read-only files.

You import new photos from cameras, CDs, memory cards, and so forth by clicking the Import button, selecting the device, and selecting specific images or all of the photos. You can edit your photos by double-clicking a photo to open the Edit Photo screen. Use the editing tools on the left-hand side of the screen. These include Basic Fixes, for simple edits; Tuning, to control the color and adjust the lighting; Effects, where you can apply any of 12 effects; and Make a Caption, for adding captions.

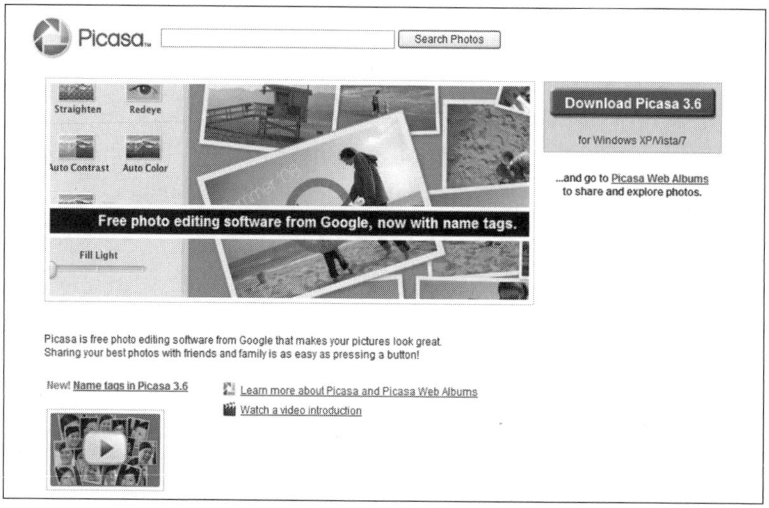

▶ **Figure 6.1.** Picasa for Windows download

▶ **Figure 6.2.** Picasa for Mac download

Steps for Video Documentary Making

Regardless of the topic or tools used, these are the basic tasks that need to be done in the production and delivery of a video documentary. Although some are obviously sequential steps, others may actually be done out of order or as many times as needed throughout the process.

- ▸ Conduct background research.

- ▸ Discuss expectations and assessment of videos.

- ▸ Brainstorm and develop a topic, keeping in mind the purpose for doing it.

- ▸ Create a storyboard or outline for the project.

- ▸ Discuss ways to communicate the story using video.

- ▸ Practice filming techniques.

- ▸ Capture the video on a video camera.

- ▸ Transfer the video (and audio, if captured) to a computer.

- ▸ Use video-editing tools to edit the video clip, and add effects such as fades, wipes, and dissolves.

- ▸ Enhance movies with music, voice-overs, and sound effects.

- ▸ Save the movie and link to it or embed it in a blog or wiki, on a web page, or post on YouTube (or TeacherTube or other video-sharing site).

Creating a Video with Windows Movie Maker

A good way to get started is to let Movie Maker (Figure 6.3) create a movie automatically using the AutoMovie feature. Then you can learn how to do your own editing and moviemaking.

1. Connect your camera to your computer and download your movies into Movie Maker.

2. In the Movie Tasks panel, under 2. Edit Movie, click Make an AutoMovie.

3. On the Select an AutoMovie Editing Style page, click on a style. Movie Maker will use this style to create your movie.

4. Under More options click Enter a Title for the Movie.

5. Type a title.

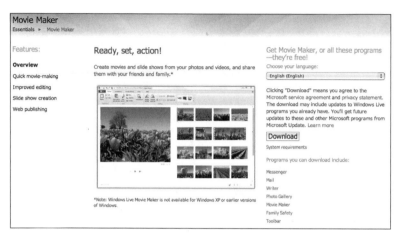

▶ Figure 6.3. Movie Maker download

❻ If you have music on your computer that you want to use as background, click More Options under Select Audio or Background Music. Click Browse, and select a song title.

❼ Click Done. AutoMovie will edit your video.

❽ Click Play on the Preview monitor.

where can you find more information about video and photo tools?

Media Literacy

Free interactive, online tools from Intel:
www.intel.com/education/tools

Creative Commons:
http://creativecommons.org

7

virtual environments

what are virtual environments?

Virtual environments can be excellent for teaching and learning! This is a very exciting step into the world of Web 2.0 and offers you and your students the opportunity to teach and learn in a new way.

Just as with any application or tool, the effectiveness and appropriateness of a virtual environment depends on what your educational goal is, what the learners are doing and why, and how you can assess their learning outcomes. In general, virtual environments are all around us, and it is important to consider them as one tool in your educational repertoire.

Multiuser virtual environments (MUVEs) have been a popular form of multimedia-based entertainment for some time. However, attention has recently turned to exploring their use to support learning, and groups have been creating MUVEs and investigating their effectiveness for both professional development and for curricular activities. Meadows (2008) defines virtual worlds as "online interactive systems in which multiple people, sometimes millions of people, share in the development of an interactive narrative" (p. 34). We know that environments such as these offer individuals and groups the possibility for creativity, collaboration, and communication.

why are virtual environments useful tools?

Students do many things these days in the world of virtual environments. They invent extensive and creative lives for themselves in which they play, build, interact, and explore. The best known and currently most popular of these environments is Second Life (SL). It is not the same as the World of Warcraft (WOW) or other game-oriented multiuser environments in which the goal is to win something or to play against others. Second Life is a 3-D user-created world that is used for multiple purposes, most particularly it is focused on social interaction.

Education is making bold steps into the world of virtual environments in several ways. Second Life was developed by Linden Lab and launched on June 23, 2003. It is accessible via any broadband Internet connection. Interested users are required to download a free Second Life Viewer, a client software package that enables individuals to create an avatar, and become a "resident" of SL. Once you become a resident, you can do many things: meet others, join groups and socialize, participate in activities and professional development opportunities, build a "location" for living, and even buy and sell property. Although joining SL is free, there is a cost for some activities.

As you create your avatar, or persona, it is possible to reinvent yourself. Your avatar is then free to wander the many three-dimensional locations, including seaside towns, educational islands, or virtual worlds that others have designed. SL users (termed residents) create most of the "in-world" environments using built-in tools (Atkinson, 2008). The result is a place to wander, socialize, build, and learn. Second Life caters to users who are more than 18 years of age, but a complementary site, Teen Second Life (http://teen.secondlife.com), is reserved for those between 13 and 17. Happily, Teen Second Life is available only to students and has stayed a safe and controlled place for educational activities.

Built into the software is a three-dimensional modeling tool based on simple geometric shapes that allows a resident to build virtual objects. This can be used in combination with the Linden Scripting Language, which can be used to add functionality to objects. More complex three-dimensional sculpted primitives (also known as sculpted prims and sculpties), textures for clothing or other objects, and animations and gestures can be created using external software. The Second Life terms of service ensure that users retain copyright for any content they create, and the server and client provide simple digital rights management functions.

Just how popular is Second Life? According to Linden Labs, more than 30 million user hours are logged each month (https://blogs.secondlife.com/ community/features/blog/2008/04/15/second-life-economy-grows-15-from-q4-to-q1). The estimate is that several million people worldwide have used SL, and typically 50,000 to 65,000 people are logged on at any given time (Baker, Wentz, & Woods, 2009). Large corporations such as IBM, Sony, Sears, and Mercedes-Benz have devoted enormous resources to create Second Life islands, and many celebrities actually have live performances through their avatars (Atkinson, 2008). Some believe that Second Life and other virtual environments will replace the Web as we have known it.

As mentioned, the number of individuals who use virtual environments has been growing exponentially, but that does not necessarily translate into its use by educators for their own development or in their professional practice. What, then, are the educational benefits or reasons that these are being used? Is it really the next big thing or the educators' silver bullet we have all been searching for? Kelton (2008) suggests that it may be something worth considering:

> Just as once many in higher education loudly proclaimed that the Internet was of no practical use and was filled with questionable material and marketing, so too do critics today have their doubts about virtual worlds. But the web grew into a vital part of our lives, and a growing number of people believe that virtual worlds will do so the same. (p. 22)

According to Dede, Dieterle, Clarke, Ketelhut, and Nelson (2007), students may no longer "see face-to-face learning as the gold standard for education" (p. 339). They continue by stating: "Their participation in multifaceted, distributed, and mediated, learning experiences outside of classrooms and courses causes them to see more traditional school learning as rather mundane because it is based solely on face-to-face learning" (p. 339).

Barab, Thomas, Dodge, Carteaux, and Tuzun (2005) suggest:

> This work sits at the intersection of education, entertainment, and social commitment and suggests an expansive focus for instructional designers. The focus is on engaging classroom culture and relevant aspects of student life to inspire participation consistent with social commitments and educational goals interpreted locally. (p. 86)

Barab et al. (2005) also state that this is "a product that is not a game, yet remains engaging, is not a lesson, yet fosters learning, is not evangelical, yet nurtures a social agenda" (p. 88).

More important, research has begun to show that students may learn in this environment. Hickey, Ingram-Goble, and Jameson (2009) reported that their research does suggest gains in learning. In two studies of Quest Atlantis, they found sixth grade students making "larger gains in understanding and achievement" than in classes that used expository text to learn the same concepts and skills (p. 187). In a study of a similar type of project, Ketelhut (2007) found that her results "suggest that embedding science inquiry curricula in novel platforms like a MUVE might act as a catalyst for change in students' self-efficacy and learning processes" (p. 99).

In addition, many educators have discovered virtual environments for their own growth and learning. At the ISTE NECC 2009 conference, one presentation was by The Virtual Pioneers, a group of social studies educators using Second Life to learn, collaborate, and share information to enhance their professional development and professional network. Teachers have created a Ning to support and collaborate with others who use Second Life (http://secondclassroom.ning.com). Once educators began to recognize the power of these environments, their explorations grew and evolved.

when do teachers use virtual environments?

Classroom Integration

Teachers are using virtual environments in a wide variety of ways to support learning outcomes. For students, educational MUVEs are designed to engage minds, promote learning, and encourage creative thinking. They have typically been designed to support inquiry-based learning and conceptual understanding. The activities that accompany these environments promote the notion that, as in the real world of complex issues, there are no simple, single, or right/wrong answers; rather, they encourage divergent and exploratory thinking. Students using educational MUVEs frequently are required to gather information offline, and usually there is an expectation of a final product that may take many forms.

One type of activity is known as epistemic games; they are "explicitly based on theory of learning in the digital age and are designed to allow learners to develop domain-specific expertise under realistic constraints" (Rupp et al., 2009, p. 4). The goal is to have learners experience what it is like to really think and act like "journalists, artists, business managers, or engineers by using digital learning technologies to solve realistic complex performance tasks" (p. 4). Designers develop a game that mimics the core experiences that learners outside the gaming environment would have in a professional practicum in a particular field. The experiences that epistemic games afford and make accessible to learners are characterized by a blend of individual and collaborative work in both real-life and virtual settings.

One example of an educational MUVE is the River City Project, described as "a multi-user virtual environment for learning scientific inquiry and 21st century skills" (http://muve.gse.harvard.edu/rivercityproject/). With funding from the National Science Foundation, researchers at Harvard have "developed an interactive computer simulation for middle grades science students to learn scientific inquiry and 21st century skills. River City has the look and feel of a videogame but contains content developed from National Science Education Standards, National Educational Technology Standards, and 21st Century Skills." The River City Project was designed to represent a virtual 19th-century American town; the town happens to be plagued by disease. The simulation requires students to work in teams, study the materials presented, and then develop a hypothesis regarding the cause of the disease. They have the ability to read documents, examine photographs, visit the hospital, and interview River City citizens. Virtual agents are available to provide guidance, but the students determine the approach they will take (Ketelhut, 2007).

Another educational MUVE currently being evaluated is Quest Atlantis (http://crlt.indiana.edu/research/qa.html), a virtual environment for students aged 9 to 12 that immerses them in educational "quests." Due to poor leadership, this city is about to become a complete disaster, and the students are invited to help by following quests established by the Atlantan Council. These involve activities such as environmental study, interviewing members of the community, studying other cultures, and developing action plans. Barab et al. (2005) have conducted research on this project; they conclude, "We now see ourselves in the business of supporting the emergence of sociotechnical structures so as to support a common intersubjective experience, not simply designing technical artifacts" (p. 104). Lim, Nonis, and Hedberg (2006) also studied this environment and found growth in learning among the students who participated.

Research suggests that educational MUVEs should not focus solely on the virtual environment; learners still require and do best when they have ongoing support from the teacher and built-in time (and obligations) for self-reflection. As with most educational computer-based games, MUVEs are more effective in supporting learning when embedded in ongoing instruction.

Other groups have set up activities in the Teen Second Life to promote international activities and global citizenship. A teen reported on her experiences in

Camp Global kids, a free summer event offered by Global Kids, Inc. (Czarnecki & Gullett, 2007). She reported her efforts to investigate public policy as related to child sex trafficking and described the funds raised in Linden dollars, which do translate into real funds to support worthy projects.

Some locations on Teen Second Life represent a collaborative effort. The Public Library of Charlotte and Mecklenburg County in North Carolina created the Eye4You Alliance (http://eye4youalliance.youthtech.info). They sought to reach teens and determined that Teen Second Life was the right way to accomplish that goal (Czarnecki & Gullett, 2007). They conducted many projects in efforts to engage and support teen learning and goals, including a Tech Virtual Museum Project where students created exhibits in real time, a College Fair, and a transitions project for teens turning 18 and transitioning into the adult Second Life grid.

Kids Connect is a program that uses SL to connect young people in different countries via media art, performance, and creative collaboration. It employs a series of workshops to teach them ways to connect and work together via performance, storytelling, and collaboration, through both physical and digital means. It includes opportunities for digital storytelling; live visual performances; theater activities, including explorations with sound; video editing and streaming; and 3-D modeling.

In the Brooklyn High School for Global Citizenship, funding from the Motorola Innovation Generation grant allowed educators to develop a new curriculum for a freshman physical science class that takes advantage of the characteristics of the virtual world in Second Life. The curriculum is designed to be well aligned to the state curriculum standards and to supplement face-to-face teaching and learning, yet their goal is to "teach the kids how to be citizen-scientists in the future" (Czarnecki, 2008, p. 14). For example, one activity required the students to tour a virtual Naples, Italy, and conduct a survey of a trash dump, which they used to make comparisons with their own real-life trash dump.

Specific educational strategies that are supported in Second Life and that work well include creating interactive workshops, scavenger hunts, and quizzes. Others include having students demonstrate their knowledge and connections through photography shows, role playing, machinima (animated movies), and contests. Guests may enter in the form of speakers, debates, or movie screenings. And finally, students can generate artifacts such as buildings, T-shirts, or other products (http://www.globalkids.org/?id=30).

Individuals involved in teaching art education are also exploring the potential in the virtual worlds. Art educators have considered the creation of art, online art exhibitions, performance art, and education about the creation of art and what it means to have visual culture (Liao, 2008). These ideas have translated into a variety of activities in which budding artists share their developing and completed works and have the opportunity to give and receive feedback on emerging efforts. Liao (2008) also suggests that the way in which avatars are created and presented is a form of art.

Imagine a "social studies class examining immigration building a virtual Ellis Island, complete with the Statue of Liberty and Lower East Side tenements" (Czarnecki & Gullett, 2007, p. 36). Consider students building an avalanche or learning math by shopping in virtual environments, or using 3-D rays in a geometry unit as students work on their angles, proofs, and demonstrations of conceptual understanding. Or perhaps consider the impact on students who can explore the most ecologically appropriate place, a green library launched in early 2009 called Emerald City. A teacher or library/media instructor can log in and allow their students to explore or hear a lecture. "One upcoming program will cover photovoltaics, the science behind converting sunlight into electricity" (Barack, 2009, p. 13).

Another school is promoting ways to encourage teens to engage in Second Life activities for curricular development; since 2005 the New York Ramapo Central School District has created six islands with about 800 users able to log on simultaneously (Czarnecki, 2008). They have approximately 1,200 students and almost 50 teachers in projects related to music, foreign language, and history. The creator of the project, Peggy Sheehy, blogs at http://ramapoislands.edublogs.org and describes her experiences as well as those of the participants. It appears that attention is given to careful validation of teens who are part of the projects, and so far no real difficulties have been reported.

Bill Freese, an instructor at Montana State University, inspired by Sheehy's work, has his preservice teaching students log in and visit three locations that are related to Montana's Indian Education for All initiative. He helps these future teachers learn skills needed to navigate and interact with that 3-D virtual learning environment. Freese reports, "Students are advised to read over the section in the text on appropriate behavior in the Second Life community. Student reaction has been positive. The best reaction comes from students who go 'in-world' together. In one case a student who went in alone and happened to begin at a location that was experiencing virtual night found the experience 'creepy.' Many students are excited by the potential 3-D virtual learning environments have for education in their classrooms in the future" (B. Freese, electronic communication, August, 2009).

Professional Development

Teachers are social, and they are universally eager to develop their connectivity on two levels. First, educators want to improve their practice, reflect on their activities, and learn from others. These goals may have encouraged them to explore virtual environments such as Second Life. But it is also true that humans, as individuals, have an innate desire to share, communicate, and grow on a personal level. People from all over the world who share interests found this environment to be richer, more creative, and more expressive than other tools, even other Web 2.0 tools.

A variety of sites have evolved to introduce and support teachers who wish to explore the qualities and characteristics of Second Life. The Teaching Village is a website for educators interested in exploring virtual worlds. Its motto is "We're better when we work together" and they support teachers as they learn. Barbara (www.teachingvillage.org/2009/07/13/why-every-language-teacher-needs-a-second-life/) writes, "Considering that I thought an avatar was a deity in Hindu Mythology, I think it's fair to say that my learning curve was pretty steep." She goes on to describe her exposure and growth in this environment and appears genuinely delighted that members of her learning community come from many countries and speak many languages.

Other sites offer introductions to all the possibilities. A list of social networks for learning and collaborating about teaching in virtual worlds is one example (www.c4lpt.co.uk/socialmedia/edunetworks.html). Second Life Bloggers (http://secondlifebloggers.ning.com) offers insights and links to others who are beginners and experts in using these tools. Gaming and Learning in Second Life (http://galisl.ning.com) is another site where educators explore and share their experiences. Their mission is "To focus and catalyze worldwide efforts of educators, commercial ventures, and organizations to harness, promote, and implement gaming for the purposes of intentional and incidental learning in Second Life." There is even a Second Life Travel Guide (http://landmarkisland.ning.com) to show others the best places to visit in this virtual environment.

The International Society for Technology in Education (ISTE) has spearheaded the efforts to bring educators together in Second Life. Each week they hold meetings and social events at the ISTE Island, and the number of individuals participating has been steadily growing. Teachers, computer coordinators, and others have planned projects, shared ideas, and developed close friendships.

web 2.0 wisdom

Making Time for Professional Development in Second Life

Ann Morgester

MY RESPONSIBILITY as the Library Curriculum Coordinator requires me to provide professional development. I have found that synchronous sessions work much more effectively for the 85 librarians in my district. This critical need can't be met effectively with the current model of limited face-to-face meetings that we have, so I have been looking for another tool that will allow the district librarians to have access to engaging professional development.

I had some limited experience with Second Life and decided to try using it to meet our training needs. I began by sending out a survey to a group of teachers and librarians, asking those with some experience to rate the difficulty of learning certain basic skills, such as walking, flying, using inventory, communicating, and so forth, on a scale of 1–5. Next, I took a group of 14 librarians taking a technology integration class into Second Life as part of the class. None of these librarians had extensive experience in Second Life and 10 didn't even have an avatar. I provided a VoiceThread tutorial on walking, flying, landing, sitting, and searching ahead of time (http://voicethread.com/share/432639/).

▶ ▶ ▶

▶ ▶

Then, with my co-teacher, I met them three times in Second Life for 90 minutes each time. The two initial in-world meetings took place at the New Media Consortium (NMC) orientation area in Second Life and Virtual Ability Island to give them more familiarity with navigating in-world. On the third meeting we had a class discussion in-world on the possible utility of Second Life for professional development with other librarians. The change in the group, from very resistant and not seeing any utility before our three meetings, to having them independently plan to pair up and work together to gain the necessary skills in Second Life, was wonderful. While recognizing that no one tool is going to meet all needs and the steep learning curve of Second Life, the participants' positive reaction and willingness to work through the inevitable technological frustrations has led me to believe that this can be an effective venue for professional development in our district.

One stated, "I like that you do not all have to be in one place for professional development and you are still communicating in real time." Another commented, "I think the expertise worldwide would be great. I would enjoy finding out what other librarians are doing around the world and being able to ask questions." In response to a question about why use Second Life instead of a blog, one participant said, "I feel a greater investment doing this with people I know than blogging— blogging is too one-sided."

Ann Morgester is a library curriculum coordinator in the Anchorage School District, Anchorage, Alaska.

Many school districts, states, and organizations have set up locations in Second Life. You will find islands for library media professionals, high school science teachers, and primary generalists. Organizations offering every type of learning abound. One school district has created some interesting ways to use Second Life for professional development.

who is using virtual environments for teaching and learning?

Of course, Second Life is not the only virtual environment for learners and children. Another very popular environment is Webkinz (www.webkinz.com). A gift of a stuffed animal used to be just that; the recipient gave it a name and perhaps talked to it. Not any more! If you purchase a Webkinz stuffed animal—and Webkinz animals come in all manner of shapes and sizes—you also get a code. The recipient goes online and registers the animal. Once there, the resident can do many of the things that those in Second Life can do, but this environment is targeted more to preteens.

You can teleport to another location, take classes in a school, own a home and start a garden, and also take your pet to the veterinarian so that it remains healthy (the instructions to parents do say that although a pet who is not cared for may become ill, none are ever allowed to die!).

An interview with a Webkinz-active 10-year-old girl resulted in this information:

> It is a lot of fun. You get away from the real world, and my friends helped me know what to do and how to do things. I have a beagle, a cat, and a salamander. I like to take care of them, and take care of my house and garden. I bathe my animals, brush their teeth, and tend to my plants in my garden. I get around by teleporting myself, and I can see if any of my friends are on when I am. You can send messages but they can only be certain safe things and no bad words. (Cassie, personal communication, August, 2009)

For other youngsters, Club Penguin is the favorite virtual environment (www.clubpenguin.com). Club Penguin tells parents that it is a virtual world for kids dedicated to safety and creativity. Although advanced features have a subscription fee associated with them, children can explore the environment for free. The website also states, "We value social involvement and encourage the kids who play Club Penguin to get involved in projects that support developing communities, and help children and families around the world" (www.clubpenguin.com/parents).

Members of Club Penguin also create their penguin avatar, and they have a wide variety of learning adventures, places to visit, and things to do. These include coloring, contests, online votes, and many other ways to engage with friends socially. Members can become tour guides and earn coins, but you must pass a test about Penguin Club to be selected. As with other virtual environments, there is a store where you can spend your coins, find penguin paraphernalia, and decorate your home.

Even though Webkinz and Club Penguin are for children, they can also be easy entry points for adults. Lisa Cundiff, from Kansas, reported that she "introduced teachers/administrators to the use of Webkinz as a way of learning basic social networking skills, information literacy, skills building, and responsibility" (L. Cundiff, electronic communication, August, 2009).

These are not necessarily the same as guided educational experiences that are completed within a school curriculum. For example, South Greenville Elementary School in North Carolina (www.pittschools.org/sge/) has 670 students. A small group of advanced students take part in a Young Einstein Club for Grades 3–5. In this project students were to plan, design, and construct a space compound, which was to be located on a distant planet named VRLAB. The students would then use virtual reality software to build the compound and walk around in it. Students would be responsible for including a specific set of objectives and criteria in their compound creation. This allowed students to construct an imaginative virtual environment while being guided by the objectives and criteria of the project.

The University of Luebeck, in Germany, designed a study in which a third grade class used virtual reality. The learners created an environment known as a "mixed reality world," in which real and virtual worlds are merged to produce a new environment where real and digital objects can co-exist. The class's goal was to incorporate computer science into the study of arts. The children used LEGO software to animate and interact with things they had previously created. They were thus able to mix the ways of thinking about these two areas and experienced true interactive learning.

Opportunities abound for students to experience educational opportunities in a virtual environment. For example, the University of Cincinnati planned a Second Life adventure to celebrate the 200-year anniversary of the publication of *On the Origin of Species* (Collins, 2008). While they planned many on-campus activities, they extended those by re-creating Darwin's historic journey, including representing indigenous species in their natural habitat. Becaused they used actual photographs, videos, and other materials collected by students on trips to the Galapagos, their Second Life site offers authentic opportunities for learners throughout the world to explore and interact while learning the history of the adventure.

What might the longer view of virtual worlds be for educators and learners in the next many years? Kelton (2008) reminds us:

> The educational aspect of virtual worlds has attracted a diversity of people and organizations. Government agencies (such as NOAA) and programs offering hazmat or other simulated training, students taking both credit and noncredit classes, and people from all around the world coming together in the same place, at the same time, to work on a shared idea or project— many of these efforts are simply not feasible in the non-digital world. (p. 22)

Although research into the use of virtual environments is only beginning to be seen in the literature base, Leese (2009) did report that freshmen were able to stay involved in their class and with their colleagues between face-to-face sessions through the use of a virtual setting and carefully structured environments. Unfortunately, we may need to wait for a robust body of research that actually provides useful information on the affordances and constraints of using these environments.

Wagner (2008) reports that users can practice new behaviors and repeat them, in safe but productive environments. This research study resulted in more engagement than expected by the instructor, and enthusiasm from the students. "Users thus create their own experiences and construct their own knowledge. Different from much of classroom learning, the experience is immersive and learning-by-doing" (p. 263).

Second Life, unlike Teen Second Life, has some of the same issues that the web has, or for that matter, that life itself has (Botterbusch & Talab, 2009). For example, individuals can have multiple or false identities, offer illicit materials, or take part in spamming. There have been some reports of harassment, vandalism, and unauthorized use of information. But in Teen Second Life, protections are firmly and carefully attended to. No vulgar language or sexually explicit content is allowed. Adults are carefully screened before being granted access into Teen Second Life, and those who are in the Teen Grid are typically involved in educational projects.

In 2008, Google experimented with Lively, which was designed to be "a free, browser-based virtual environment with tight integration to MySpace, Facebook, OpenSocial, and Google gadgets like Picasa and YouTube" (Updated Breaking News, 2008). Lively closed January 1, 2009. It is important to recognize that although Second Life is now the most heavily populated and robust virtual environment, this may not always be the case.

how do you get started with virtual environments?

It is worth the time to get familiar with Second Life (http://secondlife.com) as a start to your efforts in the virtual world. And we strongly recommend that, as an educator, you become very familiar with Second Life before you begin designing instructional activities that take advantage of its affordances. The place to begin is at Orientation Island Public, where you can learn to fly, modify your avatar, and even make sure you are appropriately dressed. You have the ability to ask questions of the numerous Second Life Mentors, who can answer them as well as show you around. You can also stop at InfoHubs where you can get information about specific aspects of thriving in Second Life.

There are three main ways to communicate: chat, instant messaging, and voice. You can chat by typing text into a text box at the bottom of your screen, much as you might do in a variety of technology environments; but it can be read by anyone in the immediate vicinity. An instant message is private and can be sent to someone online synchronously; or if they are not online, they will get your message in an e-mail. Finally, you can speak to others, but it is best to have a headset and microphone system to be effective. Worth noting is that nothing in Second Life is really private; others may save and print your chats.

Soon you will have mastered teleporting (a great way to move where you want to go quickly). You can then learn how to search for specific things you are interested in, for example, other teachers. The International Society for Technology in Education (ISTE) has an island with weekly meetings and many discussions taking place. Happily, ISTE has a docent program, so there are always volunteers ready and willing to provide you with information, resources, and introductions. That may also be a way to find others interested in topics similar to your own.

Another well-established island is Jokaydia, which was developed by two Australians. It is a community of educators and artists who are dedicated to finding ways to use Second Life in education and the arts. And the Discovery Educator Network (DEN) has also been established. In this area educators can connect and share with each other, exchange ideas, and often create innovative cross-cultural and cross-curricular projects.

Beth Kindle (2008) recommends the following as great places to begin your exploration of Second Life:

Genome Project:
http://slurl.com/secondlife/Genome/158/119/29

ISTE Island:
http://slurl.com/secondlife/ISTE%20Island/134/44/22

Jokaydia:
http://slurl.com/secondlife/jokaydia/113/150/23

NOAA:
http://slurl.com/secondlife/Meteora/175/152/27

Paris 1900s:
http://slurl.com/secondlife/Paris%201900/44/169/24

Roma (Ancient Rome):
http://slurl.com/secondlife/ROMA/215/25/22

Sistine Chapel Re-creation:
http://slurl.com/secondlife/Vassar/116/113/27

It is also worth reading Kevin Jarrett's blog about his recent sabbatical to study Second Life. Kevin has now completed his six months of immersion into all things Second Life and still helps newcomers to the ISTE Island. You can read his experiences, thoughts, and more at www.storyofmysecondlife.com/?page_id=2/.

where can you find more information about virtual environments?

There are many video introductions to Second Life. For example, www.youtube.com/watch?v=edUV0_FOl0M shows ways to move smoothly and with relative ease. Here are some more:

Information and Community for Educators using M.U.V.Es:
  http://simteach.com

New Media Consortium virtual tour:
  www.youtube.com/watch?v=S9VZKTT6gZ8

Tongue-in-cheek answers to critics of SL:
  http://torley.com/second-life-simple-answers-to-curious-remarks

For an excellent overview of SL (click on the hotlinks in the presentation to view the embedded videos), go to:
  www.slideshare.net/sreljic/aect2007sreljic

For a co-presentation on MIT's Cultura project and SL, watch this short video:
  http://willowshenlin.blip.tv

Second Life Education Wiki:
  http://simteach.com/wiki/index.php?title=Second_Life_Education_Wiki#Institutions_and_Organizations_in_SL

Educators Working with Teens:
  www.simteach.com/wiki/index.php?title=Second_Life:_Educators_Working_with_Teens

Global Kids videos:
www.holymeatballs.org/library.htm#video

Global Kids Science—Students' Houses (Machinima):
www.youtube.com/watch?v=yRkcT3PjYyM

Best Practices in Using Virtual Worlds For Education:
www.holymeatballs.org/pdfs/BestPractices.pdf

8

wikis

what is a wiki?

Wikis are web pages that students can use to write, edit, and add elements, such as images and video, to create collaborative projects. When the assignments are tailored well, the projects involve a group of students in researching, synthesizing, and analyzing information, writing about what they've learned, and evaluating and editing one another's work. The end result is a product that all members of the group believe is their best work.

The most well-known wiki in public use is Wikipedia, a collaborative encyclopedia that includes an enormous amount of information. It is constantly updated. Contributors and evaluators monitor and edit the entries, which serves as a way to authenticate the contents so that people can trust the information. The most popular wikis in education are PBworks (formerly PBwiki) and Wikispaces.

why is a wiki a useful tool?

Class assignments that include elements of project-based learning, collaboration, authentic work, and an audience can help students develop and refine higher level thinking skills. Wikis are good tools to use for such assignments.

The possibilities for classroom uses include group collaboration and problem solving, peer editing during the writing process, and electronic portfolios. Students produce a shared document online by writing, editing, and revising it in their own class, across a grade, school, district, or with others. They can work from anywhere, which means they are able to contribute 24/7 rather than being limited to the school day or class period. If they are creating work that others will use to learn about the topic, both the task and the audience are authentic.

Students read and build on each other's work in these collaborative online environments because they can do research, analyze what they've read, and synthesize it into useful knowledge before contributing their work. Then, the group reflects on it; and they discuss and edit it with the knowledge that changing anything is easy and that it can easily be changed back as previous versions are saved.

An example would be a team-writing assignment in which students research a topic in the curriculum, analyze what they find, enter their syntheses into the wiki, and consult with one another to make sure the topic is covered thoroughly and accurately. They can use peer editing to make sure the writing is clear and concise.

Because everyone in the group can add, edit, delete, or change the contents, this makes the process democratic. Changes are visible instantly, which encourages responsibility for one's actions and accountability to the group. In addition, it is possible for the teacher to track the work done by each student in a collaborative effort, which encourages a high level of contribution and quality performance. According to Lake (2009), "Students need to experience this in order to become prepared for work that can take place virtually, perhaps over long distances, often within shifting work groups."

when do teachers use wikis?

Classroom Integration

Wikis are effective tools for fostering collaborative learning. According to Tom Nelson, a technology coach at Liberty High School in Liberty, Pennsylvania's Southern Tioga School District:

> When using a wiki with students, we have them post technology projects in the wiki and then use the discussion tab to discuss the work entered. For example, a student creates and embeds a toondoo [toondoo.com is a cartoon creator] to the class wiki. The teacher posts a question on the discussion board about the project and requires all students to view the project and post a response. This helps foster the collaborative learning environment by providing the opportunity for peer-to-peer evaluation. (T. Nelson, electronic communication, August, 2009)

Integrating technology is not the end of the story. Clearly, any assignment must be based on good pedagogy. For example, in a TechLearning blog post, Jon Orech (2009c) admonishes readers that we need to rely on time-tested collaborative learning strategies and not just focus on the tools. What's new is that having the tool makes it easier to accomplish the task. He says:

> Many times in wikis, students add, but are reluctant to edit the work of others. … As a result, most wikis take on the look of a patchwork quilt, with each "panel" reflecting the ideas of a single individual. Don't get me wrong, the quilt model can fulfill some great objectives; however, for a true collaborative writing process, the final product needs to resemble, not a quilt, but a blanket. To

achieve this, teachers, once again must embrace those Cooperative Learning structures in cyberspace that they did in their classrooms. (J. Orech, blog post, March 25, 2009)

web 2.0 wisdom

Turbo-Charged Wikis: Technology Embraces Cooperative Learning

Jon Orech (February, 2009)

BY INFUSING COOPERATIVE LEARNING strategies, student-generated wikis become a much more productive activity. First, a teacher must establish a collaborative environment from the beginning of class. A wiki-based project should not be the first time students work together. Collaborative projects work well, but only if an environment of cooperation already exists.

The assignment of the project must possess two qualities. First, it must be an authentic problem or situation that must be solved collaboratively. Second, the final product must be utilized by another audience, preferably classmates to advance the learning of the entire class. In other words, the wiki cannot result in an assignment that is merely "turned in." Also teachers need to remember that the wiki is only the tool to enhance learning; the problem solving is what drives the project.

In addition, teachers need to supply a system of expectations, due dates, and a constant flow of feedback throughout the development of project. They must build in time for students to meet during class to negotiate meaning in the planning and revision stages. Assessment must be a collaborative endeavor, with students having input on the rubric criteria prior to the completion of the project, as well as an opportunity to self assess. Adherence to these strategies will ensure greater learning.

Jon Orech is the Instructional Technology Coordinator for Downers Grove South High School, Downers Grove, Illinois.

Wikis provide three options that are unlike most composing software and that offer interesting possibilities for learning and teaching. First, wikis allow people to edit someone else's work. Second, they retain previous versions that writers can revert to. Third, they keep track of everyone's individual entries and edits.

What the first option provides is the ability for true group collaboration on a document with peer editing. The second prevents the edits from writing over the original permanently and losing words, ideas, or manners of expression that might actually have been the better way to say something. Educators must teach students how to evaluate the accuracy and appropriateness of content and revert to a previous version if content has been modified incorrectly.

The third option allows teachers to track students' work; they can see exactly how much work, and of what caliber, each member of the group contributed. If the final product and the process are graded separately, teachers can review the number of contributions as well as the quality. Students, aware that teachers can see all, are motivated to do their best.

In addition to having students read other groups' completed wikis—vetted by the teacher for accuracy, of course—on topics in the curriculum and learn content from them rather than from textbooks, teachers can invite parents and the community to read the work as a culminating activity that brings in a wider authentic audience.

If students are graded on the final product, they share a common goal and would want the work to be the best possible. When they help one another by editing and making changes to each other's work, it would be for the good of the product and the entire group.

Students learn from one another and the results, both for the learner as a thinking person and for the end product, can be greater than a single isolated learner can achieve. In addition, students engaged in providing explanations to other students can learn the subjects better themselves.

When students take ownership of both their contributions and the product as a whole, they can learn to respect the contributions and thinking of others and take pride in the results. The collaboration itself can result in creativity that learners spark in one another as they work together (and challenge one another's thinking) to improve the work.

Students share control of the environment and can monitor one another. Access is open to the collaborating students by password protection, but only one person at a time can add content or edit. Peer editing means that the original copy is deleted but the earlier versions are saved, which makes it possible to revert to a previous version or reconstruct content.

Wikis can be set up to notify the person managing the wiki each time someone makes a change; if it's not appropriate, the manager (teacher or student leader) can erase it. Both monitoring and limiting access usually are enough to prevent inappropriate content and language, as well as spam.

Unlike word processors and other desktop publishing tools, most wikis provide basic editing only, which means that students focus on the message rather than the format. Entering and editing text is easy and straightforward, and there's no real learning curve for students. Again, the focus is on the subject matter because the tool is transparent.

Each student's work is saved and teachers are able to track what each one has contributed to the product, both their contributions and their corrections to another student's work. Reviewing their entire body of contributions allows teachers to see how each student's thinking, writing, and editing skills have grown over time. Because of this, some teachers are using wikis as electronic portfolios for student projects.

In "Using Wikis as Electronic Portfolios," Huff (2008) explains:

> Using inquiry-based learning, I created a wiki page to pose questions, point students to resources, and encourage them to find their own answers and solutions for creating the portfolio. Then, rather than give them step-by-step directions for creating the portfolio, I chunked the project into small deadlines and guided and supported them through the process as they asked questions, experimented with different tools, and struggled with strategies for organizing the portfolios. … I was amazed at the results: students created websites, new blogs, and combinations of the two. They weren't just stuffing papers in a manila folder: they were thinking critically and creatively, problem-solving, reflecting.

Wikis make good places to post information that both students and parents can read. Students have a way to check the specifics of an assignment in case they forget, and parents can monitor the work. For example, Karey Killiak from Millville High School in Millville, Pennsylvania, says, "We use the public wiki to post assignments, lessons, and links to resources. We use the private wikis with individual classes so that students can have discussions and post their assignments and work collaboratively on assignments" (K. Killiak, electronic communication, August, 2009).

Millville High uses wikis in almost all subject areas. In world literature, students discuss elements of an epic in the discussion tab and create original epics as a class. In 12th grade environmental science, the teacher has been using the Discussion area to create class discussions. On the public page for geometry students, the teacher has several links to applications that students access and use to solve equations. Eighth grade English students write advice for incoming seventh graders.

Professional Development

Collaboration is an advantage for educators because, traditionally, teachers have worked in isolation with little sharing among peers. Wikis, as an easy tool to use for grade-level or subject-area teams, or for any other group collaboration, provide educators with a way to post and share information, strategies, thoughts, and lessons, and to build on one another's work. They also provide a back channel for ongoing discussions among their peers about their work.

Probably the most well-known wiki-based collaborative educational project among educators is the California Open Source Textbook Project, a world history pilot project for ninth grade world history/social studies students that is based on California State Curriculum Standards. It is posted on Wikibooks at http://en.wikibooks.org/wiki/COSTP_World_History_Project/.

Administrators can use wikis with the staff. For example, principals can ask the staff to write and edit policy documents, such as Internet safety rules or hallway safety procedures, using a wiki. This gives stakeholders a truly responsible role in creating the kind of document that reflects their beliefs. The best ideas will emerge as the group collaborates toward the goal of providing the document for the school.

Professional developers can use wikis with groups of educators in workshops and in preservice or inservice courses. They can use a wiki to have the educators share best practices and discuss teaching strategies. Group members can post discussion items for class in advance, add notes during the session, and edit and use the results later.

Bill Ferriter (2009) suggests in "Learning with Blogs and Wikis":

> Consider finding a few peers to write about teaching and learning together. Divide your topic of interest into subtitles or sections. Teachers could be responsible for creating content for their area of expertise; they could generate key ideas, add links to external resources, upload appropriate documents, or embed interesting videos. Then allow users who are fluent with language to polish your final text. Find members who are sticklers for spelling and grammar and turn them loose. (p. 37)

He adds, "On a wiki, the writing process is far less intimidating than on a blog because you're not responsible for an entire selection all by yourself. Instead, you'll reflect with colleagues—which in and of itself is a powerful form of professional growth" (Ferriter, 2009).

who is using wikis for teaching and learning?

There's no shortage of great examples of teachers using wikis for collaborative student projects. Three collaborative projects that used wikis were winners of ISTE's Special Interest Group for Telecommunications (SIGTel) Online Learning Awards contest for 2007 and 2008. Following are descriptions of those award-winning projects. The other project examples were reported by educators in response to our online survey and our requests for information for this book.

Award Winners

The Mysteries of Harris Burdick Collaborative Writing Project (2008). Lisa Parisi and Christine Southard, from the Denton Avenue Elementary School in New Hyde

Park, New York, and Brian Crosby, from the Agnes Risley Elementary School in Sparks, Nevada, won for their collaborative project *The Mysteries of Harris Burdick* Collaborative Writing Project (http://classroombooktalk.wikispaces.com/Mysteries+of+Harris+Burdick).

This writing project focused on the book *The Mysteries of Harris Burdick* by Chris Van Allsburg (1984). Allsburg's book is a collection of 14 pages illustrated by Harris Burdick for 14 different unpublished books, each page with a title and one line from the book. Fourteen classes from around the world with students aged 9 to 12 collaboratively wrote a story that goes along with each page of the book, creating their own versions. Classes were paired with one or two students from the partner class, and they communicated using Google Docs, e-mail, and Skype. Collaboration was a key skill learned during this project, as students created original stories together. They also learned how to communicate effectively with students who were not sitting right next to them.

The Flat Classroom Project (2007). Julie Lindsay, from the International School in Dhaka, Bangladesh, and Vicki Davis, from the Westwood Schools in Camilla, Georgia, won an award for their Flat Classroom Project (http://flatclassroomproject.wikispaces.com).

This project was an active learning project created for students on opposite sides of the globe—Dhaka, Bangladesh, and Camilla, Georgia—to discuss and experience 10 technological trends highlighted in the Thomas L. Friedman book *The World Is Flat* (2007). This telelearning activity is original in its use of Web 2.0 tools to foster communication and collaboration and to construct web spaces and share ideas. It also champions social networking as a pedagogically valid method for learning.

International Collaborative Literature Project: From Jerusalem to Montréal (2007). Sharon Peters, from Lower Canada College in Montréal, Québec, Canada, and Reuven Werber and Karen Guth, from the Neveh Channah School in Etzion Bloc, Israel, won an award for the International Collaborative Literature Project: From Jerusalem to Montréal (http://jerusalem.wikispaces.com).

This collaborative project was created for students from Lower Canada College in Montréal and Neveh Channah School in Israel to share literature and to promote understanding between their two cultures. The project topic focuses on cities. Israeli students approached this project as Jerusalem, City of Hope, with a study of poetry, song, and speeches in Hebrew and English. Montréal students shared information and literature about their city from a variety of Jerusalem-related topics, including historical time periods, famous personalities, and political topics. Montréal students chose relevant pieces of literature representing the cultural experiences of living in Québec, with a focus on tolerance, both historically and linguistically.

Other Examples

Fifth Grade Writing. Pam Shoemaker, technology integration coordinator for Walled Lake Consolidated Schools in Walled Lake, Michigan, created a collaborative project teaming students from different schools. She says, "We wanted to figure out a way to provide students with a unique and highly motivating learning experience that would not be possible within the traditional classroom walls" (Shoemaker, 2009, pp. 16–17).

The goals were to help students become better writers, communicators, and critical thinkers while using modern technological tools. Grade 5 students in two classrooms in different elementary schools created a project wiki.

They followed this procedure: Students posted a digital image, their choice, on their page of the project wiki. They wrote about their photo and the photo of their partner in a genre according to the district's fifth grade writing unit of study planning chart. They wrote from different perspectives, and with unique styles, about the same photo. When the students were finished, each student's wiki page had the original digital photo, the student's own written response to the photo, and the partner's written response.

Students then identified similarities and differences between the two writings and met with their partners to discuss writing strategies using Skype software with webcams as videoconferencing tools.

They compared the answers to such questions as: Where did I get my ideas? Did something I read or experienced influence my writing? What skills did I work on in this piece of writing? Was this piece easy or difficult for me to write?

High School French. Dianne Krause, French teacher at Wissahickon High School in the Wissahickon School District in Ambler, Pennsylvania, created Regions of France, a wiki project for students to learn about France.

The goal was for students to research a region of France and collaborate on creating a Wikispace page for their area of France. She created the shell of the Wikispace site, wrote instructions and rubrics, and discussed these with the students. The complete assignment is on the Wikispace page (http://regions defrance.wikispaces.com).

Students researched their region, created Wikispace pages, collaborated with peers, and used other Web 2.0 resources. This project impacted their learning because they created their pages and found the information that interests them about their region. It was not teacher directed at all.

Krause says, "This was my first real Wikispace project and I underestimated the time it would take the students to do it, but it ended up being a HUGE project and worthwhile" (D. Krause, electronic communication, August, 2009).

High School English. Dan McCarthy, an English teacher at Zebra New Tech High in Rochester, Indiana, used Wikispaces to help students discuss and deal with modern problems by understanding how they relate to the same issues that appear in William Shakespeare's *The Tragedy of Romeo and Juliet*. Students researched the Internet for information to help them better understand these problems in order to better write about them. What they tried to show included how to notice these issues, how these issues started, how to understand the different classifications that were in them, and how to resolve them.

McCarthy says that students kept journals, took notes, and developed Wikispace pages. Students collaborated to plan and create a group Wikispace in which they simulated the role of psychologists who were dealing with teen problems. Students conducted surveys to find out what other teenagers thought about their topics. McCarthy says, "It was awesome." The project planning form along with standards and more information are available at http://zperiod3group4.wikispaces.com. (D. McCarthy, electronic communication, August, 2009).

Grades K–5 Research and Collaboration. Gerald Aungst's gifted students at McDonald Elementary in Warmister, Pennsylvania, use wikis in various subjects to collaborate on research and create shared documents. Aungst's purpose is to create a larger community of students to generate more ideas and deeper interaction.

Students use wiki pages to compile and share research on various topics and have the opportunity to get feedback not only from their classmates, but also from students in other buildings and from parents. Aungst sets up template pages in the wiki along with pages giving instructions for the assignments. He also has an enrichment wiki in which teachers can read and share ideas for enrichment activities (G. Aungst, electronic communication, August, 2009).

A Potpourri of Projects

Examples of wiki projects that students have developed are available at Creative Web Tools For and By Kids (http://weewebwonders.pbworks.com), a project site for Jackie Gerstein's Grade 3–5 students. She says it is a "cross-curricular, student constructivist model. Students choose their own topic, do research, and demonstrate learning with a PBWiki" (J. Gerstein, electronic communication, August, 2009).

Most of the projects involve students posting information and links to websites with information about the topic for other students. For example, in the Forensic Science Project, the student designers say, "This page is about Forensic Science, a way of using science to solve crimes and analyze evidence" (J. Gerstein, electronic communication, August, 2009).

how do you get started with wikis?

There are quite a few wikis available online, so how do you choose which to use? Whether you're the tech person in the district or a classroom teacher, if it's going to be your decision, you need to decide what you need it for in order to choose. Some are simple and some are complex. Some are free and some have costs. Some have advertising and some don't.

Fourteen Tips for Using Wikis

1. Create a culture of trust in the class.

2. Establish goals for the project.

3. Post clear instructions.

4. Establish guidelines for all processes.

5. Set deadlines (interim and final).

6. Create and display assessment rubrics.

7. Make sure project activities are meaningful.

8. Define roles for team members and work with teams to assign them.

9. Keep instructions simple for both the assignment and for the wiki pages.

10. Provide examples and suggestions.

11. Decide if the wikis should be open to the public or limited to the class.

12. Remind students of copyright and licensing issues.

13. Check work regularly.

14. Provide encouragement.

Questions to Consider Before You Decide Which Wiki is Right for You

▶ Do I need a free wiki?

▶ Is there a school or district policy about advertising on websites that students see and use?

▶ Will the school's or district's infrastructure allow access to it?

▶ Is it easy to set up and use?

▶ Does it have features that are needed, such as adding images, video, and voice?

▶ Is it age appropriate?

Once you've selected the wiki, you can start right in to set up your top wiki page. Once the group is set up in a wiki, the two primary functions are Edit and Save.

Wikispaces Tutorial

Following is a tutorial to get started with Wikispaces, which offers free, advertising-free wikis for education. Setting up a Wikispace wiki is simple. Editing is a lot like editing in Microsoft Word.

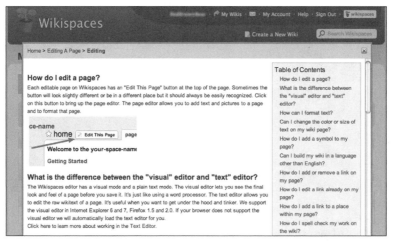

▶ **Figure 8.1.** Getting started editing your page (Wikispaces tutorial screen)

❶ Go to www.wikispaces.com/site/for/teachers/.

❷ Type a username.

❸ Choose a password.

④ Enter your e-mail address.

⑤ Answer Yes to Make a Wiki?

⑥ Choose a name for your Wikispace.

⑦ Select who can view the wiki (you can change this later):

▸ Public: Everyone can view and edit your pages

▸ Protected: Everyone can view pages but only wiki members can edit them

▸ Private: Only wiki members can view and edit pages

⑧ Certify that the space is for educational use by checking that box.

⑨ Click Join.

⑩ Your wiki page will appear, and it's ready to use.

⑪ Click on the Edit button at the top to start writing your wiki. (Entering and editing text is similar to working in a word processor.)

⑫ Click on Manage Wiki and Invite People to add new members to your wiki.

⑬ Click on Manage Wiki and Permissions to set who can view only or view and edit your wiki.

⑭ Click on Manage Wiki and Look and Feel to edit your wiki's theme or colors.

⑮ Click on the Help link anytime you need help.

where can you find more information about wikis?

Wikis in Plain English, TeacherTube Video:
http://www.teachertube.com/viewVideo.
php?video_id=20514&title=Wikis_In_Plain_English

Wiki Basics: Instructions for setting up a wiki page:
http://umwikiworkshop.wikispaces.com/Wiki_basics

7 Things You Should Know About Wikis:
www.educause.edu/eli/7ThingsYouShouldKnowAboutWikis/156807

Best Practices:
http://comm215.wetpaint.com/page/Best+Practices

MediaWiki (http://mediawiki.com) is the wiki engine that was developed for Wikipedia and other Wikimedia projects, but it is free for others to use. It is server-based, which means that it is protected and free of advertising.

Districts can set up a wiki on their own servers or use commercial wiki services such as Wikispaces (www.wikispaces.com), which offers its service free to educators and removes all advertising from its pages. Wikispaces also offers its fee-based Private Label wiki environment for a school or district, a system that provides central administration, control, and privacy. These wikis are secure because the teacher or someone at the district level determines who can view and edit.

PBworks (http://pbworks.com), formerly Pbwiki or Peanut Butter Wiki, is so named because using it is supposed to be as easy as making a peanut butter sandwich. PBworks is free for educators, and schools can password-protect their wikis.

Content management systems such as Blackboard (www.blackboard.com) offer wiki software within their systems, which makes them secure for students.

9

the future of the web—where to next?

Now that we see how to use the top web tools today, we have to wonder where technology and the resulting teaching and learning practices will be in the next few years and beyond. Although predicting the future precisely isn't possible, trends can point to logical possibilities.

The original web, now known as Web 1.0, changed the text-only information and communication capacity of the Internet into a visual experience of websites and vast libraries of data. It opened up the ability to publish to everyone. The content on a web page was predominantly text, but it was formatted to be visually pleasing and had illustrations with photos, charts, and other data. The key to its success was the ability to link to other pages and websites. The contents of those web pages were coded in hypertext markup language (HTML) or had software to allow nonprogrammers to post read-only and static information, with hyperlinks for navigation.

Today's Web 2.0 adds the element of interactivity and moves users from read-only pages to read-write. Users not only can retrieve information, but they are also able to create and share their own content easily and provide feedback on what others post, as well as add product reviews and find people with similar views. People write blogs, post images and videos, collaborate on documents, and socialize. The user experience is a democratic one. The most often used tools are the ones featured in the previous chapters.

Because of the potential, in the future people will continue to use the popular applications; however, the tools may be better integrated and transparent. Let's explore the current ideas around Web 3.0, 4.0, and X.0.

Web 3.0 is often called the semantic web and deals with the meaning of data. "Semantic web" is actually a term coined by Tim Berners-Lee, the man who is credited with inventing the World Wide Web. According to Cade Metz of *PC Magazine*, it means information cataloged as a vast database and a web "where machines can read web pages much as we humans read them, a place where search engines and software agents can better troll the Net and find what we're looking for" (Metz, 2007).

He also describes what others have identified as alternate versions of Web 3.0:

> The 3-D Web: A Web you can walk through. Without leaving your desk, you can go house hunting across town or take a tour of Europe. Or you can walk through a Second Life-style virtual world, surfing for data and interacting with others in 3-D.

> The Media-Centric Web: A Web where you can find media using other media—not just keywords. You supply, say, a photo of your

favorite painting and your search engines turn up hundreds of similar paintings.

The Pervasive Web: A Web that's everywhere. On your PC. On your cell phone. On your clothes and jewelry. Spread throughout your home and office. Even your bedroom windows are online, checking the weather, so they know when to open and close (Metz, 2007).

What's after that, or instead, or simultaneous? According to Seth Godin, who describes Web 4 in his blog of the same name,

> It is about ubiquity, identity, and connection: We need ubiquity to build Web 4, because it is about activity, not just data, and most human activity takes place offline. We need identity to build Web 4, because the deliverable is based on who you are and what you do and what you need. And we need connection to build Web 4, because you're nothing without the rest of us. Web 4 is about making connections, about serendipity and about the network taking initiative. (S. Godin, blog post, January 17, 2007)

web X.0 in education

How will the new—whatever number—web work for teaching and learning? We hope that it will be more widespread in classrooms and improve digital equity. We expect that it will be cost effective because the hardware that people will use to access it will be portable and affordable: smaller, cheaper, ubiquitous, and with web access 24/7. Schools will be able to provide the hardware for every student, which makes these devices personal and customizable.

In the not-to-distant future, teachers will be able to provide students with learning applications based on their level of understanding. They will be able to assess each task quickly and to direct students to assignments in the learning style they are most comfortable with. Students will communicate with peers, teachers, experts, and others when they need to and collaborate in teams as assignments require. Their results will appear online, with embedded images, voice, video, and more. All of the tools they need will be integrated or easy to access. Their teachers won't have to search for the right tool for the task; students will just click on the function they need and it will work. In addition, leaders will know how to support teachers as they revise and reinvent the way they teach. Clearly, this won't happen tomorrow or even next year, but we'll see a progression of more advanced and customizable tools.

Communication

Getting the message out is always the key to making a difference. As we saw in political situations in 2008 and 2009, technology tools play an increasingly critical role. In the United States' presidential election, then-candidate Senator Barack Obama was able to use the organizing potential of e-mail, video, and social networking to get people energized and politicized. In 2009, Twitter, Flickr, YouTube, and other social networking tools enabled people in Iran to rally hundreds of thousands of citizens to protest election fraud and communicate what was happening so that the world could watch despite official censorship.

The power of communication tools can be harnessed for learning when students can reach outside the walls of classrooms into the global community. For example, learning about democracy and elections by means of student posts from around the world is more powerful when current and recent events provide the context. Even history can come alive using new presentation methods. For example, was John Quincy Adams a twitterer?

> The Massachusetts Historical Society, under the Twitter tag JQAdams_MHS, is posting entries, from a diary Adams started writing the day he left Boston for St. Petersburg to serve as minister, or ambassador, to Russia. That day was Aug. 5, 1809, and the society chose Wednesday, precisely 200 years later, to post the daily entry from it. [These tweets] average 110 to 120 characters, below the 140-character limit imposed by Twitter. (Zezima, August 6, 2009)

Collaboration

We already see students who use wikis and online word processing tools to collaborate while creating and editing written documents and other media, and we see teachers who use social networks to find colleagues and form personal learning networks. Yet the use of tools such as these will grow, both so students can learn virtually and so teachers can create online textbooks and share other curricular materials online as learning tools for virtual schools.

When economic realities hinder districts from buying expensive and quickly outdated textbooks regularly, online versions offer advantages from cost, to immediacy, to a fast refresh cycle, to the ability to link to primary sources. Teachers can share their expertise to create book chapters and supplemental materials that others can retrieve as needed. As noted in Chapter 8, the California Open Source Textbook Project (http://en.wikibooks.org/wiki/COSTP_World_History_Project) is a collaborative, public/private venture created to address "the high cost, content range, and consistent shortages of K–12 textbooks in California."

Students can access these materials and learn from them. In addition, as student teams divide responsibility for researching information on specific aspects of a topic in order to produce collaborative projects, it may be possible for them to create knowledge, monitor and correct each other, and then post their results online for others to use.

In an interesting model of global collaboration, a team of animators from around the world created a five-minute animated film using the Wikipedia model, with each team member contributing shots and Facebook users voting on their favorites. The short, Live Music, was picked up and distributed by Sony Pictures Entertainment to show in theaters. The trailer is online at www.facebook.com/video/video.php?v=95080051740 (Barnes, 2009).

Mobility/Portability

Advances in chip design mean faster, smaller, and cheaper processors, which in turn mean faster, lighter, and cheaper computing devices. Netbooks are the new laptops, and while cell phones and other handheld devices lack fully functioning keyboards, students are adept at using them.

A recent report by the Joan Ganz Cooney Center states, "Advances in mobile technologies are showing enormous untapped educational potential for today's generation" (Shuler, 2009, p. 4). It highlights mobility as an opportunity to improve education by encouraging anytime, anywhere learning, reaching underserved children, promoting collaboration and communication, fitting in with learning environments, and achieving personalized learning.

Although schools in the United States are just beginning to use handheld devices in classrooms, mobile phones are used for education in "developing countries that don't have an extensive communications infrastructure but increasingly have access to cellular networks" (Shuler, 2009, p. 7).

The result of having lower cost devices available in classrooms will be in digital equity, providing access to technology for more children. Jenna Wortham of the *New York Times* cites an April 2009 report from the Pew Research Centers' Internet and American Life Project. It found that nearly half of all African Americans and English-speaking Hispanics were using cell phones (or handheld devices) to e-mail and surf the web, whereas just 28% of white Americans reported ever using a mobile device to go online. She says, "The surge is helping to close a looming digital divide stemming from the high cost of in-home Internet access, which can be prohibitive for some" (Wortham, 2009).

The result of having mobile web-accessible devices available is anywhere, anytime learning. For example, Holmes Middle School in Fairfax County, Virginia, ran a pilot iPod Touch project. According to Patrick Ledesma, the school-based technology coordinator, and Steve Jarosz, an eighth grade English teacher and department chair:

> Some teachers are using the device's Internet capabilities for accessing and posting information, while others touted the applications that facilitate data collection, educational game playing and simulations, and reading e-books. Then there are the programs for personal organization such as the calendar to keep track of important dates for assignments and projects. (Ledesma & Jarosz, 2009)

They selected the Wordpress application as their blogging platform to deliver content because it is easily readable in the handheld's Safari browser. Students blog, make comments, and discuss. Ledesma says, "The Touch really facilitates use of Web 2.0 tools with blog and podcast apps. Without these apps, it would just be a media player, but the apps really transform its usefulness in the classroom" (P. Ledesma, personal communication, August, 2009).

Ledesma surveyed students at the end of the school year and found only positive comments. These included:

▶ "I love to read, and unlimited access to classics was awesome."

▶ "When teachers reference something you can look it up [on the Internet]."

▶ "My favorite application was Vocab Daily because I would learn new words everyday."

Other students reported using the calculator in math, the Internet for research and taking notes in science and history, an application for translating foreign words into English, the calendar for recording project due dates and birthdays, and (surprising to us) the alarm clock for waking up. Commenting on the variety of uses, one student suggested, "My advice is to keep it with you at all times" (P. Ledesma, personal communication, August, 2009).

Apple's new iPad has potential as well. Building on the iPod Touch's capabilities and borrowing a page from e-readers such as Kindle and Nook, the iPad is poised to transform web interactions and expand one-to-one computing. Similar devices from HP and other hardware companies are slated to join this new category of web appliance.

While still a relatively costly consumer device with some drawbacks for school districts looking to link student work with assessment systems, the iPad has advantages for student use. According to Patrick Ledesma, "By converting the interface and quick access of a phone operating system to a tablet, combined with a larger screen and long battery life, the iPad provides quick and sustained access to applications."

As with other Web 2.0-based devices, "A wide variety of productivity and education apps, ranging from writing tools, informational resources, and subject-specific tools and games, provide both teachers and students with many new options," adds Ledesma (P. Ledesma, personal communication, May, 2010).

Personal

A browser window may have a personal start page or personal learning space that students can customize with widgets (such as mascots, photo viewers, etc.), gadgets (such as games, IM quick links, etc.), and apps (such as a thesaurus, grammar checker, spelling flash cards, etc.).

Personalizing learning, to whatever extent possible, means that students are able to find and learn what they need to know, when they need to learn it, and in a manner that suits them based on their learning styles or the way they like to approach learning. Some people learn visually; they may think in images and learn best from visual displays, including videos, photographs, slide shows, and online presentations. Auditory learners prefer listening and learn best from lectures and discussions that are podcast as well as from podcasts of their own notes to play back. Tactile/kinesthetic learners prefer touching objects, moving, performing, following directions using a hands-on approach, exploring the physical world, and manipulating objects. The interactive nature of web tools allows them to get the physical sensations they need to conceptualize information.

As the technology advances, it may be possible for students to select the method by which they learn best and have the lesson appear online. An assessment component can provide feedback to the teacher on how well they've learned the information or skill, what tasks to do next, and what approach is most likely to work.

Transparent, Integrated, Intuitive

After spending part of this book providing tutorials for the various popular web tools and examples of best practices in classrooms today, it may sound strange to say that the tools may not continue to exist in their current form. But that's precisely what may happen. From whatever user interface students choose or personal start page they customize, the tools will be transparent and intuitive. All the features will be a click away and fully integrated. This new version of the web will assemble tools so that using them is intuitive. One prototype that showed promise but might have been ahead of its time is Google Wave (wave.google.com), a communication and collaboration tool that Google released in 2009 (but stopped supporting in 2010).

The key to students' ability to use the tools well for learning continues to be teacher professional development: helping teachers to understand how students learn differently with collaboration and communication tools to which anyone can add features that provide more options when someone needs them.

For example, a group science report about South American weather patterns could work as follows: The group leader opens a wiki-like page in his personal start page and adds the names of the other students. The page would appear on all of their screens.

Each student looks at the widget for Google Earth and selects an appropriate country. As part of the exercise, each student wants to find out what the current weather is in a specific country from someone who lives there. Each could click a button to bring up a microblog box and send a tweet with the request. Followers could resend the message (currently known as RT, or retweeting) so that it reaches a wider audience.

The microblog box would offer the option of staying open to wait for replies, which are translated automatically. Each student could check the location of a responder on the Google Map widget, tally his or her responses, and include the information in the wiki or Google Docs Spreadsheet, along with any interesting comments, by copy-and-pasting the remarks and citing the author. If a reply links to a Flickr photo or YouTube video licensed for sharing on Creative Commons, a student could drag and drop it into the wiki, with attribution. At any point, any team member can insert an instant message or e-mail to any other team member or to the whole group. If someone forgets how to figure out the data, he or she can click on a gadget and use an interactive math game that teaches mean, median, and mode. Students would also have the option of checking their online textbooks for background information, as well as searching the web with a built-in intelligent search agent.

If class time is used for such an activity, the students might be on their laptops or netbooks; after school, they might work from handheld devices or cell phones. Because everything is online, whether stored on a cloud or school district server, the ongoing, editable report is always available to anyone on the team. Once the activity is completed, the group leader can post the finished product to a blog, class website, or anywhere else by clicking a make-live button and selecting where to post it. From this point, the teacher can track the contributions of each student, insert an assessment module linked to standards, and provide additional differentiated instruction modules to students whose skill in an area is weak.

Extensible: Apps, Gadgets, and Widgets

As we see from the above example, the possibilities for integrated tools are endless. Early examples include applications available on social networking sites such as Facebook. Members can add apps to integrate YouTube videos, Delicious bookmarks, and other tools. There are apps to edit photos, play collaborative games, create quizzes, engage in real-time chats, and even to create your own app. Zoho Online Office is a collaborative work space accessible from Facebook; however, this app isn't hosted within Facebook. Instead it opens a new window on the Zoho site.

For education, apps could include digital content that is integrated into a personal start page. Districts already create their own digital texts and materials. For example, when in 2005 the Vail School District in Vail, Arizona, substituted laptops for textbooks in Vail's first 1-to-1 high school, teachers created a library of original digital content so that they could select specific materials, just as they would with music on iTunes, instead of whole texts (Demski, 2009). The next step is to have them fully integrated with other apps.

Mashups as Metaphor

Mashups are interactive web applications, services, or pages that pull in content from one or more external data sources to create entirely new services. In the past, web developers, rather than nontechnical users, wrote these programs. One example is using Google Maps to superimpose crime statistics, school information, and other data to displays geared towards real estate clients. More recently, personal start pages let users add gadgets or widgets such as e-mail, calendars, newsfeeds, blogs, social networks, podcasts, games, photos, videos, weather, or other information they need.

These sites use Application Programming Interfaces (APIs) from different sites to aggregate and repurpose content in a new way. The content is automatically updated every time you visit your page. Ajax-based Pageflakes (www.pageflakes.com), iGoogle (www.google.com/ig), and Netvibes (www.netvibes.com) are examples. They also are free.

For example, iGoogle lets you create a personalized home page that contains a Google search box at the top and your choice of any number of gadgets below. Gadgets come in lots of different forms and provide access to activities and information from all across the web, without ever having to leave your iGoogle page. Gadgets allow you to do such things as view your latest Gmail messages; read headlines from top news sources; check out weather forecasts, stock quotes, and movie times; store bookmarks for quick access; and design your own gadget.

In addition, Google Apps Education Edition provides Web 2.0 tools for word processing, spreadsheets, and more. Because the interface is the web browser, tech administrators can provide e-mail, sharable online calendars, instant messaging tools, and even a dedicated website. There's no hardware or software to install or maintain (www.google.com/a/help/intl/en/edu).

Microsoft also offers free access to familiar tools. Anyone who signs up for a free Windows Live account will be able to use online versions of applications such as Word and PowerPoint, regardless of whether or not they buy the desktop versions of the software. This is Microsoft's response to Google, Adobe, Zoho, and others that offer online productivity software free for personal use (see Chapter 4 for more information on the current versions of these productivity tools). Most of these tools are likely to change over time, adding features and robustness and becoming more transparent.

Content Management Systems

Related sites specifically for education already have elements that include multiple tools and have the advantage of providing security, but there is a cost. For example, eChalk's Online Learning Environment (www.echalk.com) is a collection of web-based communication and collaboration tools that provides seamless integration with a district's existing SIS data; e-mail system; and website content, curriculum, administrative forms, and other resources.

School Fusion (www.schoolfusion.com) helps districts build fully customized websites that include content management, online calendars, classroom websites, and personal space.

Blackboard (www.blackboard.com) provides a personalized learning experience in which teachers can create and manage content, design customized learning paths for students, and evaluate student performance. It includes online learning communities that encourage peer-to-peer participation using web-based tools across schools and throughout districts. Teachers can monitor student progress with simple evaluation and analysis. They can create online professional learning communities and store and share course materials, resources, and methods online.

As an alternative, Moodle (http://moodle.org) is a free, open source Course Management System (CMS) for creating dynamic websites with tools to manage learning environments. To work, it needs to be installed on a web server somewhere, either on one at a school, district, or web hosting company. Some districts use it as their platform for online courses, and others use it to supplement face-to-face courses (known as blended learning). It includes many activity modules (such as forums, wikis, databases, and so on) for schools to build collaborative learning communities. It can also be used as a way to deliver content to students and assess learning using assignments or quizzes. Although free, having personnel to provide tech support is essential.

Intelligent Search

The amount of information is growing so fast that it is becoming necessary to build an intelligent system that leverages knowledge so that people can find what they need efficiently. The web is technically a collection of words on pages with links to connect them. Google's search engine finds the links among the words that a user types into the search box efficiently, using the number of links to that page as a measure of popularity, which determines placement in the search results a user requests. But it doesn't understand the words and can't bring any logical thought (just processing) into play.

However, advances in speed, logic, and technology bring the day of more intelligent searches closer. Will it ever be true artificial intelligence (AI)? No one is claiming that much power just yet, but improvements in object recognition, natural language, and the smart searching of a semantic web will improve capabilities. What that means for students is that searches will be more targeted and accurate, and the results will be relevant. Recent contenders in this category are Microsoft's Bing and Wolfram Alpha.

Assessment

The semantic web is all about managing content and managing data, so it is possible that schools can translate the results of students' work online into quantifiable assessments. Early examples of this are schools in Montgomery County, Maryland, that maintain running records of student reading assessments, primarily on Palm handhelds. The district believes that its ability to track test results systematically through its centralized databases helps pace both students and teachers. In one example, a teacher checks the results on her handheld to pinpoint exactly what students need to learn (Hechinger, 2009).

Although too great an emphasis on testing has the potential to stifle creativity and may even result in eliminating the teaching of the arts or other subjects not tested, a sensible approach and authentic assessment of higher-order thinking skills can result in more student creativity using web-based tools. While not yet Web 2.0 tools, there are tools that score student writing online and provide feedback for improvement.

Cloud Computing and Infrastructure

Speed and storage are the next big things to tackle. As information technology (IT) infrastructure becomes more complex, the resources needed to maintain and support it—both in equipment and personnel—become more and more sophisticated and expensive. The answer is outsourcing to online data centers that provide warehousing and management as services. According to Wikipedia, "Typical cloud computing providers deliver common business applications online which are accessed from another web service or software like a web browser, while the software and data are stored on servers."

According to a *New York Times* article on data centers:

> Much of the daily material of our lives is now dematerialized and outsourced to a far-flung, unseen network. The stack of letters becomes the e-mail database on the computer, which gives way to Hotmail or Gmail. The clipping sent to a friend becomes the attached PDF file, which becomes a set of shared bookmarks, hosted offsite. The photos in a box are replaced by JPEGs on a hard drive, then a hosted sharing service like Snapfish. The tilting

CD tower is replaced by the MP3-laden hard drive which itself yields to a service like Pandora, music that is always "there," waiting to be heard.

But where is "there," and what does it look like?

"There" is nowadays likely to be increasingly large, powerful, energy-intensive, always on and essentially out-of-sight data centers. These centers run enormously scaled software applications with millions of users. (Vanderbilt, 2009)

Welcome to cloud computing. Cloud computing means that services and information are stored and managed on servers outside of an organization, processed quickly, and available from many different devices to result in increased efficiency with reduced costs, staff workload, and energy consumption.

The more personal PC is here in the form of smart phones and mini-laptops, and wireless networks make it possible for people to be connected almost anytime and anywhere. At the same time, we're seeing the rise of cloud computing, the vast array of interconnected machines managing the data and software that used to run on PCs. This combination of mobile and cloud technologies is shaping up to be one of the most significant advances in the computing universe in decades (Hamm, 2009).

Tech companies have shifted over to the cloud a lot of the software applications that businesses typically handle for themselves. Eventually, it will all work seamlessly. While businesses are the early adopters, school districts accustomed to outsourcing some elements of their infrastructure, such as data warehousing, will see benefits from these expanded systems. In his *Business Week* article, Hamm cites a current example from the health industry that shows how it works to improve the quality of information available.

OptumHealth's eSync system assembles medical and drug records in one place and sends out alerts if it detects a potential problem. The technology allows employees to pull together pieces of vital information they didn't have before and act on them. For example, a personal-care counselor for OptumHealth was notified by the company's computing system that a patient might need counseling based on software that scans patient information and detected he recently had had stents installed. She telephoned him, and when he reported feeling pressure in his chest, she urged him to see a doctor immediately. He did—and had triple bypass surgery the next day. It might have saved his life (Hamm, 2009).

How could this translate to education? As assessment becomes more integral to learning, performance analytics, which monitors data to ensure that students are meeting learning objectives and then adapting instruction accordingly, will play a bigger role.

For a district with its data managed in the cloud, a feedback loop, much like OptumHealth's eSynch example, could provide timely interventions. The district's assessment system could alert administrators and educators when students are in danger of failing so that they can provide interventions quickly. If it alerts a teacher that a student is not performing well on a particular topic, it would prompt the teacher to provide extra help or a different way of presenting the information. In the future, the software itself might be an intelligent system capable of alerting the student and making suggestions that include different ways to learn the topic.

Schools in the Cloud

The opportunity to add data management as a Software-as-a-Service (SaaS) solution is already available. SaaS refers to computer applications that are delivered as a service rather than being physically installed on school servers or individual desktops. District administrators and educators—actually anyone with the right to know—can access the software from a PC web browser, or even from a mobile device. This means they can get the data they need when they need it. Because these applications are web based rather than housed on district servers, the service provider rather than the district's IT staff performs installation, upgrades, and maintenance.

Features of SaaS solutions include network-based access to, and management of, software from central locations rather than at each site; user access to applications remotely via the web or mobile device; centralized software updating, which minimizes the need for IT staff to download security and performance upgrades and new features; and integration into a larger network of communicating software for increased functionality as need develops. Companies such as SchoolDude and Century Consultants' StarBase suite already provide SaaS to thousands of school districts.

The potential exists for online learning to scale significantly as well. Whether full-featured curriculum programs, such as Florida Virtual School, or blended learning for credit recovery, enhancement, or as part of a traditional class, the future bodes well for schools moving into the cloud in many areas. The advent of national standards (most states have signed on) could lead to national curricula; national learning materials; and assessments to evaluate learning on individual, class, school, district, state, regional, and global levels, for comparisons as well as for individualized plans to address areas of weakness. Online books and materials already reside in the cloud in such projects as Merlot (www.merlot.org) and Curriki (www.curriki.org). Cost efficiencies will be the driver into online learning.

an old-new vision

It is possible that eventually we'll end up somewhere near Apple's vision of the Knowledge Navigator, a concept described by John Sculley, former Apple Computer CEO, in his 1987 biography, *Odyssey*. The Knowledge Navigator vision is a device that can access a large networked database of hypertext information and use software agents to assist searching for information.

Apple's Knowledge Navigator included the hardware, artificial intelligence, intuitive tools, and an intelligent agent to help you, the user, learn what you need to learn, when and how you need to learn it. One in a series of videos that Apple produced demonstrating the Knowledge Navigator more than 20 years ago showed a young student who uses a handheld version of the system to prompt him while he gives a class presentation on volcanoes, eventually sending a movie of an exploding volcano to the video "blackboard."

everything changes

Although predicting the future is at best an analysis of current trends, the only reality is that change happens regularly and evolutions can become revolutions, sometimes even in schools. Technology today is very different from the way it was in the 1970s when it transitioned from corporate mainframes to personal computing. Carr (2009) points out parallels between electricity, which went from being based at individual companies to being utility based. Similarly, technology today has moved from individual data management to utility computing as application service providers take over tasks to improve costs and efficiencies.

What does this mean for schools? It's easy to see that IT departments which today run huge operations will streamline as districts move operations offsite into the cloud. Tasks such as human resources, inventories, data processing, assessment, and reporting may soon be performed online. Large and small companies use sites such as Salesforce.com and Amazon's processing power with their Elastic Compute Cloud (Amazon EC2), and there is no reason that schools can't do so as well. Instruction, too, is moving in that direction. Many districts are using thin client and server virtualization to deliver applications. It is only one step further to move the servers into the cloud. Curricular materials are online; Web 2.0 applications are replacing—and improving on—student access to information, communications, and collaborations; and some districts are moving to virtual schooling.

What does it all mean for teaching and learning? As we said at the beginning, we want to stress that web-based tools are just ways of accomplishing what needs to be done. They may be faster and cheaper, and contain the elements of motivating students and keeping them engaged in work, but, ultimately, they have to result in increased student achievement of both basic and advanced skills. And the teacher will remain the designer of curriculum, planner of activities, and the one responsible for assessing student learning and requirements.

10

specific tools

As schools open their networks to web use and allow students greater access to online tools, some lesser-known applications have become popular because they provide capabilities that make a difference in classrooms. Educators responding to our surveys mentioned some of these tools often enough to warrant discussion of their use in enhancing student learning.

This chapter will deal with these interesting applications that readers say make a difference to their teaching, students' learning, and, in some cases, professional development. We invited educators to write about their favorite tools and how they use them in the classroom or professionally. We used the same framework as in the other chapters in the book, focusing on the what, why, when, how, and where of Web 2.0.

Among these online tools are Google Earth, Wordle, Skype, and Delicious. Here are the specific tools, listed as they appear, alphabetically:

- Audacity
- Delicious
- Diigo
- Drupal
- Evernote
- Google Earth
- Google Forms (surveys)
- Google Reader and custom RSS feeds
- Issuu
- Moodle

- Netvibes
- skrbl
- Skype
- Timetoast
- TodaysMeet
- VoiceThread
- Voki
- Webspiration
- WizIQ
- Wordle

Audacity

Al Garcia
Teacher, Online Academy, George Mason University, Fairfax, Virginia

What is Audacity?

Audacity is a free software program that serves as a multitrack audio editor and recorder. It records and works with audio files in numerous formats that include WAV, AIFF, Ogg, and MP3 files. It is intuitive and easy to use but has enough features that would be suitable even for professionals. In short, it serves as a flexible recording studio on your computer that provides the flexibility and potential for many educational opportunities.

Why Is Audacity a Useful Tool?

As a readily available and powerful multimedia project software program, Audacity supports multiple scaffolding venues both in the classroom and in the student's home. It provides high levels of motivational appeal and encourages creative development and motivation for students. It is a linking tool across content areas engaging student's higher-order knowledge capabilities. From an educator's perspective, Audacity is a 21st-century tool capable of engaging students in multiple areas.

Audacity's powerful capabilities are surprisingly easy to teach in the classroom and are supported with excellent tutorials and instructional manuals found on the distributor's website. Audacity can do all of the following and more:

- ▶ Record audio from one or more inputs and store recordings in the computer's memory as digital audio

- ▶ Edit the start time, stop time, and duration of any sound on the audio timeline

- ▶ Fade into, out of, or between clips

- ▶ Mix multiple sound sources/tracks, combine them at various volume levels, and pan from channel to channel to one or more output tracks

- Apply simple or advanced effects or filters to change the audio, including compression, expansion, flanging, reverb, audio noise reduction, and equalization

- Convert tapes and records into digital recordings or CDs

- Edit Ogg Vorbis, MP3, WAV, or AIFF sound files

- Cut, copy, splice, or mix sounds together

- Change the speed or pitch of a recording

When and *How* Do You Use Audacity?

The first project I introduced in the classroom eventually became the most popular. I asked students to research important people or characters who were part of the lessons we were studying at that time. Their task was then to produce a podcast of an interview with a famous American. We used an official-sounding Public Broadcasting introduction and the students created some interesting interviews for their podcasts. Here is a link to an example of our podcasts: http://mason.gmu.edu/~jgarciad/portfolio/artifacts/jackie.mp3.

In our Spanish level 3 class, we conducted a two-week project in which we converted the classroom into a working podcast station for the school. Students were required to fill out authentic job applications for the various positions at the station. Positions included station workers, music editors, advertising director, reporters, news editor, and announcers. Over the course of the project, they were required to produce a series of five 10-minute radio podcasts in Spanish and post them on the school website. These podcasts included relevant school news, public service announcements, advertisements, and music. It was hard work, but it provided our students with an opportunity to use their target language skills in an authentic manner.

I also used Audacity successfully as a scaffolding technique to enhance reading readiness in a target language. Specifically, I employed the podcast capability of Audacity to create Bilingual Interpretive Readings (BIR) to promote and enhance reading readiness in the target language. This was done via podcasts developed for use with specified reading assignments. The use of this technique supported student reading efforts and performance by gradually increasing their comprehension skills and their individual listening skills in the target language. Here is a link to an example of a bilingual podcast: http://mason.gmu.edu/~jgarciad/portfolio/images/El%20Misterio%20de%20 Aula%20131.mp3.

Students also used Audacity to practice their pronunciation skills in the target language. They were required to record their responses to various assignments using the target language. They also received feedback via sound files in the target language.

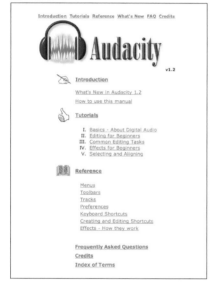

▶ The Audacity online reference manual

Students also create podcasts for use in conjunction with Microsoft PowerPoint presentations. Although PowerPoint also has the capacity to record sound files, it is not as powerful as Audacity.

How Do You Get Started with Audacity?

Go to the Audacity main website at http://audacity.sourceforge.net and download the latest stable version of Audacity. Install the program and review the tutorials. You should only require a microphone, but it is a good idea to have a USB microphone and headset combination.

Where Can You Find More Information about Audacity?

You can download copies of the User Manual and Quick Start Guide. You can access tutorials at http://audacity.sourceforge.net/help/documentation.

Delicious

Jon Orech
Instructional Technology Coordinator, South High School, Downers Grove, Illinois

What Is Delicious?

Delicious is a social-bookmarking tool. Whenever you come across a website that you want to remember later, all you do is click the Tag button (which appears on your browser after you get your Delicious account) and tag it with a few key words; it is saved. You might ask, "Why don't I just save it to my favorites?" With the web-based Delicious, your sites are accessible from any computer. Also, you can add your own annotations to any site.

That's the bookmarking aspect, so what about the social side? Delicious has a People tab that allows you to build a network with your colleagues. You can share, view, and recommend sites to them, and see what they are saving. In addition, if you run across the blog of an "expert," oftentimes his or her Delicious username is listed. You can add that person to your network as well.

Another feature is the search capability of Delicious. You can search any topic just as you would on a search engine. The difference is that Delicious will search for sites on your topic that others have already deemed valuable. Usually, the returns are quite useful.

My favorite feature is the Subscription tab. Click the tab, enter a tag word, and you have now subscribed to sites with that tag. That means if you return tomorrow, next week, or next month, Delicious will keep track of sites saved by others and constantly keep you up to date; if this sounds like an RSS feed, you are right. The difference is, again, these are sites that others thought to save.

Why Is Delicious a Useful Tool?

Two examples come to mind. If a teacher is presenting to a class and needs to have five or six sites available, all that is required is to "Tag" those sites with a particular word and search with that word, and all those sites are listed. This concept can include student participation by creating a class search engine. As students (and teachers) come across sites, they may be added to an account created for the class. That way, when it is time to research, valuable sites are gathered together.

A great student use is to create an annotated bibliography for a research paper. First, make sure all students have accounts and they are all added to your network. Then, as students do research they tag their sites with a word they share with you and write a detailed annotation as to the value of each site. Assessing student work consists of the teacher clicking a student's name, entering the tag, and viewing the sites. The teacher can also comment back; it's great for assessment for learning.

When and *How* Do You Use Delicious?

The ability to reaccess sites from any computer is quite valuable; however, I find the social aspect to be the true gem. To illustrate, using my personal learning network, let me take you through a Delicious session that was part of my professional development.

As I logged on, I noticed I had an item in my in-box. A colleague had sent me a site on open-source textbooks because she knows I am doing research on that topic. I checked my Digital Storytelling subscription and found a new article and a new site explaining an upcoming worldwide storytelling project. I also checked other colleagues' lists, and I particularly appreciated those who annotated each source carefully. Building a network and sharing is how the power of Delicious is unleashed.

Delicious works for students, too. In one classroom, students were completing a collaborative research project that involved searching in Google, printing sources, and writing a paper together. One student was searching, but not in Google; she was using Delicious.

When asked, she said that she learned about Delicious in her English class and had noticed that the sources she found were more relevant to her research. After bookmarking a site, she sent it to her project partner via Delicious. She included a note in the annotation field explaining how the source would contribute to their argument. The interesting point is that she did this on her own.

When the teacher saw what was happening, she stopped class and let the student show everyone what she was doing. Many other students went to Delicious to open an account so that they could get the same kind of results.

► Jon Orech's Delicious page

How Do You Get Started with Delicious?

Go to http://delicious.com. Open an account, read the tutorial, and make sure to download the shortcut buttons to your browser. There are different instructions for Internet Explorer and Firefox. (Hint: for your username, pick something identifiable. I'm jorech: feel free to add me to your network!)

Where Can You Find More Information about Delicious?

Article:
"Top 10 Ways to Use Delicious":
www.lifehack.org/articles/technology/top-10-ways-to-use-delicious.html

Video:
Getting Started with Delicious:
www.youtube.com/watch?v=NGXElviSRXM

Diigo

Vicki Davis
Teacher, Westwood Schools, Camilla, Georgia

What Is Diigo?

Diigo allows you to bookmark websites, index them with tags, and mark up and annotate web pages with highlights, comments, and sticky notes. You can also create groups and share your bookmarks with others. You can even use a tag "dictionary" that serves as a list of categories which can be used to index and share information that you can export as live updates for web pages, wikis, and so forth. Diigo empowers you to share your bookmarks easily via Twitter, your blog, or other social media.

Why Is Diigo a Useful Tool?

Social bookmarking, or the ability to bookmark and share those bookmarks with others, has been around for quite some time, but Diigo groups have some very powerful features. One feature is the ability to use a tag dictionary that allows you to create a taxonomy or a consistent cataloging system while still being able to enjoy the "folksonomy" of simply tagging items with whatever words you wish. When you send something to a group using the handy Diigo Firefox plug-in (which I highly recommend), these standard tags pop up automatically so that you can select them with a click instead of racking your brain for the proper tags to type in.

Diigo also has tools that allow us to aggregate and share bookmarks, their tags, and current information using link rolls and tag rolls; my favorite feature has to be the auto blog post. Everything that I tag "education" is rolled together and posted automatically to my Cool Cat Teacher blog, and I can send it to my blog and to Twitter automatically.

There are other powerful features, including Diigo Lists (creating lists and making web slides out of them that you can run like a PowerPoint presentation but with the added ability to interact live with the sites) and Diigo

Communities (which allows you to follow information on websites or categories of interest to you).

When and *How* Do You Use Diigo?

I really understood the use for social bookmarking when I began using Diigo myself. Now I use it with my 9th and 10th grade classes as part of our award-winning Flat Classroom and Digiteen projects. I also use it to share links on my blog. It does so much more than bookmarking; it creates massive indexed catalogs of current information that can be shared in many powerful ways.

I have a special, approved educator account and can create "profileless" profiles for students if they are under age 13. They can use all the features of Diigo and share with their classmates and yet exist in a world cordoned off from all other Diigo users. This protects students, upholds the law, and provides ways to share.

▶ Diigo message page

One important aspect of this is that by having some standard tags, you can use the RSS feed to populate wikis or any web page with common research topics. For example, on Digiteen, we have nine aspects of digital citizenship and have set up nine tags (plus a few extras); when a student uses the tag called digital safety, it not only goes to Diigo but also to the wiki page on that topic. This means that we can research digital citizenship and, as we bookmark the pages to the appropriate categories, we are sending current information to our wiki pages on Digital Citizenship according to our nine categories. It is a powerful research tool!

How Do You Get Started with Diigo?

Go to www.diigo.com and click on the Join Now button. Create an account. You can also watch a video about Diigo.

Where Can You Find More Information about Diigo?

You can see my Diigo list on using Diigo as a Web 2.0 research tool at www.diigo.com/list/coolcatteacher/research2/.

Other sources of information:

Diigo Tutorial on Diigo's YouTube channel:
www.youtube.com/watch?v=0RvAkTuL02A

Educator group:
http://groups.diigo.com/groups/educators

Digital citizenship group:
http://groups.diigo.com/groups/ad4dcss

Drupal

Steven Burt
Content and Research Manager, Clarity Innovations, Portland, Oregon

What Is Drupal?

Drupal is an open-source content management system. It is free software that allows individuals or groups to manage all sorts of content on the web, including blogs, discussion forums, images, podcasts, files, and much, much more.

Why Is Drupal a Useful Tool?

Drupal is a platform, a foundation of sorts, for building a school or district web presence. One of its greatest strengths is its extensibility, which is its capacity to interface with all sorts of Web 2.0 tools and data sources. Once installed on a server, Drupal creates a website that can be customized with just about any sort of look and feel that allows any number of users and visitors to add or moderate content in just about any form.

Drupal is useful for just about any content you want to display on the web for public consumption or for a private group. Some educators use it as a tool for the school's or district's home page, while others use it to create digital portfolios with students and blogging platform for teachers. It can even be used as a parent-communication tool. Educators can set up their own pages, integrate Web 2.0 tools, and create an interactive online presence. They can create virtual brochures with static pages of their classroom or school content.

When and *How* Do You Use Drupal?

Students and parents expect schools to have interactive websites. I've helped schools set up their sites using Drupal because the platform can be extended in all sorts of directions where teachers and students can exchange and interact with information in a very rich manner. Here are examples of how a few schools and teachers are using Drupal.

▶ The Skyline School website

A very straightforward example is the Skyline K–8 school site, www.skylinek8. org. Their principal, Ben Keefer, wanted a website to keep the community and his students informed as to what is happening in the school. The site has a clean interface with only essential information: news and updates from the office, monthly newsletter, staff pages, and general information.

Drupal's content and blog modules allow users such as the principal, librarian, and staff to have their own pages. Although Drupal refers to these types of pages as blogs, teachers don't have to allow comments or other collaborative tools. Instead, they use them as simple home pages where they can post information about what is going on in their classroom.

The previous example provided features of a school site, but Drupal can manage district sites (the district site and all of the schools). This can provide a consistent theme and interface (both for visitors and for users adding content) as well as integrate work flow and permissions. One such example of a sophisticated work flow is the district site for the Eugene, Oregon, 4J School District. This is a large district with thousands of students and dozens and dozens of content contributors (at the school and district level).

For them and districts like them, Drupal is an excellent fit, as it can manage all the various departments in such a way as to create a custom work flow (who can publish to the site, what reviews and approvals are necessary, and when the content goes live). This process can be structured using Drupal at a very granular level. This way, many users in disparate locations can create content that goes into a work flow which other editors can review and post to the site—all without the hassle of e-mailing attachments and reminders. For districts that want to allow departments to manage their own portion of the site, Drupal can handle that as well.

▶ The Eugene 4J School District website

For instance, on the Eugene 4J website there are more than 15 different departments, each of which has varying needs for information dissemination and access. To develop a site such as this from scratch or by using other content management system tools, each section would often be treated as nearly an entirely different site that couldn't "talk" to the other areas of the site. Drupal provides a way to divide the content areas of the site and specify which users can add content. From there, editors can approve content (e.g., post it live to the site) and even modify the menu system—all from a Web interface without ever having to know any code.

District websites built on Drupal offer advantages to other content management tools, and even to building it on your own. Some schools worry that using a free open-source tool is risky. They ask, "Who will support it?" and "What if it stops working?" However, what holds it all together (PHP with a database, often MySQL) are industry standards that are well supported and, frequently, ones that many school technologists already know.

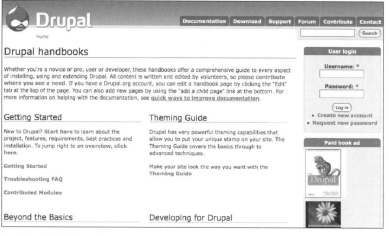

▶ Drupal User Manual page

How Do You Get Started with Drupal?

Unlike web-based tools, such as Google Docs, Drupal is server based. This means it has to be downloaded from Drupal and installed on a server before you can begin to use it. One of the easiest ways to get started is to use a low-cost, third-party hosting company (I've used www.site5.com and www.siteground.com, with good results). Their systems include an automatic installer for Drupal; you can literally click two or three buttons and have an install of Drupal ready to go. From there, it is really a question of acquainting yourself with resources on Drupal, whether through Drupal's groups, the main site, www.drupal.org, or even Twitter (lots of developers and users post about it).

The first steps usually involve choosing a theme that you like (many theme templates are available for free) and then configuring the site in terms of permissions and access. It may sound very challenging, but like many technical tools that are a bit complicated due to many moving parts, as long as you follow the tutorials you shouldn't have too many issues.

Where Can You Find More Information about Drupal?

There are many companies that provide information about Drupal and its use in education. Clarity Innovations (www.clarity-innovations.com), specializes in developing rich websites based on Drupal for learning organizations.

Bill Fitzgerald of Funny Monkey (www.funnymonkey.com) does most of his work with Drupal, focusing on using Drupal as a platform for student digital portfolios.

The Drupal community (www.drupal.org) is one of the most active and prolific open-source communities. There are new modules (add-ons) constantly in development that can be adapted for use by educators.

Evernote

Steven W. Anderson
Instructional Technologist, Stokes County Schools, Danbury, North Carolina

What Is Evernote?

Evernote is an online organizational tool that allows you to clip text, images, audio, and PDF files from the web and save them to one location. The information can be shared across several platforms and devices.

Why Is Evernote a Useful Tool?

When students are assigned any type of research in school, the first place they go is the Internet. And why wouldn't they? Students have access to vast amounts of information from the archives of the Smithsonian to the research notes of those working on the pyramids in Egypt.

One problem is that students often have a hard time organizing information. For example, I assigned a research project on the elements of the periodic table. Students visited the computer lab, and by the end of the hour they had used up three packs of paper and an ink cartridge in the printer. Students printed entire web pages so that they could have the notes to compile later. I learned that they needed to cut and paste into a document to save on the amount of paper we were using. That worked, but they couldn't save recordings of interviews or other audio resources.

Evernote makes organizing notes and information for research easy. After a simple and free registration process, students can save text, pictures, audio, and PDF files from the web. The program is available for several platforms, including PC, Mac, iPhone/iPod Touch, Blackberry, and Palm Pre.

Students can download the software, use the web version of the program, or just use the bookmarklet to save information. (A bookmarklet is a shortcut you add to your bookmarks or favorites toolbar in your Internet browser.) When you are on a page you want to save, simply click the Evernote bookmarklet, enter the name of the page, determine some tags, and add any other notes.

Once saved, you will have access to the information as if you had used the other methods.

Once information is clipped from the web and saved, students can go in, either online or offline, and review the information. They can remove information they don't need with a simple edit, combine clips, and even start to write their research papers or reports online or offline.

One of the best features is that highlighted and clipped text keeps all the links intact and clickable inside the program, so it is easy to continue researching. Another great feature is that when students clip items from a web page, the address is also clipped, so the reference information is there for students to use to cite their sources.

When and *How* Do You Use Evernote?

I have seen Evernote used in several different types of classrooms. One high school teacher uses it with her American history students to organize a year-long project highlighting major topics in American history. Within their Evernote Notebook, they have a page for each topic that is part of their project. As they conduct their research, they organize pictures, text, quotes, audio, and other information for topics such as the American Revolution, the presidency, the Civil War, the growth of trade, immigration, the role of America on the world stage, and others. Then, at the end of the year, they have 15–20 pages, all organized, annotated, and clickable, to demonstrate their understanding of the progression of American history.

In an elementary classroom, the teacher uses Evernote to teach her students the right and wrong ways to conduct research and how to organize their thoughts. The program acts as their digital "brain," where they can think, write, organize, and learn, as she puts it. For example, in a unit on weather, students choose a type of cloud. They then use their Evernote notebook to gather, clip, and organize images and text from the web.

Using exercises just like this throughout the year, a teacher is able to easily teach what is good information and what is not, and students can easily delete pieces of unnecessary information in their Evernote notebooks. The teacher can also teach research organization skills because students can move information around in their notebooks to make it more cohesive. Finally, the students learn about proper citation of sources, because as they snip information from the web the address of the information is also saved. The exercise turns into an excellent teaching tool for citing sources.

▶ Evernote registration screen

How Do You Get Started with Evernote?

Getting started with Evernote is as easy as visiting www.evernote.com and signing up for a free account. Students will need to provide a username, password, and e-mail address. The free account gives you 40MB of space to save per month. A premium account ($5/month, $45/year) gives you 500MB a month.

According to Evernote, the free space provides approximately 20,000 text notes, or 400 mobile snapshots, 270 web clips, 40 audio notes, or 11 high-resolution photos per month.

Where Can You Find More Information about Evernote?

Evernote Videos and Tutorials:
  www.evernote.com/about/what_is_en/video/

Expand Your Brain with Evernote (Adam Parish, Lifehacker.com):
  http://lifehacker.com/5041631/expand-your-brain-with-evernote

7 Ways to Use Evernote (Joel Falconer, Stepcase Lifehack):
  www.lifehack.org/articles/technology/7-ways-to-use-evernote.html

Evernote Tutorial (Evernote.com):
  www.youtube.com/watch?v=3tvpmTvWJnU

Google Earth

Lisa Parisi
Teacher, Denton Avenue School, Herricks UFSD, New York

What Is Google Earth?

Google Earth (http://earth.google.com) is a free download that, according to Google, enables the user to "view satellite imagery, maps, terrain, 3-D buildings, from galaxies in outer space to the canyons of the ocean."

Why Is Google Earth a Useful Tool?

Google Earth is invaluable as a tool to enable students to view their own area as well as areas where collaborative partners live. They are able to study the geographic features of specific places easily. The site also has such features as Real Time Earthquakes, World Oil Consumption, and Global Awareness hot spots.

New features are added with each version. Some examples provided by Google show what is new in version 5.0. With Google Earth 5.0 students have the ability to see global changes with decades of historic imagery. If you've ever wondered how your neighborhood has changed throughout time, Google Earth now gives you access to the past. With a simple click, check out suburban sprawl, melting ice caps, coastal erosion, and more.

You can also virtually dive beneath the surface of the ocean. In the new ocean layer, you can plunge all the way to the floor of the sea, view exclusive content from partners such as BBC and National Geographic, and explore such 3-D shipwrecks as the Titanic.

You can track and share your paths with others. Take placemarks a step further and record a free-form tour on Google Earth. Simply turn on the touring feature, press record, and see the world. You can even add a soundtrack or narration to personalize the journey.

When and *How* Do You Use Google Earth?

We have used Google Earth in our fifth grade classroom for many projects. We open it up each time we meet a new collaboration classroom, viewing their school and comparing their geographic features to ours.

We also have used it to track the daily progress of a United Nations mission by sea (using the longitude and latitude coordinates to find the ship each day until it reached port in Africa); watched the fires in Victoria, Australia, while we discussed how to help from our part of the world; and learned about the crisis in Darfur.

Our favorite experience with Google Earth was tracking our "trip" on the Oregon Trail during our Westward Expansion unit. We found the start point and ending point, placing markers at each. We then examined the terrain along the trail and the towns at which we would be stopping. As we hit each town, river crossing, or mountain pass, we uploaded our original pictures, diary entries, and videos about our simulated experience in that place.

This was a great way for students to view the physical terrain of the Oregon Trail. But there was more. We had middle school students from Paul Bogush's class join us as collaborators on this project.

Paul is a middle school social studies teacher in Connecticut who loves using technology to connect his classroom to others. He had his students use Google maps and Google Earth to add research information about a chosen aspect of the Oregon Trail.

Each student completed a Google Map/Google Earth file on such topics as specific pioneers, laws of each territory, and Indian encounters. Our students were able to learn so much more about the Oregon Trail and pioneers simply by viewing their files and following the placemarks in each map.

How Do You Get Started with Google Earth?

Google Earth is a free download; so start with the download (http://earth. google.com). At that point, the easiest thing to do is find places on the map. Type in the city or country, and Google Earth will "fly" you to the site.

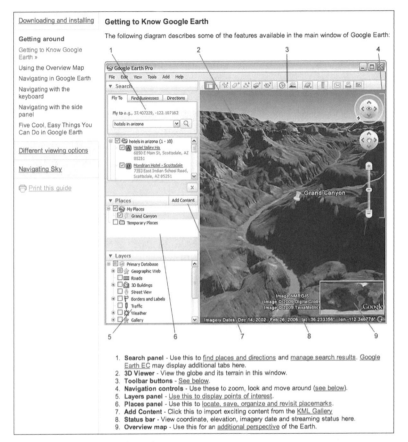

The following diagram describes some of the features available in the main window of Google Earth:

1. **Search panel** - Use this to find places and directions and manage search results. Google Earth EC may display additional tabs here.
2. **3D Viewer** - View the globe and its terrain in this window.
3. **Toolbar buttons** - See below.
4. **Navigation controls** - Use these to zoom, look and move around (see below).
5. **Layers panel** - Use this to display points of interest.
6. **Places panel** - Use this to locate, save, organize and revisit placemarks.
7. **Add Content** - Click this to import exciting content from the KML Gallery.
8. **Status bar** - View coordinate, elevation, imagery date and streaming status here.
9. **Overview map** - Use this for an additional perspective of the Earth.

▶ Getting to know Google Earth

Where Can You Find More Information about Google Earth?

For basic tips and tricks from Google, visit Google Earth for Educators. There are reader contributions and materials for using Google Earth in all areas of the curriculum: www.google.com/educators/p_earth.html.

There are ideas, examples, classroom-based resources, and ideas for using Google Earth as a tool, as well as a forum for discussions, in this classroom Google Earth wiki: http://classroomgoogleearth.wikispaces.com.

Using Google Earth in the math curriculum provides standards-based lesson ideas, examples, and downloads for mathematics that embrace active learning, constructivism, and project-based learning using Google Earth: http://realworldmath.org/Real_World_Math/RealWorldMath.org.html.

Google Forms (Surveys)

Esther Eash
Director of Libraries and Technology Integration, EdisonLearning, Inc., Wichita, Kansas

Pamela Livingston
Education Technology Analyst and Google Certified Teacher, EdisonLearning, Inc., New York, New York

What Are Google Forms (Surveys)?

Google Forms is an online tool to generate survey forms. You can create the form and use it to get information about whatever categories you include. You can e-mail the form in the body of a message or send it as a link; you can also embed it in, or link to it on, web pages. As respondents submit results, the data automatically populates a Google Spreadsheet and generates a results summary.

Why Are Google Forms (Surveys) a Useful Tool?

Google Forms are free, flexible, and easy to use for teachers and students who want to create forms as well as for those who will fill them out. With little effort, Google Forms creates a professional-looking form that can be embedded in an e-mail or website or shared via a unique URL that can be posted to Listservs, Twitter, or websites. Google Forms gives real-time, immediate feedback. With the built-in results summary, you can view and analyze the data easily. Teachers can also add additional columns or download the data in CSV, HTML, text, Excel, Open Office, or PDF format to analyze further or to incorporate into presentations or other work.

When and *How* Do You Use Google Forms (Surveys)?

We do professional development workshops and also work with teachers and students directly. Some uses we make of Google Forms are for evaluations, quizzes, and anonymous assessment.

I use Google Forms to create an on-the-fly survey at the start of a professional development session to find out about the workshop participants ahead of time.

Similarly, classroom teachers can find out what their students know before teaching a unit or a project. After I've held a workshop, I create a survey to find out how participants viewed the material and the presentation and to get important and quick feedback. I can make it anonymous or have it include names.

Classroom teachers use Google Forms for different purposes. Some do a quick check of student learning after a unit or a presentation and are able to differentiate instruction to address what they find out afterward. For example, some teachers create quick quizzes to check students' understanding and compile results.

Others teachers survey students in order to get full participation as opposed to oral brainstorming, which often leaves out the quieter students. For example, teachers and administrators in one school created a survey about bullying in which students were able to answer anonymously so the educators could find out the real scoop in a way that wasn't public or embarrassing to any students.

Math teachers used a candy graphing survey with students to teach probability. This project gave them a new take on the M&M or Skittles counting exercise in which students are given a bag of multicolored candy and are to guess how many of each color it contains, then actually count and compare to their guesses. They got instant graphing and analysis of results across the entire group. Previously the individualized responses had to be compiled. The input and compiling are now instantaneous and the whole class can see the results. View the form here: https://spreadsheets.google.com/viewform?formkey=dEd HcE5OcjlGaVdESkZ1OUJKOTVxTnc6MA.

When language arts teachers teach students how to write a 10-word summary, they create the Google "So What?" form to save time and get right to the whole-class sharing. It requires students to choose 10 words carefully to summarize their understanding. Groups or teams sometimes work on a summary together. The teacher brings up all the 10-word summaries for whole-class discussions. See the form at: https://spreadsheets.google.com/viewform?formkey=dGxzanBoMG00MXB6blUteGRadXVfc2c6MA.

We used Google surveys to poll national and international students about their use of 1-to-1 computing. More than 700 responses from the United States and internationally were received after a post on Twitter and several Listservs. A group of eighth grade students in Michigan evaluated the results, discovered trends, found differences, correlated results, researched the schools and countries that responded, critiqued the questions and the form, and created a presentation that showed their findings. Students worked in teams of four, turned their work into VoiceThreads, and asked other students to participate. Go to http://spreadsheets.google.com/viewform?key=0AoR2js1w6jsScHFpemc 1ZklEVEJnR0dHUDJYU0ptTnc&hl=en for details.

► Google Forms support pages

How Do You Get Started with Google Forms (Surveys)?

Google Forms is a free online application tool. You will need to have a Google account. (It's free.) After logging into your account, click on Google Help > Google Docs Help > Google Spreadsheets > Working with Data Forms. You can create a form from the Docs list or by first creating a spreadsheet and using it to create a form.

Where Can You Find More Information about Google Forms (Surveys)?

Google Forms Help:
http://docs.google.com/support/bin/topic.py?hl=en&topic=15166

Fantastic Forms:
http://markcallagher.com/?p=315

Quick Takes:
www.portical.org/Presentations/quick_takes

Google Reader and Custom RSS Feeds

Jon Orech
Instructional Technology Coordinator, South High School, Downers Grove, Illinois

What Is Google Reader?

Google Reader (http://reader.google.com) is an aggregator. It gathers and centralizes your Google selections of news, information, and more into a single reader that is available to you on a mobile device or a computer. Google Reader also enables you to follow what others are reading and have selected.

What Is an RSS Feed?

An RSS feed enables a user to "subscribe" to a news source, blog, or web page that is continually updated. Instead of searching a site each day, the RSS feed, collected by Google Reader (or other aggregator), gathers new articles and centralizes them.

RSS is valuable especially for keeping abreast of current issues. A constant flow of information on a news topic can help students to acquire and synthesize information. While working on a project, researchers are not only able to get feeds from news sources, but to create custom feeds as well.

Let's say two students are researching global warming and decide to get news feeds from national sources. Miguel gets his from Fox and Ashley gets hers from CNN. Needless to say, these two students are going to receive considerably different information on the topic. The problem? The information is coming from a single source. The solution? Create a custom RSS feed. Google's RSS feed provides the tools.

Why Is a Google Custom RSS Feed a Useful Tool?

This tool has several functions. First, it filters all news on a given topic directly to the user. Second, the user can edit the list of sources and keep only the most valuable. Third, the user can limit his feed to receive news posts only from specific countries. News from these varied sources can raise questions that lead to incredible learning experiences. These questions might include:

▶ "What would cause them to believe this?"

▶ "What does this information suggest about the culture?"

▶ "What is their opinion of our country?"

▶ "How much can we trust their news sources?"

▶ "And, therefore, how much can we trust ours?"

Hopefully, all of these questions will lead to some reflection and, maybe, some empathy, tolerance, and acceptance. At the very least, students will have a broader base of research to synthesize.

When and *How* Do You Use Custom RSS Feeds?

Students researching topics from the swine flu to steroids in baseball will have a constant flow of news releases on that topic. From there, they can "star" articles to keep for later, or, better yet, add them directly to their Delicious social bookmarking page with one click.

One of the teachers at South High School requires students to respond to at least one article a week via a personal blog. All of this information is used to help create a semester-long "advocacy" research project. Students select a current issue that directly affects them. During the course of an entire semester, students research (through databases, interviews, and web research) all sides of the issue and develop a persuasive project to speak on behalf of, or advocate for, a particular position. Sample topics might include a change in the minimum age for driving, hydrogen fuel cell cars, traumatic brain injury research, open borders, space exploration, or epilepsy awareness in schools. The custom RSS feed sends them a steady flow of current news on their topic.

We can take this one step further. Chances are these news sources, although varied, will reflect a very Americanized view of the situation. Some educators have stressed the need to create global citizens with a sense of empathy and awareness of cultures, beliefs, and attitudes worldwide. In addition, some research projects call for a more international view. One way to increase understanding is to add another step to the creation of the custom feed by including a country code in the search. To do this, add to your search words "site:" followed by the two-letter country code (a list of these codes can be found at http://code.google.com/apis/adwords/docs/developer/adwords_api_countries.html).

This way, you will get returns ("feeds") only from news sources in that country (just one of many advanced search features on Google). Some possibilities include "Economy" from a Chinese point of view ("site: CB") or "Kim Jong-il" from the North Korean perspective ("site: KP"). To get multiple perspectives from two opposing countries, try two feeds, same topic, such as "Gaza Strip" from the Israeli ("site: IL") and Palestinian ("site: PL") perspectives.

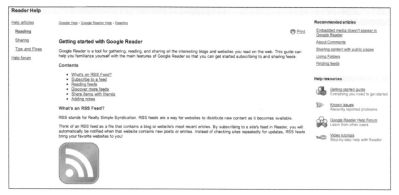

▶ The Google RSS Reader "getting started" page

How Do You Get Started with Custom RSS Feeds?

To create an account the student must first have a Google account and must be familiar with the function of Google Reader (any other aggregator will work as well.) After a typical Google search (hopefully, using advance search features), click the News link on the top left.

Then click the Sort By Date link. This will show the most recent news articles on the topic. From here, click the Add a News Gadget for "____" located on the bottom of the page. This will lead to the familiar Add to Google Reader page. Click the link. Your students now have a custom feed on the topic from a variety of sources.

To use RSS, begin by having students open a Google account. From there, navigate to Google Reader. Students can then add any existing feed they wish. The trick in creating the custom feed is the topic, as well as the search words. This strategy is designed to follow current events and trends of a given issue, as opposed to a historical topic. Choosing words that best focus on the topic results in superior feeds.

Where Can You Find More Information about Custom RSS Feeds?

To get an introduction to RSS, try the CommonCraft Video "RSS in Plain English" at www.commoncraft.com/rss_plain_english/.

Alan November also has some great insights about the procedure of custom feeds at http://novemberlearning.com.

Issuu

Elizabeth Helfant
Coordinator of Instructional Technology, Mary Institute Country Day School,
Independent School, St. Louis, Missouri

What Is Issuu?

Issuu is a digital publishing platform in which students can create beautiful digital editions of their work by uploading their publications.

Why Is Issuu a Useful Tool?

Issuu is a useful tool to publish student work in online magazine form. The work can be literally anything that students have created. Students prepare their work in any file format. They are instructed to complete the work as if they are professional publishers and to print their final copy to PDF. The PDF is simply uploaded to Issuu (www.issuu.com), and Issuu publishes the work in magazine style format. Issuu also provides an embeddable widget of their work that can be pasted into a blog post and reviewed and commented on by their peers.

When and *How* Do You Use Issuu?

We use Issuu to publish a variety of student works. One of our favorite uses of it is in the creation of short poetry booklets containing original writings and images. However, our absolute favorite is for the final publishing step in the creation of graphic novels and comic books. Our comic book projects have included a retelling of *Antigone*, a retelling of *The Odyssey* from another character's point of view, and an overview of U.S. history events. Students enjoy creating graphic novels and comic books. Using Issuu provides them with a terrific opportunity to be creative and to think critically in order to engage their audience and relay the important information in an interesting, yet informative way.

One of the most effective uses for Issuu is in the creation of a graphic novel. Students can tell an original story, retell a story from another perspective or in another time period or environment, or summarize a story or event.

In U.S. History, students were assigned one of 55 significant, historical events. They were told to turn the event into a comic section of 4–6 pages that would be combined with the work of their classmates to create a graphic novel survey of American history that would be published on Issuu. In English class, students were told to use comic format to retell *The Odyssey* from the perspective of a character other than Odysseus. Another English class used the graphic novel assignment to retell the story of *Antigone*.

Students used a mind-mapping tool (e.g., bubbl.us or Mindomo) to brainstorm and storyboard, or they collaborated on the storyboard using Google Docs. Sharing during the designing phase allowed teachers to provide feedback to deepen student work. Students designed their project and thought about the written text and images that they wanted to use to convey their meaning.

Once students developed their idea, they had to create images for each of the frames in their comic. Some took photos with their cell phones, sent them to Flickr, and edited them. Some used a digital camera to take well-framed shots and then used editing software. Students who wanted to use drawings instead of photos drew images on their tablet PCs using ArtRage or InkArt1.3, or they drew images and scanned them into the computer.

Once the images were created, students created the graphic novel and added dialogue and text. The best tool for this is ComicLife, from plasq. It isn't free, but it is reasonably priced and has a free 30-day download, which is enough time to complete a project. ComicLife allows users to easily select a comic layout for each page in their graphic novel. Students added captions, title, and conversation bubbles. Finally, they printed their graphic novel to a PDF and uploaded the PDF to Issuu. Issuu generated the online comic and provided an embed code to display it on the class website.

The teachers who did this project with their students were Scott Small (U.S. History), Carla Federman (U.S. History), Tex Tourais (English), and Bridgette Leschorn (English).

How Do You Get Started with Issuu?

The main part of an Issuu project is the creation of the student work for publication. Once the document is ready for publication, go to http://issuu.com and click on Sign Up. You can also watch a video. Fill out the form and click the

Submit button. Students can upload any kind of document, and Issuu will turn it into an online publication in magazine, presentation, or paper modes.

▶ The Issuu upload page

Where Can You Find More Information about Issuu?

Issuu:
> http://issuu.com

Sample projects

http://issuu.com/ekay/docs/athena_book_final_actually

http://issuu.com/ehelfant/docs/team_devon

http://issuu.com/ehelfant/docs/team_harmony

http://issuu.com/ehelfant/docs/team_oz

Resources to help

Comic Life (Download the free 30-day trial):
> http://plasq.com

HeroMachine (Generate comic strip characters):
> www.ugo.com/channels/comics/heromachine2/heroMachine2.asp

Sumo Paint (Online paint program):
> www.sumopaint.com

Flickr (Photo storage and sharing site):
> www.flickr.com

Moodle

Miguel Guhlin
Instructional Technology Services, San Antonio ISD, San Antonio, Texas

What Is Moodle?

Moodle is a course management system, providing educators with the benefits of a website but with many more learning activities that can be built in for students. Teachers can easily arrange instructional materials and activities as well as facilitate discussions online.

Moodle allows teachers to create a safe online learning center for themselves and their students to work in. It allows them to post class materials and extend learning beyond the classroom walls. For many, Moodle is a one-stop shopping solution that can include blogs, wikis, podcasts, quizzes, and survey questionnaires that print incredible graphs. Moodle also allows teachers to post grades and create online forums, with attachments.

Why Is Moodle a Useful Tool?

Moodle is invaluable for students because it provides them with a safe, virtual environment that enables them to engage with content and with each other as they learn. Teachers find it indispensable because it extends their physical classroom into an online virtual space. Moodle has a variety of features, including discussion forums; a built-in grade book; and ways to post learning activities, hand in assignments via the Internet, and embed interactive activities such as crossword puzzles and quizzes created by others.

Moodle is also customizable, and educators can add new modules and themes. I've listed a few examples of what you can do.

Share questionnaires with students, parents, and anyone on the Internet

Moodle's questionnaire module enables you to quickly design a survey, share it with others, and then graph the data with horizontal, multicolored bar charts. You can download the data in Excel for further number crunching, which is great for students to work with; you and your students can then save the raw data and open it in popular spreadsheet programs.

Create task-based activities

Using Half Baked Software's Hot Potatoes tool (which is free and available for Windows and Macintosh), teachers can quickly and easily design crossword puzzles, multiple-choice quizzes, text-entry quizzes, jumbled-word exercises, fill-in-the-blank exercises, and matching exercises. These activities are automatically scored in Moodle—saving the teacher the effort—and grades are put into the grade book.

Podcast with Moodle

Students can record their audio and share it as a podcast by adding a podcast module to Moodle. In my school district, our Bilingual/ESL Department is using iPods to facilitate second language learning using podcasts on iPods or MP3 players. Teachers load content from sources such as United Streaming and other third-party vendors, and students create their own content using the Audio Recorder Module in Moodle (there are other modules, too). Using the podcast module in Moodle, both students and teachers can post their podcasts and subscribe to others in iTunes or via RSS readers (e.g., Google Reader).

When and *How* do you use Moodle?

The most widespread use of Moodle in our district began with conducting literature circles online. When we think of literature circles, we think of kids sitting in a circle reading books and sharing their thoughts on it based on the role they are assigned. Discussing books helps students build connections, sets a purpose for reading beyond the intrinsic motivation we all prize, and motivates them. It also helps them read, observe, question, discuss, answer questions, and write about what they are reading. It's a fantastic activity, rich with opportunities for reflective learning. Students can post online book talks to persuade other group members to choose their book for literature circles, vote on book selections, and use the Moodle discussion forums to discuss their book, upload images, and more. Several thousand students are involved in using online literature circles as a result of Moodle.

Writing teachers want to provide students with immediate feedback. However, using traditional notebooks can be a bit of a deterrent because there are too many for teachers to carry around. Using Moodle, students can submit their writing via the Assignment Module in Moodle. Writing teachers are able to score the writing samples as well as provide feedback without printing out the writing. This makes providing feedback for many student writers much easier than before and without using precious resources such as paper and ink, which are limited in my district.

Finally, Moodle is catching on as a tool to facilitate online professional learning for district staff. More than 300 educators have participated in online professional learning that has been facilitated 100% online via Moodle. You can see examples of courses online at http://intouch.saisd.net/plc/.

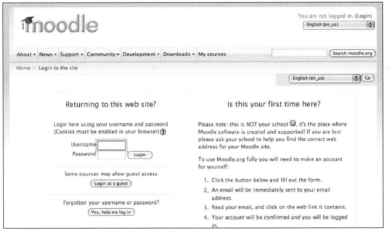

▶ The Moodle login page

How Do You Get Started with Moodle?

To get started with Moodle, you can work with your school district or organization to set up a web server and install Apache, PHP, and MySQL on it. These tools create the environment that Moodle needs, because it is part web page, part database. You can get everything to start with online at http://moodle.org.

Where Can You Find More Information about Moodle?

For basic tips and tricks for Moodle, visit Moodle Habitudes. You will find a wealth of resources online at http://mguhlin.net/moodle/.

There are videos and ways to use Moodle in schools, as well as help on how to set it up online, at http://moodletutorials.org. You can also find a discussion of how to use Moodle in schools online at http://moodle.org/mod/forum/view.php?id=4792/.

Furthermore, join the live conversation available via Twitter using the #moodle hashtag (search on Moodle via http://search.twitter.com) to find what people are sharing about Moodle use.

Netvibes

Jeff Utecht
Elementary Technology and Learning Coordinator, International School, Bangkok, Thailand

What Is Netvibes?

Netvibes is a content aggregator site. It pulls information from a variety of sources on the web and displays them on a single site for viewing. Think about having all your favorite sites in one place, on one page. That is Netvibes.

Why Is Netvibes a Useful Tool?

Imagine if you could pull all the web resources you use in your class to one place. Imagine if you could give students one URL that had all the websites, blogs, newspapers, and images that you wanted them to use for a research project. Imagine if you could read the content of 200 sites on one page.

Netvibes has many uses in the classroom, from following student blogs, to creating sites for students, to using as a resources hub. Netvibes allows you to create your own site for free and without ads.

When and *How* Do You Use Netvibes

We're using Netvibes at our school as a way to keep track of student blogs and link students to other blogging classrooms around the world. Going to our site (www.netvibes.com/isbg5) will show how fifth grade teachers and students are developing a one-stop shop for all their blogging and connecting needs. Tabs on the site represent teachers at the school who have their students blogging. From here the teacher can track, read, and quickly respond to students who are writing on their blogs.

Teachers also allow class time for students to read each other's blogs. By using Netvibes the students have access not only to other classmates' blogs but also to bloggers in other rooms around the world. They can read, respond, and browse in a safe environment, set up by teachers, using educationally appropriate links teachers have approved and put there.

If students have individual Netvibes pages, teachers can "Share a Tab" of information with a student by simply entering their e-mail address into the share-tab box. The tab and all the content on that tab will then be copied over to the student's Netvibes site. For example, a teacher could create a tab of content related to a science topic; find RSS feeds, news articles, links, games, and so forth; and add them all to their science tab. Once they have gathered the content they want, they then enter the student's e-mail address, and all that information is transferred to the student's account.

Netvibes has many widgets that students add to their own personal page to help keep them organized at school. For example, some use a simple to-do list to remind them of due dates and class assignments, a calendar to allow them to keep their own schedule of events in their lives, and a digital notepad to jot down quick notes to themselves. Students can even sign up for a service such as box.net, which lets them upload files and store them on the web as a way to manage their own documents.

The power of Netvibes is in the individualization of each account. Allowing students to customize their own learning environment is a powerful way to start teaching the power of the web.

▶ The Netvibes Start page

How Do You Get Started with Netvibes?

Getting started with Netvibes is simple and straightforward. Head to www. netvibes.com and click Sign Up in the upper right-hand corner of the site. Once you follow the sign-up process your personal page will be created for you. Now the only thing you have to do is add content by clicking on the big green Add Content button in the upper left-hand corner. Once there, explore the possibilities and widgets that Netvibes has to offer.

When you've explored a bit, make a public site. Next to the Add Content button will be a button that reads Pages. From there you can create and name your public site, turning any or all of your tabs public for the world to see. You can make some of your tabs public while keeping other tabs private, so don't think it's an all or nothing deal. You can have the best of both worlds!

Where Can You Find More Information about Netvibes?

The best place to get more information about Netvibes is on their tour page. From there you can quickly learn all you need to know to get started using this powerful site with your students and school. Go to http://tour.netvibes. com/overview.php.

skrbl

Samantha Morra
Glenfield School Technology Coordinator, Montclair Public Schools, Montclair, New Jersey

What Is skrbl

Online whiteboards can be created instantly using a tool called skrbl. These whiteboards can be used for collaboration using computers in the classroom, across town, or anywhere there is an Internet connection.

Why Is skrbl a Useful Tool?

So easy to use, skrbl is great for collaboration and brainstorming. You simply go to the website (www.skrbl.com) and click on Start skrbl Now. This generates a multiuser whiteboard, and you can type words or draw. You can project it, or use it with an interactive whiteboard. Collaborating is one of skrbl's most useful features because you and your students can work with others on other computers. When you generate the whiteboard, it assigns a specific URL to that board. You share that URL with your students, and then they can add to it. You can have your entire class on one board at the same time. You can also upload pictures and files if you are signed in, and students can work with those. There is nothing to download or install. One of the amazing things about using this tool is how the information the students put up evolves as students post.

When and *How* Do You Use skrbl?

I use skrbl with my students to generate ideas for projects. Recently, I asked a class to generate ideas for a research project about a global or local issue that concerned them. Students added their responses to the board. We went over the topics, rearranged them, and discussed them. The students went home that night and shared the board with an adult. They were instructed to come back to class with three facts about one of the topics. This was going to be the launching point for their research. Comparing and contrasting information was made interesting using skrbl.

I once had a class brainstorm a list of all the technology and machines that they use on a daily basis. That included cell phones, calculators, washing machines, and so forth. Then they had to find out how people did similar things 100 years ago. They had to research whether the object had a different name, learn a little about how it worked, and use the board to post what they found out. For some reason, the adding machine fascinated them, and it sparked some great conversations and research.

I also work with other teachers. I worked with one middle school language arts teacher on using a skrbl board to investigate literature. Her class was reading *The Crucible*, by Arthur Miller. We drew a line down the middle of the board. On one side students had to write events in the story, and on the other side they had to write information about the life and times of Miller. If they saw a connection, they could draw a line from one side to the other. Their final assignment was to write an essay about how *The Crucible* reflected the life and times of Miller.

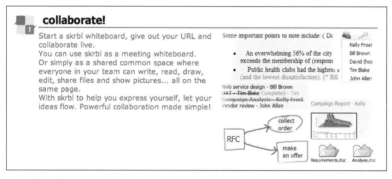

▶ Information page about skrbl

How Do You Get Started with skrbl?

It is very easy to get started with skrbl. You go to www.skrbl.com and click on Start skrbl Now. You do not need to register to use it, but if you sign in, you can save your skrbls. It is free up to 10 MBs, and they do not delete your boards.

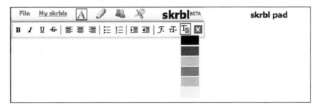

▶   The skrbl start screen

These easy-to-use tools for drawing, writing, editing, and formatting text on the skrbl pad are tools that students in any grade can use.

Where Can You Find More Information about skrbl?

Virtually all of the information you need about skrbl is on www.skrbl.com. The FAQs are at www.skrbl.com/faq.html.

Skype

Kevin Jarrett
Technology Facilitator, Northfield Community School, Northfield, New Jersey

What Is Skype?

Skype (www.skype.com) is a free program that turns your computer into a worldwide videoconferencing system featuring text (instant messaging) capabilities, file transfers, and even the ability to call landline telephones.

Why Is Skype a Useful Tool?

Skype is a powerful, easy-to-use software application that can effortlessly connect classrooms and communities around the world. Its combination of voice, video, and instant messaging (IM) technologies enables classroom teachers such as Cheryl Lykowski (http://globalexplorers.wikispaces.com), who teaches fifth grade in Bedford Public Schools (http://bedford.k12.mi.us) in Bedford, Michigan, to create rich, cross-curricular interactions with students around the globe. She and her students have been connected with a school in Colombia. They have collaborated on lessons, shared information about each other's culture and school practices, created podcasts, and conducted multiple projects.

From its inception in 2003, Skype has rapidly grown to become one of the world's most popular Internet applications. Today, more than 443 million people worldwide have Skype accounts. On any given day, more than 42 million of them are online and communicating with each other.

New features are added with each version. For example, with Skype 4.1, classrooms can collaborate in real time with other classrooms. Students can make calls using audio only, video with audio, or text (instant messaging). They can send files of any kind directly over the Skype connection in real time. Students can send text messages while another user is offline, and that person will get them once he or she signs in again. Skype also supports voice mail but there is an extra cost.

Users can share their screens, even between different platforms, to illustrate ideas, work collaboratively, or demonstrate software. No special software is required other than the Skype connection. Skype is available in many languages, which opens up a wide range of curricular possibilities for students to communicate and learn.

When and *How* Do You Use Skype?

We are starting to use Skype more and more in our district. For example, last year we Skyped with a Guatemalan immigrant who came to the United States 12 years ago and who is now a network engineer and administrator for a very large school system in Alabama. Third grade students working on a unit about immigration interviewed him about his experience coming to this country. They asked him about his impressions of the United States and about living here, building his career, and starting and owning his own business. Students found it to be an extremely powerful and memorable experience.

This year, classrooms in our elementary school will be collaborating with schools in New York, South Carolina, Georgia, and New Zealand. One third grade class will conduct a "read-aloud" collaboration and compare and contrast cultural interpretations of the texts. A fourth grade class will be developing "Study Buddies," and they will initially assist each other with math and science subjects at various times during the day. Multiple classrooms are planning to Skype with authors of books they read in class. All of these activities are free!

How Do You Get Started with Skype?

Skype is a free download, so start with the download (www.skype.com/download). During the installation process, the software will guide you through setting up your account (called a Skype ID). Afterward, a wizard will help you test your microphone, speakers, and webcam (if installed) by making a test call to the Skype Call Testing Service. The instructions are visual and simple to follow.

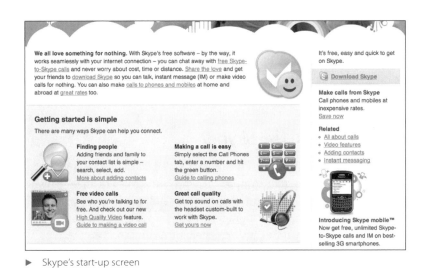

▶ Skype's start-up screen

Caution: Educators in districts with restrictive firewalls or other controls on Internet-based programs or the installation of software on local machines should consult with people in their district responsible for information technology before trying to use Skype. Firewall and client computer configuration changes may be necessary for Skype to work properly in such environments.

Where Can You Find More Information about Skype?

Once an educator has a Skype account, the next step is to find other Skype-using educators to collaborate with. One such directory is available at http://skypeinschools.pbworks.com/Directory/. Another great place to locate possible collaboration partners is Lucy Gray's Global Education Collaborative Ning (http://globaleducation.ning.com).

Usually, once educators make connections to others using Skype, ideas for projects, lessons, and collaborations flow freely. For those who need a head start, this blog post presents many great suggestions: www.teachingdegree.org/2009/06/30/50-awesome-ways-to-use-skype-in-the-classroom/.

Timetoast

Steven W. Anderson
Instructional Technologist, Stokes County Schools, Danbury, North Carolina

What Is Timetoast?

Timetoast is an online, interactive timeline creation tool.

Why Is Timetoast a Useful Tool?

At some point or another most students will have to make a timeline, either as a requirement of an assignment or as a way to understand, organize, and remember information.

In my class, students have made timelines on various topics. In some cases, they were organizing all the major battles during World War II, describing the events surrounding the Civil Rights movement, or even creating a timeline of the major events in their lives.

Before they had access to the Web, students would purchase poster board, brightly colored paper, and markers to create timelines. Now there is a Web 2.0 way—Timetoast—for them to not only create timelines but also make them interactive.

In addition, timelines created in Timetoast look good, and they also have features that make them useful for learning. For example, students can enter images and text about an event on the timeline, and they can add links to further information about the event and even cite resources. Students can share their timelines on various social networking services such as Twitter, Facebook, Reddit, and Delicious. They can also embed them in blogs, wikis, or class and school web pages, or share them with a direct link.

When and *How* Do You Use Timetoast?

One of the best examples I have seen of students using Timetoast is in a middle school history class. Students had been investigating the travels of various explorers and world travelers (Lewis and Clark, Christopher Columbus, Magellan, etc.). The students conducted research and created lists of web resources. For example, they referred to diaries that these explorers maintained during their travels. Using the diaries, students were able to create dynamic timelines that included images, quotes, and links that described the journeys of their travelers.

Timeline Categories

Music

Britney Spears, T252 Unit 2, S.L.A.M, KeSha, Jazz in America , Concerts I rocked out at, more...

Film

WarBones, Disney Timeline, Disney Cartoon Premieres , Jewish Life Cycle, henrry, Classic Disney Movies, more...

Science and Technology

Volcanoes: Nature's Way of Letting Off Steam, Le réseau messicole au fil du temps, Summer in full bloom, ANTECEDENTES DEL E-LEARNING, The History of TV, EDUC 8840 TIMELINE, more...

Business

First BankAmericano: Dead, but Not Buried, Innovation Project, VANQUISH MX TIMELINE, tylerdavis, Stephen Brockelman, Creative Highlights, Eli Lilly, more...

Politics

The Books I've read as of January 2010, Afghan detainees: After Colvin's testimony, Tidslinje, Three Cups of Tea, Gordon Brown's Week That Was, more...

Biography

SA Timeline, Joe Autobiograghy, A Canadian Life, Dwayne Michael Carter, Jr By: Tyler G, Ned Kelly, more...

Art and Culture

Disney Movies between 1990-2000, Fernand LEGER sa vie, Celebrating Northeast Michigan, Dr. Seuss' Books, 2010 Fiscal Year, more...

Personal

Mrs. White's Life, Nûçeyên Zêdetir Diğer Haberler زبر واعی, Obra Social São João Bosco, My Life, RDLA Effective Writing Instruction, more...

▶ Some Timetoast categories

How Do You Get Started with Timetoast?

Getting started with Timetoast is as easy as setting up an account. Go to www.timetoast.com and enter a username, password, and e-mail address. From there you have full access to the site to create as many timelines as you need or want.

Where Can You Find More Information about Timetoast?

About Timetoast:
www.timetoast.com/about

"Timetoast Creates Interactive Timelines to Share Memories and History" (Ben Parr, Mashable, April 3, 2009):
http://mashable.com/2009/04/03/timetoast/

"Butter Up Your Lessons with Timetoast"
(S. Anderson, blog post, February 23, 2009):
http://web20classroom.blogspot.com/2009/02/butter-up-your-lessons-
with-timetoast.html

"Introduction to Using Timetoast" (Radford Education):
www.youtube.com/watch?v=NeYmDGohxUc

TodaysMeet

Mike Hasley
Secondary Social Studies Specialist, Henrico County Public Schools, Henrico, Virginia

What Is TodaysMeet?

TodaysMeet is a microblogging website that allows a teacher to create a chat room or back channel where students can post messages with 140 or fewer characters. Teachers can create private chat rooms in which students ask questions of one another and of the teacher, and teachers can get immediate feedback about student comprehension.

Why Is TodaysMeet a Useful Tool?

Back channeling is a particularly useful tool in the classroom. TodaysMeet allows the teacher to get quick responses and instant feedback without the need to have anyone registered. Students can share insights, ask questions, and get immediate answers when they don't understand something. The conversation is private to your class or to whomever you invite, and you have a chat room that is focused on one relevant topic.

In addition, the chat room that the teacher sets up can be used during the school day, or left open for a specified time period for students to go back to at home, possibly weeks later. This allows for synchronous and asynchronous conversations about the topic.

When and *How* Do You Use TodaysMeet

I began using it with teachers in a class I taught on Internet tools in the classroom. I was trying to show them how they can make a basic lecture more interesting and relevant for students.

When the teacher needs to lecture about a topic or do a presentation, students can use the chat room to help further their understanding of a topic. It makes the lecture more interactive because students can ask each other questions and a teacher can read the back channel later and answer the questions in the next class.

For a Fishbowl activity, while the inner circle of students are discussing the topic at hand, the outer circle can be in a TodaysMeet chat room discussing the same topic, or carrying on their own conversation among themselves about the topic.

Teachers can invite outside professionals, academics, and anyone else they want to join in the conversation. This chat room can be as open as the teacher likes. Invite experts, administrators, and even parents to take part in the conversation.

Teachers can create a chat room for a pre- or post-discussion among students on a point the teachers want to highlight in the class. For example, if a teacher is going to talk about the Reverend Dr. Martin Luther King, Jr., students can watch his "I have a dream" speech on YouTube in advance and go to a TodaysMeet room to share their impressions of the speech. Then, in class the next day, the teacher can spark a deeper discussion about the speech.

Teachers can set up a chat room for a study review from home. The teacher sends the study room URL to the students, who then visit the TodaysMeet room at the scheduled time of night (or asynchronously) and ask their teacher questions about the content they're studying.

Administrators can use TodaysMeet during meetings or staff development sessions so that participants have a back channel to ask questions. Administrators can answer the questions at the session or afterward.

How Do You Get Started with TodaysMeet?

A simple four-step procedure (less than a minute) is all that is required for teachers.

❶ Go to http://TodaysMeet.com.

❷ Name the room.

❸ Choose how long you want the room to exist.

❹ Create your room.

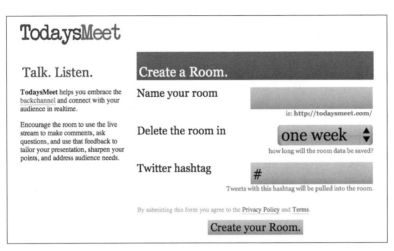

▶ The TodaysMeet start screen

Once the teacher has set up a room, students will then:

❶ Go to the unique web address the teacher created

❷ Type their names

❸ Start typing in the room

Note: Warn the students that their comments are public to the class, so sticking to the purpose of the chat room is essential.

Where Can You Find More Information about TodaysMeet?

Go to http://todaysmeet.com and http://todaysmeet.com/about to learn more about back channeling and TodaysMeet.

VoiceThread

Bob Sprankle
Technology Integrator, Wells-Ogunquit Community School District, Wells, Maine

What Is VoiceThread?

VoiceThread is an online tool that takes media presentations to a new level by allowing for conversation. Users can create a VoiceThread with voice, video, text, or images and invite others to add to the presentation with voice, video, or text. It is an incredibly simple tool and easy to set up and get going in a matter of minutes.

Why Is VoiceThread a Useful Tool?

VoiceThread is a tool that allows student (and teacher) work to be transformed into a conversation with an authentic global audience. Student work used to be shared in the hallway on a bulletin board, where others in the building could only view the work. VoiceThread allows anyone in the world to not only view the work, but to also interact with the creator by leaving reflections, comments, questions, or kudos. Rather than limiting students with feedback from only one teacher in the classroom, many other educators and students can be invited into dialogue around the work. Feedback can be typed, recorded by voice or video, uploaded as audio, or even recorded by phone. Commenters can even "draw" on the slides in order to illustrate a point.

When and *How* Do You Use VoiceThread?

I've used VoiceThread with students in a variety of ways. One of the most powerful uses is for assessment purposes. For example, I've had my second graders use VoiceThread to report what they've learned about using another piece of software, Google Earth. Because students can "speak" their reflections, I get more in-depth thoughts from most students at this level than I would with a written or typed response.

One of my favorite uses of VoiceThread was when students gave feedback to a software company that asked us to beta test a new product. Rather than the CEO of the company hearing only a summary of ideas from me, the teacher, he was able to listen to each and every student. The students were thrilled and empowered that they were able to speak directly to the CEO and help shape the evolution of the product.

This year I plan to use VoiceThread with third graders to create electronic portfolios. The students will post all of the work they do in the computer lab within their own VoiceThreads. Their teachers, parents, and other family members will be the only ones allowed to view the VoiceThreads and will be able to record comments, questions, and kudos.

I've used VoiceThread as a homeschool connection tool to explain to parents what is offered at our website and give them information about the technology curriculum. I've also used VoiceThread with other educators to provide tutorials, or as a forum for discussions of practice and pedagogy.

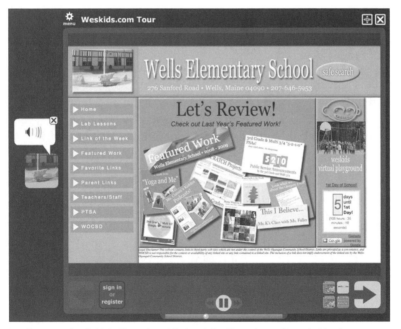

▶ An example of a VoiceThread-enabled website. Note the audio and video icons on the left of the browser window.

How Do You Get Started with VoiceThread?

VoiceThread offers free and paid educator subscription options. Head to http://voicethread.com to sign up, and then dig into the excellent tutorials that VoiceThread offers at http://voicethread.com/support/.

▶ The VoiceThread start page

Where Can You Find More Information about VoiceThread?

VoiceThread includes a plethora of information with the above-mentioned tutorials and on the company's help page found at http://voicethread.com/help/faq/. They also display exemplary educational uses of VoiceThread on their Library page (http://voicethread.com/library). They keep you up-to-date on their blog (http://voicethread.com/blog), where they announce new features such as their latest acquisition of more than 700,000 New York Public Library images and the learning modules that accompany them. The blog also provides further tutorials and documentation of the effects of VoiceThread on learning.

Voki

Christine Southard
Special Education Teacher, Herricks UFSD, New Hyde Park, New York

What Is Voki?

Voki is a free online service and Web 2.0 tool that allows you to create person-alized speaking avatars. These avatars can then be embedded in any online space that accepts html, such as a website, blog, or wiki.

Why Is Voki a Useful Tool?

Voki is a great motivational tool to use with students because of its creative nature and visual appeal. From a teacher's perspective, a Voki is an ideal tool for educators to use with younger students to improve their literacy skills.

Prior to working in the program, students must research the characters, people, or topics, or all three, that they intend to speak about using their avatar. Students can then write and edit scripts based on their research. Scripts can be centered on writing lessons that focus on the author's purpose, and they can also be used as opportunities for editing. Rereading scripts prior to recording gives students the opportunity to improve their fluency.

When and *How* Do You Use Voki?

Voki is a useful tool because you can have students create speaking avatars for just about any subject. Students can portray themselves as a Voki and reflect their opinion or knowledge on a particular topic. Students can also create Vokis to role-play a variety of fiction and nonfiction characters. Language teachers can have students create Vokis to practice their language skills. The options are limitless.

I have seen a few teachers use a Voki avatar embedded in their website or blog to introduce themselves to students at the beginning of the year. Teachers have also used Vokis to introduce students to a new lesson or unit and have embedded the avatar in a school website or wiki.

In our fifth grade class, we log in the students under our Voki account while they are in school. Then the students go through a number of prompts to create the look of their Voki. They have a variety of characters to choose from, including animals, real and fictitious people, and some odd and interesting characters. Students can also choose a background setting from Voki or upload their own. This is a great opportunity to discuss the importance of setting. Students can then add their own voice to the Voki by using the phone (with teacher supervision), a microphone, or the text-to-speech option within Voki, or by uploading an audio file.

In our classroom, we usually allow our students to choose to use a Voki as a response to an activity. For example, in a unit on time zones, a number of children chose to use Vokis to describe what they were doing at various Greenwich Mean Times (GMT). They wrote their scripts and then pasted their text and chose a speaker within Voki. We embedded their final products in our timezoneexperiences wiki. Here are some examples from our wiki:

> (Girl) Student Example:
> http://timezoneexperiences.wikispaces.com/Zero+O%27Clock

> (Girl) Student Example:
> http://timezoneexperiences.wikispaces.com/Fifteen+O%27Clock

> (Boy) Student Example:
> https://timezoneexperiences.wikispaces.com/Three+O%27Clock

Because Voki is a presentation tool, students are more actively involved in the learning processes of writing prior to using the application. Whatever the topic students are going to speak about, they must research, brainstorm, organize, write, and edit a script that fulfills the needs of the assignment. Prior to recording their Voki, students must practice their fluency skills by rereading their script and tailoring their tone of voice to the topic and intended audience. However, there is a text-to-speech option within the Voki application that will speak for you.

▶ The Voki create screen

How Do You Get Started with Voki?

Go to Voki.com and create a login for yourself. Choose and customize your avatar, pick a background setting, and then give your Voki a voice. Embed the final product in your website or blog.

Where Can You Find More Information about Voki?

www.voki.com

Webspiration

Barbara Bray
Educational Consultant, My eCoach, Lafayette, California

What Is Webspiration

Webspiration is a tool for concept-mapping tool (also called mind mapping and idea mapping). It uses the power of visual learning and outlining to enhance thinking and collaboration skills. The people who designed the concept-mapping tool, Inspiration, put this version on the web as Webspiration.

Concept and idea mapping are processes where one or more participants, using brainstorming techniques, create maps using keywords that are representative of specific concepts. The result of a concept-mapping session is a concept map: a series of words laid out in a graphical representation with reciprocal connections, links, images, and resources. By looking at how the relationships between words or concepts have been outlined, students can understand them. The web interface allows learners to jump in and use existing templates or start brainstorming online.

Why Is Webspiration A Useful Tool?

Students will need the digital-age skills of visual learning and critical thinking in collaborative environments. Visual learning techniques are graphical ways of representing information that help students to think clearly and to process, organize, and prioritize new information.

Webspiration unleashes creativity, strengthens organizational skills, and transforms ideas and information into knowledge in the form of idea mapping, webbing, and concept mapping. Webspiration uses a variety of visual diagrams for creative thinking, planning, understanding concepts, and improving retention. Visual diagrams provide a high-level view revealing patterns, interrelationships, and interdependencies. They also help students understand complex information by slicing that information into smaller parts that can be more easily understood and learned.

Webspiration is a valuable tool for visual literacy. Learning science, technology, social studies, mathematics, health and nutrition, history and geography, and arts and crafts relies on visual texts such as maps, diagrams, graphs, timelines, or tables. Students can use visual texts and transfer them into Webspiration to understand and explain them.

When and *How* Do You Use Webspiration?

Students use Webspiration to map out ideas, organize with outlines, and collaborate online with teams or colleagues. They create concept maps, mind maps, idea webs, and other powerful visual thinking models in Diagram View. They build organized outlines, plans, and reports with Outline View.

I worked with primary students in Florida who did a collaborative weather report as part of their cross-age, cross-curriculum Enhancing Education Through Technology (EETT) grant. The kindergarten classes created weekly weather reports for their area using the data that was collected from the weather station that middle school students created and monitored. The teachers decided they wanted to continue this project as a collaborative online project with several schools where students developed a weekly report. The students used Webspiration, with daily symbols representing that day's weather. Each class included a video podcast, images, or files about that week.

Eleventh grade students collaborated on the progress of the H1N1 flu virus and other current events using Google Trends and Webspiration. The students worked in groups of four and created a timeline for their event. They updated it as newsbreaks several times during the week. They included links to news reports, embedded streaming video, and even uploaded a podcast giving their perspective.

Eighth grade students took on the roles of leaders during the Constitutional Congress. In each of their positions, they defended a bill, argued different positions, and redefined what it meant to be part of history during that time. They enhanced their face-to-face debate by using Webspiration to keep track of the arguments in the debate. Think of Webspiration as a collaborative back channel where all the students are invited to contribute during a presentation, debate, or activity.

Third grade students created and posted their family tree, using pictures of the different members of their family. Working with the teacher, each student invited different family members to contribute to the symbol on the family tree that represented them.

I have always used Webspiration for brainstorming, especially using RapidFire to come up with ideas quickly. I invite other professional developers, coaches, and colleagues to brainstorm with me using Webspiration. This is a great tool to enhance any workshop or presentation. Because it is online and has tools such as chat, this is a great collaborative planning tool. Last time I used it, we were able to develop a workshop agenda in diagram form that allowed presenters to add more details to their section. When it was done, each of us was able to export it as a diagram and an outline.

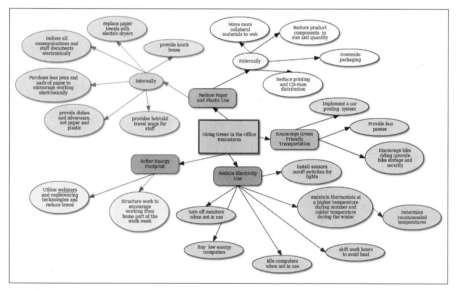

▶ A completed Webspiration concept map

How Do You Get Started with Webspiration?

Go to http://mywebspiration.com and sign up for a free account, then click on Diagram on the starter screen to open a new diagram. Enter a title for your document. The title becomes the central topic or main idea for your diagram. To add a new idea quickly, click on the workspace and begin typing. A new symbol to hold your text is automatically created.

Where Can You Find More Information about Webspiration?

http://mywebspiration.com

WizIQ

Serge Danielson-Francois
Librarian, Divine Child High School, Archdiocese of Detroit, Dearborn, Michigan

What Is WizIQ

WizIQ (www.wiziq.com/about_us.aspx) is a virtual classroom environment that allows faculty to work with groups of learners independently. Two
versions of the web-hosted videoconferencing software are available to the
public. We opted for the premium version of WizIQ so that faculty can share
audio and video controls with their students to archive sessions for remote
asynchronous access.

The free version is fully functional, but it is unidirectional: the teacher can
address the class, but the students cannot use audiovisual tools to address each
other or the teacher. With the free version, only one person can "broadcast,"
either the teacher or the student.

The premium version allows for "distributed cognition," with every participant contributing some expertise. For example, many people can share the
microphone and whiteboard tools in a serial fashion. The cost was $49.95 for
one year when we signed up.

Why Is WizIQ a Useful Tool?

WizIQ is a useful tool because it allows students to experience videoconferencing and faculty to remain innovative and engaging. At Divine Child, we are
committed to ensuring that the Web 2.0 tools we integrate into the classroom
have greater applicability than just the classroom. We believe that digital-age
learning should be authentic and have a personal and professional echo for our
students and our faculty.

Students are able to subscribe to WizIQ without much fuss and to take classes
from professionals outside our school. Prior to the Advanced Placement (AP)
U.S. History test, some of our students used a WizIQ tutorial (one example

is www.wiziq.com/tutorial/22231-The-Offical-APUSH-Cram-Packet) to quiz each other and review key points.

Premium online tutoring for the exam was available, but our students chose to use free resources, including SlideShare presentations, as a discussion starter for their review sessions. We welcome the challenge of ensuring that our class offerings exceed the standard of service available on the web. WizIQ allows our faculty to gauge the effectiveness and creativity of their lesson plans and their learning resources.

When and *How* Do You Use WizIQ?

We have used WizIQ for our spring term exam review and encouraged students to contact faculty during prearranged evening office hours. Faculty members are able to group students according to ability and offer a targeted review for students who are struggling with similar questions. We have also used WizIQ for tutoring during the summer when one faculty member is able to work several times a week with a student on academic probation. Finally, we have used WizIQ to breathe new life into our summer reading program by providing students with the opportunity to discuss required titles in a small group setting.

Students who read *The Catcher in the Rye* in the summer meet online to discern the truth of Holden Caulfield's unreliable narrative. They share links to the SparkNotes plot summaries and character profiles (www.sparknotes.com/lit/catcher), which are freely available online, and discuss possible questions teachers might pose on book tests at the beginning of the school year. We make a point of highlighting the fact that faculty will focus on material not available online. Students are also encouraged to use Flickr and Google Earth to explore in greater depth the setting for the novel. As is our custom, we like to cluster use of Web 2.0 tools to maximize engagement and learning. We also value having students work through complex material in peer-to-peer settings.

How Do You Get Started with WizIQ?

To get started with WizIQ, faculty and students will need to create a username and choose a password at www.wiziq.com. Institutions will need to decide whether potential use of this Web 2.0 tool warrants investment in a yearlong premium subscription.

▶ The WizIQ start screen

Where Can You Find More Information about WizIQ?

More information on WizIQ is available at www.wiziq.com.

Wordle

Samantha Morra
Glenfield School Technology Coordinator, Montclair Public Schools, Montclair, New Jersey

What Is Wordle

Wordle creates word clouds from text. These clouds, or visual representations of text, give prominence to words that appear more frequently in the text.

Why Is Wordle a Useful Tool?

Wordle is much more than just about creating pretty pictures with words. It is a great visualization tool that can become a catalyst for discussion and insight. It is about understanding and discovering patterns in text and generating conversations among students and teachers.

When and *How* Do You Use Wordle?

When I first discovered Wordle, I decided to share it with my middle school students. We were discussing the power of words and images, and it seemed like a perfect fit.

We went to the federal government's Our Documents website (www. ourdocuments.gov), which has the text of all the documents that are important in United States history. We selected the text of the Declaration of Independence. Then we went to Wordle (www.wordle.net) and created a word cloud with it. Students could see instantly which words were most important.

Next, I gave students the assignment to choose another one of the "100 Milestone Documents" on the Our Documents site and analyze the Wordles they produced. Students enjoyed this exercise and learned more about the power of words.

The conversations they had about the assignment were amazing. One student chose the Gettysburg Address. He said he chose to make the colors gray because it was about war, and it was sad. Another student chose Andrew Jackson's "Message to Congress On Indian Removal." As she read it over, she commented that the words *whites* and *civilized* were together and the words *Indians* and *savage* were together. This sparked a discussion about racism and the creation of our country. I could not get my students to leave when the bell rang. I knew this was one site I wanted to share with other teachers.

In addition to teaching, I conduct staff development workshops for teachers in my district. We usually create a word cloud with the Declaration of Independence or a piece of literature. It never ceases to amaze me how Wordle just clicks (pardon the pun) with so many teachers, no matter what their level of technology. Out of all the tools I cover, teachers start using Wordle first after they leave my workshop.

One of the social studies teachers in my school always asks her students to create an interesting cover for their reports. She likes to encourage creativity, but some students complained that they could not draw and hated that part of the assignment. Her technology skills were not that strong, but she heard about Wordle. She gave them the option of copying and pasting their reports into Wordle, making adjustments for layout and color, and using that as the cover. Many of her students chose that option. One student put her report into Wordle and saw that "also" was the largest word. She showed it to her teacher and said, "I guess I use 'also' too much." The teacher made a lesson out of it, and now the students are much more aware of the word choices they make. This teacher now uses Wordle with all of her students, and it has become a word variety self-assessment tool.

How Do You Get Started with Wordle?

You go to the Wordle site at www.wordle.net. There is no login or member-ship. You can just copy any text from a Word file, the web, or any other source, and make it into a word cloud by pasting it into the box. As you press the create button, there is a magical moment where unwieldy text is trans-formed into an image on the screen. The larger words can help the viewer identify the main ideas from the text quickly and easily. You can also enhance your word clouds by changing the font, layout, and colors.

▶ A Wordle image from the U.S. Declaration of Independence

Where Can You Find More Information about Wordle?

You can find Wordle at www.wordle.net.

I also find the Wordle group on Diigo a valuable source for information: http://groups.diigo.com/groups/wordle/. It is a great way to collaborate with other educators about the use of Wordle. It is also a great place to find examples, tips, and innovative ways to use Wordle in education.

11

an assortment of web 2.0 tools

This book has examined the ways educators are using Web 2.0 tools for instructional practices and professional development. This chapter presents a collection of these tools, many of which are discussed earlier in the book, so readers can find tools they need quickly and easily. It's also a way to see the range of tools available for classrooms today.

We recognize two important things: First, tools will come and go, and web addresses will change. We apologize for that in advance. Second, we know that each of you is a creative, adventurous educator; thus, we encourage you to use these tools in a way that is meaningful for you and your students. There are no Web 2.0 tool police! Be creative, have fun, and maximize the instructional value.

tool categories

We hope you will find this list useful. Since there are almost 200 tools listed here, we organized them into the following 24 categories:

- Annotation and Note Taking
- Audio and Podcast Tools
- Blogs
- Calendars
- Collaborative Writing Tools
- Idea or Mind Mapping
- Educator and Student Communities
- Communication and Online Discussion Tools
- Content Management Systems and Learning Spaces
- Online Whiteboards
- Maps
- Microblogging and Microblog Readers

- Photo Editing and Photo Sharing
- Presentation and Video-Editing Tools
- Publishing and Drawing Tools
- Portals and Social Bookmarking
- Quiz and Activities Generators
- RSS
- Timelines
- Videoconferencing
- Video Sharing
- Virtual Worlds
- Wikis
- Other Tools

tools

Annotation and Note Taking

Awesome Highlighter (www.awesomehighlighter.com). Awesome Highlighter lets you highlight text (like on real paper) on any web page and then gives you a short link to the page, which you can share or e-mail.

Evernote (http://evernote.com). Evernote allows you to write a note or capture something from a web page and save it so that it is indexed and searchable by keywords, titles, and tags.

Notely (www.notely.net). Notely is a collection of tools to help you get organized. It includes a scheduler, calendar, note taker, to-do list, task list, homework planner, and more.

SpringNote (http://springote.com). SpringNote allows you to create pages, work on them with others, and share files. You can create either a personal notebook to keep track of things or group notebooks to collaborate on projects.

Audio and Podcast Tools

Audacity (http://audacity.sourceforge.net). Audacity is free, open source software that you download to record and edit sounds.

Audiopal (www.audiopal.com). Audiopal lets you record your voice or use built-in voices and incorporate the audio into a web page, blog, or social networking site.

Chirbit (www.chirbit.com). Chirbit allows you to record, upload, listen to, and share sound; create micropodcasts and short audio clips; and incorporate these into websites such as Twitter and Facebook.

Gabcast (http://gabcast.com). Gabcast allows you to record your voice using a phone or VoIP to create podcasts, post audio to a blog, create audio greetings, and host conference calls.

Digital Podcast (Educational) (www.digitalpodcast.com/browse-educational-20-1.html). Digital Podcast (Educational) is a collection of topics that range from lessons in languages, relaxation, and history alive, to lessons in film-making. It allows you to add your own podcasts, tag them, and share them with the world.

The Education Podcast Network (http://epnweb.org). The Education Podcast Network brings together a wide range of podcast programming designed to support educational goals for teachers and classrooms. Topics include educational curricular content and professional development opportunities, including those that explore issues of teaching and learning today. It allows educators to offer podcasts for inclusion in the network; organizers vet all suggested additions for appropriateness. Once accepted, podcasts are available to anyone interested in the topic.

iSpeech (www.ispeech.org). iSpeech is a text-to-speech converter that transforms your blog into a talking blog so that people can listen to the text on the page.

Kids Podcasts (http://kids.podcast.com). Kids podcasts (and family podcasts) provide education and entertainment through a wide variety of stories, radio broadcasting, and information. It allows you to add students' podcasts and make them available to anyone.

MyPodcast (www.mypodcast.com). MyPodcast.com provides software to record, publish, and air podcasts. It offers explicit directions on how to get started, set up equipment, download recording software, and more.

Podomatic (www.podomatic.com). Podomatic allows you to create, find, and share podcasts, customize a podcast page, get audience data, share video and photos, and be part of a podcast community.

Podbean (www.podbean.com). Podbean allows you to create podcasts in three easy steps and upload, publish, manage, and promote your podcasts. It also allows you to store and manage podcast subscriptions.

Read the Words (www.readthewords.com). Read the Words allows you to convert text to speech, including words you type in, uploaded files, and web pages, and embed the results in e-mail or a web page.

Talkr (www.talkr.com). Talkr converts text to speech and allows you to listen to text-only blogs on your iPod. You can tell Talkr which feeds (machine-readable blogs or news sources) you want by subscribing to them.

Vaestro (www.vaestro.com). Vaestro is audio forum software that you can use on your website to talk to others, host interactive podcasts, or use like an audio blog to communicate with groups of people.

Vocaroo (http://vocaroo.com). Vocaroo allows you to record your voice and send voice messages. You can install a widget on your website or blog to allow visitors to record and play back their own voices.

Voki (www.voki.com). Voki allows you to create personalized speaking avatars and use them on your blog, on your profile, and in your e-mail messages.

YackPack (www.yackpack.com/education.html). YackPack provides voice and text messaging for communication among teams. It works like a discussion board to help people focus on a topic and share ideas. You can record, embed, or link voice messages.

Yodio (http://yodio.com). Yodio provides an audio player to embed on websites so that you can create and listen to sound along with your photos or presentations, as well as share narratives such as an audio postcard or narrated photo album or storybook.

Blogs

Blogger (www.blogger.com). Google's Blogger provides a platform for blogs so that students can share their thoughts in writing, photos, and videos. They can post from the web or mobile phone and can personalize their blogs with themes, gadgets, and more.

Class Blogmeister (www.classblogmeister.com). Class Blogmeister is a blogging engine or online publishing tool that was developed specifically for classroom use so that students can publish assignment-based writing. Teachers set up and maintain accounts and are responsible for them.

CoverItLive (www.coveritlive.com). CoverItLive allows you to turn live blogging into an online event by streaming live onto your web pages or blog so that others can hear from you in real time. You can add pictures and videos.

Easyjournal (www.easyjournal.com). Easyjournal provides software for you to keep a blog or journal online and includes a broad range of features and personalization capabilities.

Edublogs (www.edublogs.org). Edublogs allows teachers to create and manage student blogs that include useful features for podcasting and displaying videos, photos, and more. It includes step-by-step instructions and video tutorials.

ePals (www.epals.com). ePals is a K–12 online community with school-safe e-mail and blog tools for students to connect, collaborate, and learn. It features a global community of connected classrooms and collaborative learning projects.

Gaggle (www.gaggle.net). Gaggle provides e-mail, blogs, chat rooms, message boards, and digital lockers for students.

LiveJournal (www.livejournal.com). LiveJournal provides the tools to express yourself, share, and connect with others online. You can use LiveJournal as a private journal, a blog, a discussion forum, or a social network.

Posterous (www.posterous.com). Posterous provides a simple way to put many things online using e-mail. You can share thoughts, photos, audio, and files by e-mailing them to post@posterous.com; they create a blog and provide a URL. You can send documents, photos, and MP3 and video files.

21Classes (www.21classes.com). 21Classes allows teachers to create, host, and manage a virtual classroom or blog to communicate with their students and encourage student writing and communication. Students can upload text and photos, or insert videos into their blog posts.

TypePad (www.typepad.com). TypePad provides a platform for control over what, when, and how you publish content to your blog. You can customize the look and feel of your blog design, publish different types of media, and manage comments.

Weebly (www.weebly.com). Weebly allows you to create a classroom website and blog with a drag and drop interface, as well as host a domain, at no cost. Teachers can manage their students' accounts, accept homework assignments online, and keep parents up to date.

WordPress (www.wordpress.com). WordPress.com is a state-of-the-art, open-source publishing platform that requires you to have a hosting account, a database, FTP, and other features, which many schools and districts do have. WordPress adds the missing features so that you can set up blogs with a choice of design, three gigabytes of file storage, integrated statistics, a spam blocker, and versions in more than 50 languages.

Calendars

Assign-A-Day (http://assignaday.4teachers.org). Assign-A-Day is a free tool designed to enhance teacher and student communication through an online teacher-managed calendar. Teachers create a calendar for each of their classes and add assignments for the students to view. Students view their teachers' calendars to see assignments for classes they might have missed, or to get an overview of the class.

Google Calendar (www.google.com/intl/en/googlecalendar/overview.html). Google Calendar lets you share your schedule and view the schedules of others who choose to share theirs, send invitations and track RSVPs, sync with desktop applications, and work offline or on a mobile phone.

30 Boxes (www.30boxes.com). 30 Boxes provides an online calendar, social event organizer, and reminder of important events. You can connect with friends and share significant dates.

Collaborative Writing Tools

Buzzword (https://buzzword.acrobat.com). Adobe's Buzzword is a new online word processor that you can use to collaborate with others. Students can write, edit, and comment on documents; add images; and share with others. Teachers can control access levels and versions, track edits by contributor, and keep track of changes.

EtherPad (http://etherpad.com). EtherPad is a web-based word processor that allows people to work together in real time, edit the same document simultaneously, and see changes instantly reflected on everyone's screen.

Google Apps Education Edition (www.google.com/a/help/intl/en/edu). Google Apps Education Edition is a free suite of hosted communication and collaboration tools designed for schools and universities. It includes e-mail, messaging, calendars, word processing, spreadsheet, forms, and presentation software.

HyLighter (www.hylighter.com). HyLighter provides a collaboration plug-in for collective thinking and editing as contributors interact. Instead of actually changing the original document, as in a wiki or online editor, or redlining, as in Track Changes, it points to the locations in the document where reviewers have made comments or recommended changes.

MixedInk (www.mixedink.com). MixedInk takes an approach to collaborative writing in which people weave their best ideas together. An organizing group runs each topic and invites others to join. It was designed for short texts that get attention, such as an op-ed, mission statement, or open letter.

Scribd (www.scribd.com). Scribd is the place where you can publish, discover, and discuss original writings and documents. People can share their writing or find others' works. It is a platform for readers, authors, publishers, and others seeking to express themselves, share ideas, and exchange information.

TextFlow (http://textflow.com). TextFlow is a collaborative tool that allows concurrent work of several users, all working on their own versions of the document.

Thinkature (www.thinkature.com). Thinkature places instant messaging inside a visual, shared work space. You can use it as a collaboration environment, a meeting room, a personal web-based whiteboard, or something else. Students can communicate by chatting, drawing, creating cards, and adding content from the web in real time.

YourDraft (www.yourdraft.com). YourDraft allows you to create and share content instantly as well as edit collaboratively. The WYSIWYG editor allows fast and flexible drafting. You can give others the right to edit your page or only to read your page and add replies.

Zoho Writer (http://writer.zoho.com). Zoho Writer provides sharing and collaboration. Post your documents online and share them with those in the group for collaboration in real time. You can upload documents from the desktop, Google Docs, or anywhere on the web and download and save them to your computer.

Idea or Mind Mapping

Bubbl.us (http://bubbl.us). Bubbl.us is a web application that lets you brainstorm online. Students can create colorful mind maps, share and work in teams, embed a mind map in a blog or website, e-mail and print a mind map, or save it as an image.

Debategraph (www.debategraph.org). Debategraph is a wiki debate visualization tool that lets you present the strongest case on any debate that matters to you, openly engage the opposing arguments, create and reshape debates, make new points, rate and filter the arguments, monitor the evolution of debates via RSS feeds, and share and reuse the debates online and offline.

Gliffy (www.gliffy.com). Gliffy is online diagram software used to create professional-quality flowcharts, diagrams, floor plans, technical drawings, and more. The online diagram editor makes it easy to create diagrams, drawings, and mind maps.

Mind42 (www.mind42.com). Mind42 is a browser-based, online, mind-mapping tool that allows you to manage and keep track of ideas alone, in teams of two, or in a large group. Students can brainstorm and collaborate and then immediately get an updated view of all the collected ideas.

MindMeister (www.mindmeister.com). MindMeister provides web-based mind mapping with real-time collaboration to allow global brainstorming sessions. Students can create, manage, and share mind maps online. They can access them anytime, from anywhere. They can work on the same mind map simultaneously and see each other's changes as they happen.

Mindomo (www.mindomo.com). Mindomo is a visual tool that lets you organize your ideas and work and gain insights into the relationships between various parts of a problem to formulate a solution. Teachers can plan and track projects, manage tasks and priorities, and define goals and objectives as students learn visually.

Webspiration (www.mywebspiration.com). Webspiration allows you to combine the power of visual thinking and outlining to enhance thinking, learning, and collaboration. Students can use Webspiration to map out ideas, organize with outlines, and collaborate online with teams or colleagues.

Educator and Student Communities

Badoo (http://badoo.com). Badoo is a worldwide socializing site that supports members meeting new people and friends in and around their local areas. It includes the interactions and activities of most social networks, but it focuses on expanding social circles locally. One of Badoo's strengths is the control users have over the exposure of their profiles; it also has instant messaging and uploads of photos and videos.

Bebo (www.bebo.com). Bebo is a popular social networking site that connects you to individuals and information globally. It combines community, self-expression, and entertainment in a way that allows you to share, with selected others in your network, digital content which you create yourself or which you admire.

Classroom 2.0 (www.classroom20.com). Classroom 2.0 is a social network for those interested in Web 2.0 and collaborative technologies in education. The site, built on a Ning, hosts discussions; and educators can find and connect with colleagues.

Curriki (www.curriki.org). Curriki is a community of educators, learners, and experts who create free, open-source instructional materials for a repository that will benefit teachers and students.

Engrade (www.engrade.com). Engrade is an online classroom community with a free set of web-based tools that allow you to manage classes online and provide parents and students with 24/7 real-time class information that's private and secure. It includes an assignment calendar, online messaging, grade book, attendance book, and progress reports.

Friendster (www.friendster.com). Friendster is a global online social network with more than 110 million members worldwide. It is focused on helping people stay in touch with friends and discover new people and things that are important to them. Friendster prides itself in delivering an easy-to-use, friendly, and interactive environment where users can connect easily with anyone around the world.

Hi5 (http://hi5.com). Hi5 is a global social entertainment network primarily for youth. It is available in more than 50 languages. It is a highly interactive social experience and ranks as one of the fastest growing youth sites, particularly for social media.

LinkedIn (www.linkedin.com). LinkedIn is a widely interconnected network of professionals (50 million!) from around the world. You can connect your network of trusted colleagues to others' networks, in a safe environment and set up collaborations, consultations, and interactions. LinkedIn represents 170 industries and 200 countries.

MySpace (http://myspace.com) and **Facebook** (www.facebook.com). MySpace and Facebook are websites that connect people through personal expression, content, and culture. With a global community of millions of users, they provide forums for personal profiles, photos, videos, messaging, games, and music. Individuals find old friends, establish new friendships, and interact at multiple levels.

Ning (www.ning.com). Ning provides a social platform that allows people to join and create Ning Networks. Creators control the layout and have a wide choice of features—videos, photos, chat, music, groups, events, and blogs—in addition to a latest-activity feature, member profile pages, friends, messaging, e-mail notifications, RSS support, and third-party applications.

SchoolNet Global (www.schoolnetglobal.com). SchoolNet Global is a social network designed to bring educators and their students together for collaborative educational projects in 34 countries.

WizIQ (www.wiziq.com). WizIQ is an online teacher community for learning and collaboration. Students and teachers can find, share, download, and upload PowerPoint presentations on educational subjects and topics. Teachers can teach and learn live in WizIQ's virtual classroom.

Communication and Online Discussion Tools

Chatzy (www.chatzy.com). Chatzy provides a chat service that allows its users to create chat rooms, send out invitations to people they know, and communicate privately in these chat rooms. It is often used as a back channel for side conversations during presentations.

FlashMeeting (http://flashmeeting.e2bn.net). FlashMeeting is an online meeting application that allows a dispersed group of people to meet from anywhere in the world with an Internet connection. Someone books a meeting and informs participants, who can then click on the link to enter the meeting at an arranged time.

Mikogo (www.mikogo.com). Mikogo is a cross-platform desktop sharing tool, ideal for web conferencing, online meetings, or remote support.

OpenHuddle (www.openhuddle.com). OpenHuddle allows you to interact, in whatever way you want, with as many people, or as few, as you would like. You can choose from and use video, audio, text chat, and a drawing board in whatever way you see fit. Teachers can invite students into a "huddle" and start discussions with as little required hardware as a webcam and a headset or microphone.

Scribblar (http://scribblar.com). Scribblar is an online collaboration tool to use for training and tutoring, working with images, brainstorming, and demonstrating. It includes a real-time multiuser whiteboard, image upload and download, text chat, and live audio.

Skype (www.skype.com). Skype is a free, downloadable tool that allows you to make free phone calls (with or without video) from your computer to another Skype user. You use your Internet connection to turn your computer into an Internet phone.

SnapYap (www.snapyap.com). SnapYap is a video communication tool that allows you to participate in live video calls, record video messages, and send and receive video e-mails with just a webcam and an Internet connection. Users can launch video calls in their web browsers.

Tinychat (http://tinychat.com). Tinychat provides audio and video web communication services in disposable conference rooms for up to 400 people and 12 live audio-video streams. It provides disposable, private, encrypted, person-to-person audio-video calls.

TodaysMeet (http://todaysmeet.com). TodaysMeet is a back-channel communications tool to help you connect with others in real time. People can use the live stream to make comments, ask questions, and provide feedback. It helps you tailor your presentation, sharpen your points, and address audience needs.

Voxli (https://voxli.com). Voxli provides online voice conferencing for up to 200 people at a time. You send the URL of your voice conference through e-mail or instant messenger and use Push to Talk to control when you are speaking, even if you are outside the browser.

YackAll (http://yackall.com). YackAll provides a way to communicate with a group while on the go. It provides a means to have a continuous long-running conversation no matter when it is or where the participants are located.

Yuuguu (www.yuuguu.com). Yuuguu offers cross-network instant messaging, instant screen sharing, real-time collaboration, web conferencing, and remote support.

Content Management Systems and Learning Spaces

Drupal (http://drupal.org). Drupal is a free, open-source software package that allows you to publish, manage, and organize a wide variety of content on a website. You can use it for a school or community web portal, discussion site, social networking site, personal website or blog, and more.

Haiku (www.haikulearning.com). Haiku is a learning management system that allows you to organize, manage, and deliver course content, assignments, and assessments. You can securely conduct discussions, exchange messages, take attendance, and collect and grade homework.

Moodle (http://moodle.org). Moodle is a course or learning management system. Educators can use this free web application to create effective online learning sites with dynamic content. To work, it needs to be installed on a web server.

NineHub (http://ninehub.com). NineHub.com provides a free learning management system that is hosted on this Australian site. You can create your system or online class without technical knowledge.

Online Whiteboards

CoSketch (http://cosketch.com). CoSketch is a multiuser online whiteboard that provides you with the ability to visualize and share your ideas as images quickly. Anything you paint will show up in real time for all other users in the room. You can save a sketch as an image for embedding on forums, blogs, and so forth.

Dabbleboard (www.dabbleboard.com). Dabbleboard is an online collaboration application that appears as an online whiteboard that has a new type of drawing interface that's easy to use. Students can draw or work together easily.

Scriblink (http://scriblink.com). Scriblink is a free digital whiteboard (with no registration) that users can share to collaborate online in real time. Features include privacy, dynamic tools, and file options such as printing, saving, and e-mailing work, uploading images, and in-screen chat or VoIP conferencing.

skrbl (www.skrbl.com). skrbl is a tool that allows you to create instant online whiteboards that students can use for collaboration via computers in the classroom or anywhere there is an Internet connection.

Twiddla (www.twiddla.com). Twiddla is a no-setup, web-based meeting space that allows you to mark up websites, graphics, and photos or start brainstorming on a blank canvas. You can co-browse websites using a shared, real-time whiteboard, mark it up, share files, and chat.

Maps

Google Earth (http://earth.google.com). Google Earth lets you "fly" anywhere on Earth (and beyond) to view satellite imagery, maps, terrain, and 3-D buildings, from mountain peaks to the canyons of the ocean. You can even tour the solar system and distant galaxies. You can explore rich geographical content, save your toured places, and share with others.

Google Maps (http://maps.google.com). Google Maps allows you to enter addresses to locate places geographically and get directions from one place to another.

Google Sky (www.google.com/sky). Google Sky provides a way to browse and explore the universe. You can find the positions of the planets and constellations and even watch the birth of distant galaxies as seen by the Hubble Space Telescope. Google Maps has teamed up with astronomers at some of the largest observatories in the world to provide these views of the sky.

Quikmaps (www.quikmaps.com). Quikmaps is a free mash-up service. It enables you to draw directly onto a Google Map. You can view it online, on your website, in Google Earth, or on your GPS. You can scribble on it, do line tracing, add text labels, and save a map to your desktop.

Microblogging and Microblog Readers

Edmodo (www.edmodo.com). Edmodo is a private microblogging platform built for teachers and students, with the privacy of students in mind. Teachers and students can share notes, links, and files. Teachers also have the ability to send alerts, events, and assignments to students and can decide to post an item to a public timeline.

Plurk (www.plurk.com). Plurk is a microblogging site that allows you to chronicle and share information, ideas, thoughts, and activities and then communicate them to others using Plurk.

TweetDeck (www.tweetdeck.com). TweetDeck provides a personal browser for staying in touch with what's happening online by connecting you with your contacts across Twitter, Facebook, and more.

Twitter (http://twitter.com). Twitter is a microblogging site that provides a real-time, short messaging service (SMS) that works over multiple networks and devices. You can use it to follow the sources most relevant to you and access information online or via short messaging service as it happens—from breaking world news to updates from friends.

Twitterific (http://iconfactory.com/software/twitterrific). Twitterrific is a Mac application that lets you read and publish posts or tweets to the Twitter website.

Twitteroo (http://rareedge.com/twitteroo). Twitteroo is a PC application that lets you update your Twitter status from your desktop, get Twitter notifications, view Tweets, and more.

Photo Editing and Photo Sharing

BeFunky (www.befunky.com). BeFunky is an online photo editor that provides digital effects tools to turn photos into special effect digital artwork. You can save images to a private or public space.

Blabberize (http://blabberize.com). Blabberize allows you to upload a photo and a sound clip and use their technology so that the mouth moves to make it look like the image is talking.

Flickr (www.flickr.com). Flickr is a free online photo management and photo sharing application. You can upload an image, edit it, organize your photo collections, share the images with others, and create cards, photo books, and other items.

Fotoflexer (http://fotoflexer.com). Fotoflexer is an online image editor that allows you to create interesting effects and provides the tools to retouch and enhance images.

Photobucket (http://photobucket.com). Photobucket is a video site that provides free web-based versions of Adobe's video remix and editing tools.

Photoshop (Online) (www.photoshop.com). Adobe provides Photoshop.com, an online image editor that has many of the same tools as their commercial software so that you can edit images professionally.

Photo Story (www.microsoft.com/windowsxp/using/digitalphotography/PhotoStory/default.mspx). Microsoft's free downloadable software allows you to create a presentation from digital photos, with narration, effects, transitions, and music.

Photosynth (http://photosynth.net). Photosynth allows you to take a collection of photos of places or objects. It analyzes them for similarities and displays them in a reconstructed three-dimensional space.

Picasa (http://picasa.google.com). Picasa is Google's free photo-editing software that you can use to edit and enhance images, share them with others, and organize them into albums on your computer using the desktop application. Picasa is available for PC and Mac and requires downloading.

Pixlr (www.pixlr.com). Pixlr is a free online photo editor that allows you to make quick fixes to your images using a wide range of editing tools.

Scrapblog (www.scrapblog.com). Scrapblog is an online scrapbooking site that allows you to turn your photos into a personalized scrapbook. You select a kit and upload images, and the software creates the scrapbook, which you can print or share.

Presentation and Video-Editing Tools

Animoto (http://animoto.com/education). Animoto provides an assortment of tools for you and your students to create videos with images, video clips, and music. You can sync music and images for high production values and then share it in several ways.

Empressr (www.empressr.com). Empressr is a free online storytelling tool that allows you to create, manage, and share rich media presentations online. Upload your video, images, and audio to get started creating slide shows.

Jing (www.jingproject.com). Jing is screen capture software that allows you to share a snapshot of a project, collaborate on it, narrate it, or add comments. You can select a window or region and Jing will record up to five minutes of video of everything that appears in that area. Point to things with your mouse, scroll, flip through photos, click around in a website or application, and Jing captures it. Teachers and students can create tutorials.

Movie Maker (http://download.live.com/moviemaker) and **Windows Live Movie Maker** (http://explore.live.com/windows-live-movie-maker). Movie Maker is a downloadable video-creating and video-editing software that is a part of Microsoft's Windows Live.

Museum Box (http://museumbox.e2bn.org). Museum Box provides the tools for you to build up an argument or description of an event, person, or historical period by placing items in a virtual box. You can display anything from a text file to a movie. You can also view the museum boxes submitted by other people and comment on the contents.

PhotoShow (www.photoshow.com). You can create photo shows and stories online and view them at this site or post them to others. You add pictures and videos you want to include in your show, view an automatically generated slide show, customize it, and then share it.

PreZentit (http://prezentit.com). PreZentit allows you to create presentations online either alone or with a group of people who are working on the same presentation at the same time. Presentations can be private or public, and you can download them and show them offline.

Prezi (http://prezi.com). Prezi's free online presentation tool allows you to create public-only presentations online that you can show either online or offline. You can create groups; import images, videos, and other media files; share and collaborate; edit; download the results; and embed them in blogs and on websites.

Sketchcast (http://sketchcast.com). Sketchcast allows you to communicate online by recording a sketch and including your voice. You can embed the sketch in your blog or website for people to play back, and you can also point people to your sketchcast channel (or let them subscribe to your sketchcast RSS feed).

Sliderocket (www.sliderocket.com). The free version of Sliderocket is an online presentation maker that includes authoring tools, uploading of PowerPoint slides, an asset library, printing, publishing, and online support.

Slideshare (www.slideshare.net). Slideshare provides an online tool for sharing presentations. You can upload your PowerPoint presentations, Word documents, and Adobe PDF Portfolios and share them publicly or privately. You can add audio to make a webinar or embed slide shows in your blog or website.

Slidesix (http://slidesix.com). Slidesix is an online presentation tool that allows you to upload and share your PowerPoint, Keynote, and OpenOffice (www.openoffice.org) presentations. You can record audio and video narration and attach external videos online, manage presentations and groups, and create a widget to share Slidesix presentations on your blog.

280Slides (http://280slides.com). 280Slides allows you to create presentations, access them from anywhere, and share them. You can upload existing documents, work online, save them online, download to PowerPoint, and publish online.

VCASMO (http://vcasmo.com). VCASMO provides a multimedia presentation solution for creating a photo-video slide show, presentation, training, seminar, conference, meeting, or live event. Features include a variety of file formats, the synchronization of music, a simple editor, the option to save privately or publicly, and more.

VIDDIX (www.viddix.com). VIDDIX provides a video platform that allows users to add all kinds of web content to their video timeline. You can interact with your audience and choose from two types of players: overlay and dual screen.

VoiceThread (http://voicethread.com). VoiceThread is a tool for having conversations about media. Teachers can organize student discussions about various types of media, such as images, video, and presentations. Students can navigate around an image and add comments, create digital stories, and collaborate and share stories with others.

Vuvox (www.vuvox.com). Vuvox provides a media creation tool with a choice of ways to create. You can use Collage to produce dynamic interactive panoramas, Studio to build a presentation, Express to include online albums and RSS feeds, and Cut-Out Express to use photos as frames for slide shows.

Zentation (www.zentation.com). Zentation provides you with video and slides to create online presentations that simulate a live experience to use for webinars, webcasts, training, and virtual events. You can synchronize your YouTube video and PowerPoint slides and get a simple outline for viewers. Viewers can use a comment section to blog about your presentation.

Zoho Show (http://show.zoho.com/login.do). Zoho Show provides an online tool for making presentations that includes pre-built themes, clip art, and shapes. It has features such as drag-and-drop that make it an easy application to use. You can access it from anywhere, share and collaborate, present remotely, and embed the presentation in your blog or website.

Publishing and Drawing Tools

Calameo (http://en.calameo.com). Calameo allows you to upload documents in all major formats and convert them into digital publications. You can share your published work on the site or embed it in a website or blog.

Comicbrush (www.comicbrush.com). Comicbrush provides a simple way to create, publish, and share a comic. Their stock artwork includes a collection of comic backgrounds, characters, and props that you can mix with your own photos. You can add speech balloons, text, your own artwork, and more, and then publish your comic to the web.

Comic Creator (www.readwritethink.org/files/resources/interactives/comic). Comic Creator provides tools for students to compose their own comic strips for a variety of contexts (pre-writing, pre- and post-reading activities, response to literature, and so on). Students can choose backgrounds, characters, and props, and compose dialogue.

Formatpixel (www.formatpixel.com). Formatpixel allows you to create an online magazine, fanzine, brochure, catalogue, portfolio, and more. You can design projects, lay out text, upload images, add interactivity, and customize the appearance by moving, inserting, or deleting pages to create multipage presentations.

Glogster (http://edu.glogster.com). Glogster provides tools in their EDU zone for students to create interactive online posters using photos, images, graphics, videos, and sound. They can add links to other websites and embed their work in web pages, wiki pages, or a blog.

GoAnimate (http://goanimate.com). GoAnimate enables you to create computer-animated stories, satires, and sentiments that can be shared online. The site offers features to customize animations, and you can include items from GoAnimate's library of ready-made characters, backgrounds, props, sound effects, and music.

Issuu (http://issuu.com). Issuu provides a digital publishing platform for stories, books, reports, and other documents. You can create a digital edition of any writing by uploading your work to produce an online publication that simulates the look of a professional magazine.

Kerpoof (www.kerpoof.com). Kerpoof provides tools for students to create artwork; make animated movies; tell a story; make printed cards, T-shirts, and mugs; and view the stories and movies of others. It includes instructions for making a picture using Picture Maker and a movie using Animation Studio.

LetterPop (www.letterpop.com). LetterPop provides tools to create newsletters, presentations, invitations, picture collages, and more. You can browse templates and drag and drop the one you want, type in ideas, upload pictures, and save your work.

MakeBeliefsComix (www.makebeliefscomix.com). MakeBeliefsComix provides the tools to create comic strips. It promotes creativity, tests new ideas, and provides ways to communicate through art and writing by offering a choice of characters with different moods that users can write words and thoughts for.

OpenZine (www.openzine.com). OpenZine provides a social publishing platform with browser-based tools to create work and display it as well as to share, control, and manage ideas. You create a cover and images online; add shapes, text and effects; and gather your information to create the Zine by mixing and matching content from multiple sources (with approval).

Pikistrips (sponsored by Comeeko) (http://pikistrips.com). Pikistrips allows you to create comic strips, upload photos, add bubble comments, and then make them available to others. You can also create items (T-shirts, for example) that can be purchased, if you choose.

Pixton (http://pixton.com). Pixton is a remixable, animated, comic website on which schools can create private, customizable, classroom sites as well as develop print-based materials. Students can create, share, and remix comics around content topics and also focus on grammar and spelling.

Plotbot (www.plotbot.com). Plotbot offers collaborative screenwriting software for educators or students to develop their own plays.

Scrapblog (www.scrapblog.com). Scrapblog is an online scrapbook creation tool with drag-and-drop ability that allows you to add photos, personal touches, and share your creation. Students can keep their Scrapblogs private or make them public.

Scribd (www.scribd.com). Scribd is a social publishing site where you can share work, manage documents, create reading lists, and publish creative materials instantly. You can create a classroom or a school community and invite others to read and view your work. You can index all works by search engines if desired.

Sketchfu (http://sketchfu.com). Sketchfu is an online drawing site with the features of sophisticated drawing programs. Individuals may save and publish their drawings. Students can create free accounts and save their work to share, publish, and print.

Stripcreator (www.stripcreator.com). Stripcreator is a website that allows you to create and save your own comic strips. You can print, export, and share these comics, or you can keep them private.

Stripgenerator (http://stripgenerator.com). Stripgenerator allows you to create individual comic strips or a comic strip blog to explain, explore, or expand on your comic strip. You can save strips and make them public, or you can keep them private for specific groups of individuals.

Tikatok (www.tikatok.com). Tikatok is an online publishing environment for children. They can start with a blank book or use one of many "story starters." After including drawings, decorations, and designing all aspects of the book, they can then save it. For a small fee they can create a hardcover or paperback book.

Toondoo (www.toondoo.com). Toondoo provides you with tools to create your own comic strips and then publish, share, and discuss them.

Tux Paint (www.tuxpaint.org). Tux Paint is a free drawing program for children aged 3 to 12 (PK–6). It has an easy-to-use interface and includes sound effects (which can be disabled) and an online cartoon mascot who guides children as they use the program. It is also available in several languages. Students can print drawings or turn off this feature.

Portals and Social Bookmarking

Delicious (http://delicious.com). Delicious is a social bookmarking site that allows you to tag, save, manage, and share web pages from a server that stores such information. You can share tags with the general community or with an approved group of individuals. These resources are available from any computer. You can also access others' favorite tagged recommendations.

Diigo (www.diigo.com). Diigo is a resource to annotate, archive, organize, and share web resources; build a personal learning network by sharing those resources; and create a collaborative group for developing knowledge, assignments, or activities. These can be public or private.

Edutagger (www.edutagger.com). Edutagger is a social bookmarking site designed for K–12 learners and educators. It supports you in tagging and storing your web links online, sharing them with others, and keeping them within an educational environment.

Fleck (http://fleck.com). Fleck is a social bookmarking site that allows you to collect and share websites as you come across them. It also allows you to use Twitter to share your bookmarks by shortening the URL and sharing it with others. You can also point out sections of a website by adding a notation for others to see or asking questions for students to respond to.

iGoogle (www.google.com/ig). iGoogle lets you create a personalized home page that contains a Google search box at the top and your choice of any number of gadgets below. Gadgets come in lots of different forms and provide access to activities and information from all across the web. For example, you can view Gmail messages, read news headlines, store bookmarks, and more.

Jog the Web (www.jogtheweb.com). Jog the Web is a bookmarking and tracking site. It allows teachers to organize and lead students through topic-related web pages for safe, guided exploration. Educators can create "tracks" of content or explore other educators' already created sets of websites.

Netvibes (www.netvibes.com). Netvibes provides a free web service that you can use to bring together media sources and online services as a start page online or personal portal. You can include blogs, news, weather, videos, photos, social networks, e-mail, and more. Everything is automatically updated every time you visit your page.

Pageflakes (www.pageflakes.com). Pageflakes provides a social personalized home page where you can customize the web using "flakes," which are small, movable versions of all of your web favorites that you can arrange on your personal home page. You can also participate in the Pageflakes community, sharing your page as a "pagecast" with a private group or with the world and connecting with others.

StumbleUpon (www.stumbleupon.com). StumbleUpon is a web-sharing site that enables you to preselect a group of keywords or specific friends and see only the sites that are highly rated and match your choices. You can also rate sites you see, and others will have the option of viewing those. It is considered community-based surfing and can be organized for students as well.

TrailFire (www.trailfire.com). TrailFire is a bookmarking and commenting website that allows you to create a "trail" of websites to guide others to specific locations and place commentary or questions on those websites. You can also explore others' trails to find new sites on specific content.

Quiz and Activities Generators

Google Forms (http://docs.google.com). Google Forms provides you with a tool to generate online survey forms. You can create the form and use it to get information on whatever categories you want. You can e-mail the form; send it as a link; and embed it in, or link to it on, web pages. The results are displayed in a spreadsheet.

MyStudiyo (www.mystudiyo.com). MyStudiyo allows educators to create professional looking quizzes, surveys, or homework challenges and add them to a website or blog. Multiple-choice or rating forms are available, but other models of quizzes are being developed.

Quia (www.quia.com). Quia provides educators with the ability to create, share, and use online learning activities that are available in a searchable format. Activities include games, quizzes, surveys, and other types of learning materials.

Quizlet (http://quizlet.com). Quizlet allows educators to create online flash-cards or find flashcards others have created. Users receive immediate feedback on their answers and can reuse the cards multiple times. This site is appropriate for all grade levels for test preparation, practice, and reviews.

Wordle (www.wordle.net). Wordle is a tool for generating "word clouds" from text that you provide. The clouds—word images—give greater prominence to words that appear more frequently in the source text. You can print them out or save them to the Wordle gallery to share.

RSS

Bloglines (www.bloglines.com). Bloglines provides one location for searching, subscribing, and sharing aggregates of your personal web preferences. The service is available in many languages and brings your selected news and information to you on any computer.

Google Reader (http://reader.google.com). Google Reader allows you to blend your Google selections of news, information, and more into a single reader that is available to you on a mobile device or a computer. You can also follow what others are reading and have selected. Educators can subscribe to national or international news, keep students current on specific topics, and have access to multiple resources.

Timelines

Dipity (www.dipity.com). Dipity allows you to create a timeline on a particular event, track current events, or use others' timelines. Students must be 13 or older. Current events are routinely tracked as well. You can view timelines graphically, as a list, or in a map format.

Timetoast (www.timetoast.com). Timetoast is an online interactive time-line creation tool with which you can design your own or search for others' timelines on many topics. You can publish these timelines on Twitter or other social networking sites.

XTimeline (www.xtimeline.com). XTimeline is a web-based system for creating timelines and customizing them with pictures, videos, and more. A large database of timelines is available to use or customize for students.

Videoconferencing

Skype (http://skype.com). Skype is an integrated system for making web-based telephone calls using audio and video. It also allows text messaging. Educators can invite authors, experts, and others into their classroom using Skype, as long as both parties have free accounts.

Ustream (www.ustream.tv). Ustream is a live, interactive video broadcast platform that allows anyone with an Internet connection and a camera to engage an audience by creating a broadcast channel. It is considered a one-to-many site but also allows viewer-to-viewer interaction. It provides a back channel to interact with talk shows, sports events, or political events, as well as music performances.

Video Sharing

Next Vista (www.nextvista.org). Next Vista for Learning is a free, online library of short, teacher- and student-made videos for learning. Teachers and students are invited to view or create videos on serious topics for others to use. Teachers can create discussions around the topics to guide student learning.

SchoolTube (www.schooltube.com). SchoolTube is designed as a safe media-sharing website that approves all materials prior to posting. Tags help educators search for appropriate videos and allow creators to assist others with the use of their materials.

TeacherTube (www.teachertube.com). TeacherTube is an online repository for videos by and for teachers. These videos are appropriate for classrooms and can also be used to assist parents in supporting their children's learning.

Xtranormal (www.xtranormal.com). Xtranormal provides a simple way to create movies. You type something, and the site turns it into a movie online and on your desktop. Students can create a story and pick the set, actor, sounds, and animation, and it appears instantly as a movie.

YouTube (www.youtube.com). YouTube is a video-sharing website where you can upload and share videos as well as watch others' videos. Some schools and districts use security software to allow access to the educational aspects of this public forum.

Virtual Worlds

Club Penguin (www.clubpenguin.com). Club Penguin is a virtual world for children; it is dedicated to creativity and safety. Participants create a penguin avatar and wander around this virtual world. They enjoy collaborative and individual games and filtered chats. With a subscription, participants gain access to other specialized activities. This site works to foster global citizenship and community service.

Second Life (http://secondlife.com). Second Life is an online, 3-D, virtual environment that can be used for education, professional development, social networking, and more. Many institutions have "islands" in Second Life where you can join others, create a virtual community, and even take courses.

Teen Second Life (http://teen.secondlife.com). Teen Second Life is an international gathering place for teens aged 13–17 to make friends and to play, learn, and create. Teens can create and customize a digital self, called an "avatar," and can participate in a variety of virtual educational experiences.

Webkinz (www.webkinz.com). Webkinz is an online social environment for owners of Webkinz pets. These are plush animals that come with a unique secret code. With it, you enter Webkinz World, where you can care for your virtual pet, answer trivia questions, earn KinzCash, and play learning and other games.

Wikis

PBworks (http://pbworks.com). PBworks offers a web publishing and wiki site for educators to collaborate and share their content. A Basic Edition is free and allows public or controlled access to your class or collaborative wiki.

Wetpaint (www.wetpaint.com). Wetpaint is a collaborative website creator. While not specifically for education, it does promote collaboration in creating websites that include the features of wikis, blogs, forums, and social networks for groups that want to create a community based on whatever topic is chosen.

WikiEducator (www.wikieducator.org). WikiEducator is a collaborative community to plan educational projects around the world, develop free content for teachers and students, and create open education resources for all to share.

Wikispaces (www.wikispaces.com). Wikispaces is a wiki and publishing site in which you can embed documents, images, and audio and video files. The creator of each wiki controls access, and educational information is extensive.

Other Tools

EduRatings 2.0 (http://er2.weebly.com). EduRatings 2.0 is a way to stay current and get end-user feedback on new tools. It is an interactive website designed to help educators find the best free Web 2.0 applications for instruction, communication, and professional development.

iRows (www.irows.com). iRows allows students and teachers to create collaborative spreadsheets, generate graphs and charts, and solve problems.

LibraryThing (http://librarything.com). LibraryThing is an online book club. Individuals catalog their books, annotate reasons for their views, and find recommendations from others with similar tastes.

Scratch (http://scratch.mit.edu). Scratch is a programming language designed for students age 8 and up so that they can develop stories, games, music, and more. The goal is to teach students digital-age learning skills. Educational resources and strategies are also available to assist in using this tool.

TinyURL (http://tinyurl.com). TinyURL allows you to create short URLs that stand for long ones. They make it easier to share websites with others, and the URLs never expire.

A
references

A

ACMA. (2007). *Media and communications in Australian families: Report of the media and society research project*. (Report by Australian Communications and Media Authority), Canberra: Australia. Retrieved June 17, 2009, from www.acma.gov.au/WEB/STANDARD/pc=PC_310893

Anderson, C. (2009). *Free: The future of a radical price* [Kindle reader version]. New York, NY: Hyperion.

Atkinson, T. (2008). Second Life for educators: Inside Linden Lab. *TechTrends, 52*(2), 18–21.

B

Baker, S. C., Wentz, R. K., & Woods, M. M. (2009). Using virtual worlds in education: Second Life as an educational tool. *Teaching of Psychology, 36*(1), 59–64.

Barab, S., Thomas, M., Dodge, T., Carteaux, R., & Tuzun, H. (2005). Making learning fun: Quest Atlantis, a game without guns. *Educational Technology Research and Development, 53*(1), 86–107.

Barack, L. (2009). Green libraries grow in SL. *School Library Journal, 55*(1), 12–13.

Barnes, B. (2009, July 16). An animated film is created through Internet consensus. *The New York Times*. Retrieved from www.nytimes.com/2009/07/16/movies/16mass.html?_r=1&ref=arts

Belshaw, D. (2007, February 15). Using Twitter with your students [Blog post]. Retrieved from http://teaching.mrbelshaw.co.uk/index.php/2007/02/15/using-twitter-with-your-students

Belshaw, D. (2009). Twenty-nine interesting ways to use Twitter in the classroom, Screen 1. Retrieved April 15, 2010 from www.ideastoinspire.co.uk/twitter.htm

Bialo, E., & Sivin-Kachala, J. (2009, March, 31). K–12 Survey on Web 2.0: Safe schools in a Web 2.0 world initiative. In G. Solomon (Moderator), *Opportunities and Challenges for Web 2.0 in Schools*. Technology & Learning webinar sponsored by Lightspeed Systems, March 31, 2009. Available from www.lightspeedsystems.com/researchsurvey

Botterbusch, H. R., & Talab, R. S. (2009). Ethical issues in Second Life. *TechTrends, 53*(1), 9–12.

Brenda. (2008, March 27). Re: Teacher's use of podcasts as teaching tool! [Blog comment]. Retrieved from http://www.classroom20.com/forum/topics/649749:Topic:122802

C

Carr, N. (2009). *The big switch: Rewiring the world, from Edison to Google*. New York, NY: W.W. Norton & Company.

Cloud computing. (2010). In Wikipedia. Retrieved May 5, 2010, from http://en.wikipedia.org/wiki/Cloud_computing

Cohen, N. (2009, June 21). Twitter on the barricades: Six lessons learned. *The New York Times*. Retrieved from www.nytimes.com

Collins, C. (2008). Looking to the future: Higher education in the metaverse. *Educause Review, 43*(5), 52–63.

Convergence. (2009). In Wiktionary. Retrieved from http://en.wiktionary.org/wiki/convergence

Creative C ommons. (2010). In Wikipedia. Retrieved May 5, 2010, from http://en.wikipedia.org/wiki/Creative_Commons

Crook, C. (2008). *Web 2.0 technologies for learning: The current landscape—opportunities, challenges and tensions*. (Research report from Becta, Coventry, UK). Retrieved from http://partners.becta.org.uk/upload-dir/downloads/page_documents/research/web2_technologies_learning.pdf

Curious, S. (2009, January 11). Listening and learning: Mark Smilowitz's classroom teaching podcasts. [Blog post]. Retrieved from http://siobhancurious.wordpress.com/2009/01/11/listening-and-learning-mark-smilowitzs-classroom-teaching-podcasts/

Czarnecki, K. (2008). Virtual environments and K–12 education: A tour of the possibilities, Part I. *Multimedia & Internet Schools, 15*(4), 14–18.

Czarnecki, K., & Gullett, M. (2007). Meet the new you. *School Library Journal, 53*(1), 35–39.

D

Dalton, B., & Proctor, P. (2008). The changing landscape of text and comprehension in the age of new literacies. In J. Coiro, M. Knobel, C. Lankshear, & D. Leu, (Eds.), *Handbook of research on new literacies* (pp. 287–324). New York, NY: Lawrence Erlbaum Associates.

ddeubel. (2007, August 30). Re: Social networking [Blog comment]. Retrieved from www.classroom20.com/forum/topics/649749:Topic:45491

Dede, C., Dieterle, E., Clarke, J., Ketelhut, D. J., & Nelson, B. (2007). Media based learning styles. In M. M. Moore, W. Anderson, & W. G. Anderson (Eds.), *Handbook of Distance Education* (2nd ed., pp. 339–352). New York, NY: Routledge.

Demski, J. (2009, June 1). Free at last. *THE Journal.* Retrieved from www.thejournal.com

Dodge, T., Barab, S., & Stuckey, B. (2008). Children's sense of self: Learning and meaning in the digital age. *Journal of Interactive Learning Research, 19*(2), 225–249.

F

Ferdig, R. (2007). Examining social software in teacher education. *Journal of Technology and Teacher Education, 15*(1), 5–11.

Ferriter, B. (2009). Learning with blogs and wikis. *Educational Leadership, 66*(5), 34–38. Retrieved from www.ascd.org/publications/educational_leadership.aspx

Friedman, T. L. (2007). *The World Is Flat* (Rev. ed.). New York, NY: Farrar, Straus and Giroux.

Friedman, T. L. (2009, April 21). Swimming without a suit. *The New York Times.* Retrieved from www.nytimes.com

G

Godin, S. (2007, January 17). Web 4 [Blog post]. Retrieved from http://sethgodin.typepad.com/seths_blog/2007/01/web4.html

Green, H., & Hannon, C. (2007). *Their space: Education for a digital generation* [Pamphlet]. Available from www.demos.co.uk/publications/theirspace

H

Hamm, S. (2009, June 15). Cloud computing's big bang for business. *Business Week, 24,* 42–48. Video accessed from www.businessweek.com/magazine/toc/09_24/B4135cloud_computing.htm

Harris H., & Park S. (2008). Educational uses of podcasting. *British Journal of Educational Technology, 39*(3), 548–551.

Hechinger, J. (2009, June 12). Data-driven schools see rising scores. *The Wall Street Journal.* Retrieved from http://online.wsj.com/home-page

Hickey, D. T., Ingram-Goble, A. A., & Jameson, E. M. (2009). Designing assessments and assessing designs in virtual educational environments. *Journal of Science Education and Technology, 18*(2), 187–208.

Hollis, J. (n.d.). Sharing educational content using a blog [Blog post]. Retrieved May 6, 2009, from www.guide2digitallearning.com/blog_jim_hollis/sharing_educational_content_using_blog

Huff, L. (2008). Using wikis as electronic portfolios [Blog post]. Retrieved from www.guide2digitallearning.com/technology_curriculum_integration/using_wikis_electronic_portfolios

J

Jakes, D. (2005, December 1). Making a case for digital storytelling. Retrieved from www.techlearning.com/article/4958

Jenkins, H., Clinton K., Purushotma, R., Robinson, A.J., & Weigel, M. (2006). *Confronting the challenges of participatory culture: Media education for the 21st century.* Chicago, IL: The MacArthur Foundation. Retrieved from www.projectnml.org/files/working/NMLWhitePaper.pdf

Johnson, L., Levine, A., Smith, R., & Smythe, T. (2009). *The 2009 Horizon Report: K–12 edition.* Retrieved May 9, 2009, from www.nmc.org/pdf/2009-Horizon-Report-K12.pdf

K

Kelton, A. J. (2008). Virtual worlds? Outlook good. *Educause Review, 43*(8), 15–22.

Ketelhut, D. J. (2007). The impact of student self-efficacy on scientific inquiry skills: An exploratory investigation of River City, a multi-user virtual environment. *Journal of Science Education and Technology, 16*(1), 99–111.

Knittle, B. (2008). *An introduction to Second Life for educators.* Retrieved from www.bethknittle.net/IntroToSLforEd.pdf

L

Lake, D. (n.d.). *Web 2.0 tools in context.* Retrieved August 3, 2009, from www.guide2digitallearning.com/tools_technologies/web_2_0_tools_context

Lave, J., & Wenger, E. (1991). *Situated learning. Legitimate peripheral participation.* Cambridge, UK: Cambridge University Press.

Ledesma, P., & Jarosz, S. (2009, June 24). Adding a touch of technology [Online exclusive]. *Teacher Magazine.* Retrieved from www.teachermagazine.org

Leese, M. (2009). Out of class—out of mind? The use of a virtual learning environment to encourage student engagement in out of class activities. *British Journal of Educational Technology, 40*(1), 70–77.

Lemke, C., & Coughlin, E. (2009). *Leadership for Web 2.0 in education: Promise and reality.* (Report by Consortium for School Networking). Retrieved from www.cosn.org/Portals/7/docs/Web%202.0/CoSN%20Report%20042809Final%20w-cover.pdf

Lenhart, A., Madden, M., Smith, A., & Macgill, A. (2007). *Teens and social media.* (Report by Pew Internet Project). Retrieved from www.pewInternet.org/~/media//Files/Reports/2007/PIP_Teens_Social_Media_Final.pdf.pdf

Levy, A. (n.d.). Creating classroom podcasts. Retrieved July 26, 2009, from www.teachersnetwork.org/NTNY/nychelp/technology/podcast.htm

Liao, C. L. (2008). Avatars, Second Life, and new media art: The challenge of contemporary art education. *Art Education, 61*(2), 87–91.

Lim, C. P., Nonis, D., & Hedberg, J. (2006). Gaming in a 3D multiuser virtual environment: Engaging students in science lessons. *British Journal of Educational Technology, 37*(2), 211–231.

Livingstone, S. (2008). Taking risky opportunities in youthful content creation: Teenagers' use of social networking sites for intimacy, privacy and self-expression. *New Media and Society, 10*(3), 459–477.

Lum, L. (2006, March 9). *The power of podcasting.* Retrieved from www.diverseeducation.com/artman/publish/article_5583.shtml

M

Meadows, M. S. (2008). *I, Avatar: The culture and consequences of having a second life.* Berkeley, CA: New Riders.

Metz, C. (2007, March 14). Web 3.0. *PC Magazine.* Retrieved from www.pcmag.com/article2/0,2817,2102852,00.asp

Mishra, P., & Koehler, M. J. (2006). Technological pedagogical content knowledge: A framework for teacher knowledge. *Teachers College Record, 108*(6), 1017–1054.

Mr.Balch. (2009, May 24). Re: Calling All Teachers!!! [Blog comment]. Retrieved from http://www.google.com/support/forum/p/sites/thread?tid=1b9ad8f1959c2f4d&hl=en

Mulryne, K. (2010). Twenty-nine interesting ways to use Twitter in the classroom, Screen 4. Retrieved April 15, 2010 from www.ideastoinspire.co.uk/twitter.htm

N

National School Boards Association. (2007). Creating & connecting: Research and guidelines on online social and educational networking. Alexandria, VA: Author. Retrieved from www.nsba.org/SecondaryMenu/TLN/CreatingandConnecting.aspx

O

Orech, J. (2009a). Why I Tweet [Blog post]. (n.d.) Retrieved from www.guide2digitallearning.com/blog_jon_orech/why_i_tweet

Orech, J. (2009b). Turbo-charged wikis: Technology embraces cooperative learning [Blog post]. (February 16, 2009). Retrieved from www.guide2digitallearning.com/teaching_learning/turbo_charged_wikis_technology_embraces_cooperative_learning

Orech, J. (2009c). Collaboration [Blog post]. (March 25, 2009). Retrieved from www.techlearning.com/blogs/16752

Owen, M., Grant, L., Sayers, S., & Facer, K. (2006). *Social software and learning.* (Report from Futurelab, Bristol, UK). Retrieved from www.futurelab.org.uk/resources/documents/opening_education/Social_Software_report.pdf

P

Parkinson, A. (2009, February 21). Twalter-egos [Blog post]. Retrieved from http://livinggeography.blogspot.com/2009/02/twalter-ego.html

Partnership for 21st Century Skills. (2004). *P21 framework definitions.* Retrieved April 28, 2010, from www.ocmboces.org/tfiles/folder1041/P21_Framework_Definitions.pdf

Partnership for 21st Century Skills. (2009). *Media literacy.* Retrieved July 6, 2009, from www.21stcenturyskills.org/index.php?option=com_content&task=view&id=349&Itemid=120

Perez, J. C. (2009, February 25). Facebook to improve how members discover applications. *PCWorld.* Retrieved from www.pcworld.com/businesscenter/article/160235/facebook_to_improve_how_members_discover_applications.html

Podcast. (2010). In Wikipedia. Retrieved April 15, 2010, from http://en.wikipedia.org/wiki/Podcast

R

Rupp, A., Choi, Y., Gushta, M., Mislevy, R., Thies, M. C., Bagley, E., Nash, P., Hatfield, D., Svarovsky, G., Shaffer D. W. (2009). *Modeling learning progressions in epistemic games with epistemic network analysis: Principles for data analysis and generation.* (Paper presented June 25, 2009, at the Learning Progressions in Science conference (LeaPS), Iowa City, Iowa). Retrieved from http://epistemicgames.org/eg/wp-content/uploads/leaps-learning-progressions-paper-rupp-et-al-2009-leaps-format1.pdf

Rushkoff, D. (2005). *Get back in the box: Innovation from the inside out.* New York, NY: HarperCollins.

S

Sculley, J. (1987). *Odyssey: Pepsi to Apple: A journey of adventure, ideas, and the future.* New York, NY: HarperCollins.

Shareski, D. (2009, April 30). A slightly different approach [Blog post]. Retrieved from www.techlearning.com/blogs.aspx?id=20074

Shoemaker, P. (2009). Wikis + webcams + writing = WOW: A multimedia approach to writers workshop. *MACUL Journal, 29*(3), 16–17. Retrieved from www.macul.org/site/files/09journalconf.pdf

Shuler, C. (2009). *Pockets of potential: Using mobile technologies to promote children's learning.* Retrieved July 3, 2009, from www.joanganzcooneycenter.org/pdf/pockets_of_potential.pdf

Siemens, G. (2004). *Connectivism: A learning theory for the digital age.* Retrieved from www.elearnspace.org/Articles/connectivism.htm

Six degrees of separation. (2010). In Wikipedia. Retrieved April 15, 2010, from http://en.wikipedia.org/wiki/Six_degrees_of_separation

Social network service. (2010). In Wikipedia. Retrieved April 15, 2010, from http://en.wikipedia.org/wiki/Social_network_service

Stone, B., & Wortham, J. (2009, June 8). New software, new iPhone, new Steve? Live-blogging the Apple extravaganza. *The New York Times.* Retrieved from www.nytimes.com

Surowiecki, J. (2004). *The wisdom of crowds: Why the many are smarter than the few and how collective wisdom shapes business, economies, societies, and nations.* New York, NY: Doubleday.

T

Tapscott, D., & Williams, A. D. (2006). *Wikinomics: How mass collaboration changes everything.* New York, NY: Portfolio Group.

tbarrett. (2008a). GeoTweets—Inviting your network into the classroom [Blog post]. (2008, January 18). Retrieved from http://tbarrett.edublogs.org/2008/01/18/geotweets-inviting-your-network-into-the-classroom

tbarrett. (2008b). Plan, tweet, teach, tweet, learn, smile [Blog post]. (2008, March 7). Retrieved from http://tbarrett.edublogs.org/2008/03/07/plan-tweet-teach-tweet-learn-smile

Technology's impact on learning. (2009). Retrieved May 9, 2009, from www.guide2digitallearning.com/question_month/technology_s_impact_learning

Trotter, A. (2009, January 7). Students Turn Their Cellphones On for Classroom Lessons. *Education Week.* Available from www.edweek.org

U

Updated Breaking News: Google announces Lively (2008, July 8). *Virtual Worlds News.* Retrieved from www.virtualworldsnews.com/2008/07/breaking-news-g.html

V

Van Allsburg, C. (1984). *The mysteries of Harris Burdick.* New York, NY: Houghton Mifflin.

Vanderbilt, T. (2009, June 8). Data center overload. *The New York Times.* Retrieved from www.nytimes.com

W

Wagner, C. (2008). Learning experience with virtual worlds. *Journal of Information Systems Education, 19*(3), 263–266.

Waiksnis, M. (2009, August 10). What is Your Favorite? [Blog post]. Retrieved from http://edleaderweb.net/blog

Walker, L. (2009, March 29). Nine great reasons why teachers should use Twitter. [Blog post]. Retrieved from http://mrslwalker.com

Web 2.0. (2010). In Webopedia. Retrieved April 15, 2010, from www.webopedia.com/TERM/W/Web_2_point_0.html

Wortham, J. (2009, July 22). Mobile Internet use shrinks digital divide. *The New York Times.* Retrieved from www.nytimes.com

Z

Zezima, K. (2009, August 6). John Quincy Adams, Twitterer? *The New York Times.* Retrieved from www.nytimes.com

national educational technology standards

Web 2.0 tools are effective tools for students, teachers, and administrators to use to reach their goals in addressing technology standards and improving student achievement.

National Educational Technology Standards for Students (NETS•S)

All K–12 students should be prepared to meet the following standards and performance indicators.

1. **Creativity and Innovation**

    Students demonstrate creative thinking, construct knowledge, and develop innovative products and processes using technology. Students:

    a. apply existing knowledge to generate new ideas, products, or processes

    b. create original works as a means of personal or group expression

    c. use models and simulations to explore complex systems and issues

    d. identify trends and forecast possibilities

2. Communication and Collaboration

Students use digital media and environments to communicate and work collaboratively, including at a distance, to support individual learning and contribute to the learning of others. Students:

 a. interact, collaborate, and publish with peers, experts, or others employing a variety of digital environments and media

 b. communicate information and ideas effectively to multiple audiences using a variety of media and formats

 c. develop cultural understanding and global awareness by engaging with learners of other cultures

 d. contribute to project teams to produce original works or solve problems

3. Research and Information Fluency

Students apply digital tools to gather, evaluate, and use information. Students:

 a. plan strategies to guide inquiry

 b. locate, organize, analyze, evaluate, synthesize, and ethically use information from a variety of sources and media

 c. evaluate and select information sources and digital tools based on the appropriateness to specific tasks

 d. process data and report results

4. Critical Thinking, Problem Solving, and Decision Making

Students use critical-thinking skills to plan and conduct research, manage projects, solve problems, and make informed decisions using appropriate digital tools and resources. Students:

 a. identify and define authentic problems and significant questions for investigation

b. plan and manage activities to develop a solution or complete a project

c. collect and analyze data to identify solutions and make informed decisions

d. use multiple processes and diverse perspectives to explore alternative solutions

5. Digital Citizenship

Students understand human, cultural, and societal issues related to technology and practice legal and ethical behavior. Students:

a. advocate and practice the safe, legal, and responsible use of information and technology

b. exhibit a positive attitude toward using technology that supports collaboration, learning, and productivity

c. demonstrate personal responsibility for lifelong learning

d. exhibit leadership for digital citizenship

6. Technology Operations and Concepts

Students demonstrate a sound understanding of technology concepts, systems, and operations. Students:

a. understand and use technology systems

b. select and use applications effectively and productively

c. troubleshoot systems and applications

d. transfer current knowledge to the learning of new technologies

National Educational Technology Standards for Teachers (NETS•T)

All classroom teachers should be prepared to meet the following standards and performance indicators.

1. Facilitate and Inspire Student Learning and Creativity

Teachers use their knowledge of subject matter, teaching and learning, and technology to facilitate experiences that advance student learning, creativity, and innovation in both face-to-face and virtual environments. Teachers:

a. promote, support, and model creative and innovative thinking and inventiveness

b. engage students in exploring real-world issues and solving authentic problems using digital tools and resources

c. promote student reflection using collaborative tools to reveal and clarify students' conceptual understanding and thinking, planning, and creative processes

d. model collaborative knowledge construction by engaging in learning with students, colleagues, and others in face-to-face and virtual environments

2. Design and Develop Digital-Age Learning Experiences and Assessments

Teachers design, develop, and evaluate authentic learning experiences and assessments incorporating contemporary tools and resources to maximize content learning in context and to develop the knowledge, skills, and attitudes identified in the NETS•S. Teachers:

a. design or adapt relevant learning experiences that incorporate digital tools and resources to promote student learning and creativity

b. develop technology-enriched learning environments that enable all students to pursue their individual curiosities and become active participants in setting their own educational goals, managing their own learning, and assessing their own progress

   c. customize and personalize learning activities to address students' diverse learning styles, working strategies, and abilities using digital tools and resources

   d. provide students with multiple and varied formative and summative assessments aligned with content and technology standards and use resulting data to inform learning and teaching

3. Model Digital-Age Work and Learning

Teachers exhibit knowledge, skills, and work processes representative of an innovative professional in a global and digital society. Teachers:

   a. demonstrate fluency in technology systems and the transfer of current knowledge to new technologies and situations

   b. collaborate with students, peers, parents, and community members using digital tools and resources to support student success and innovation

   c. communicate relevant information and ideas effectively to students, parents, and peers using a variety of digital-age media and formats

   d. model and facilitate effective use of current and emerging digital tools to locate, analyze, evaluate, and use information resources to support research and learning

4. Promote and Model Digital Citizenship and Responsibility

Teachers understand local and global societal issues and responsibilities in an evolving digital culture and exhibit legal and ethical behavior in their professional practices. Teachers:

   a. advocate, model, and teach safe, legal, and ethical use of digital information and technology, including respect for copyright, intellectual property, and the appropriate documentation of sources

b. address the diverse needs of all learners by using learner-centered strategies and providing equitable access to appropriate digital tools and resources

c. promote and model digital etiquette and responsible social interactions related to the use of technology and information

d. develop and model cultural understanding and global awareness by engaging with colleagues and students of other cultures using digital-age communication and collaboration tools

5. Engage in Professional Growth and Leadership

Teachers continuously improve their professional practice, model lifelong learning, and exhibit leadership in their school and professional community by promoting and demonstrating the effective use of digital tools and resources. Teachers:

a. participate in local and global learning communities to explore creative applications of technology to improve student learning

b. exhibit leadership by demonstrating a vision of technology infusion, participating in shared decision making and community building, and developing the leadership and technology skills of others

c. evaluate and reflect on current research and professional practice on a regular basis to make effective use of existing and emerging digital tools and resources in support of student learning

d. contribute to the effectiveness, vitality, and self-renewal of the teaching profession and of their school and community

National Educational Technology Standards for Administrators (NETS·A)

All school administrators should be prepared to meet the following standards and performance indicators.

1. Visionary Leadership

Educational Administrators inspire and lead development and implementation of a shared vision for comprehensive integration of technology to promote excellence and support transformation throughout the organization. Educational Administrators:

    a. inspire and facilitate among all stakeholders a shared vision of purposeful change that maximizes use of digital-age resources to meet and exceed learning goals, support effective instructional practice, and maximize performance of district and school leaders

    b. engage in an ongoing process to develop, implement, and communicate technology-infused strategic plans aligned with a shared vision

    c. advocate on local, state, and national levels for policies, programs, and funding to support implementation of a technology-infused vision and strategic plan

2. Digital-Age Learning Culture

Educational Administrators create, promote, and sustain a dynamic, digital-age learning culture that provides a rigorous, relevant, and engaging education for all students. Educational Administrators:

    a. ensure instructional innovation focused on continuous improvement of digital-age learning

    b. model and promote the frequent and effective use of technology for learning

    c. provide learner-centered environments equipped with technology and learning resources to meet the individual, diverse needs of all learners

    d. ensure effective practice in the study of technology and its infusion across the curriculum

    e. promote and participate in local, national, and global learning communities that stimulate innovation, creativity, and digital-age collaboration

3. Excellence in Professional Practice

Educational Administrators promote an environment of professional learning and innovation that empowers educators to enhance student learning through the infusion of contemporary technologies and digital resources. Educational Administrators:

    a. allocate time, resources, and access to ensure ongoing professional growth in technology fluency and integration

    b. facilitate and participate in learning communities that stimulate, nurture, and support administrators, faculty, and staff in the study and use of technology

    c. promote and model effective communication and collaboration among stakeholders using digital-age tools

    d. stay abreast of educational research and emerging trends regarding effective use of technology and encourage evaluation of new technologies for their potential to improve student learning

4. Systemic Improvement

Educational Administrators provide digital-age leadership and management to continuously improve the organization through the effective use of information and technology resources. Educational Administrators:

    a. lead purposeful change to maximize the achievement of learning goals through the appropriate use of technology and media-rich resources

    b. collaborate to establish metrics, collect and analyze data, interpret results, and share findings to improve staff performance and student learning

c. recruit and retain highly competent personnel who use technology creatively and proficiently to advance academic and operational goals

d. establish and leverage strategic partnerships to support systemic improvement

e. establish and maintain a robust infrastructure for technology including integrated, interoperable technology systems to support management, operations, teaching, and learning

5. Digital Citizenship

Educational Administrators model and facilitate understanding of social, ethical, and legal issues and responsibilities related to an evolving digital culture. Educational Administrators:

a. ensure equitable access to appropriate digital tools and resources to meet the needs of all learners

b. promote, model, and establish policies for safe, legal, and ethical use of digital information and technology

c. promote and model responsible social interactions related to the use of technology and information

d. model and facilitate the development of a shared cultural understanding and involvement in global issues through the use of contemporary communication and collaboration tools

index of web 2.0 tools and portals

This is a partial index the purpose of which is to direct the reader to specific tools and communities. The table of contents (pages vii–x) will direct the reader to concepts.

Page references in **bold** indicate Chapter 10 main discussions. Page references in *italic* indicate Chapter 11 mini discussions.